Advance praise for
The No-Cry Sleep Solution for Newborns

Yet again, Elizabeth Pantley spins her baby magic! She continues to tower above her competitors by showing us, more than anything, her uncanny ability to hone in on what babies really need, and how best to give it to them. Stressing with sensitivity the uniqueness of different families, she still manages to teach us how to take advantage of our own infant's innate capacities to sleep, but while doing so, reminds us to be open to the messages our babies whisper to us.

—James J. McKenna, Ph.D.
Director, Mother-Baby Behavioral Sleep Laboratory
Fellow, American Association for the Advancement of Science
Department of Anthropology, University of Notre Dame
www.cosleeping.nd.edu

It was a genuine pleasure to read such a well-presented, honest and evidence-based book. This is a complex area, and it is commonly difficult to separate opinion from evidence-based observations. *The No-Cry Sleep Solution for Newborns* manages to make these distinctions very clearly, and provides sensitive and compassionate ideas of what does or might work, together with clear descriptions of the reality of caring for a young infant.

Recognizing the important information in scientific studies of infant sleep, this is the first book I have seen that translated many of these insights into a usable form for parents. Further, Pantley recognizes that everyone is different, and thus a range of options is more valuable that a single "one size fits all" approach. I will be pleased to commend this book to parents as a very valuable contribution to their bookshelf.

—Professor Peter Fleming Ph.D.
Professor of Infant Health and Developmental Physiology,
School of Social and Community Medicine, University of Bristol
Consultant Paediatrician, University Hospitals Bristol

Expectant and new parents, take heed! This is the one sleep book you need to read *before* your little one arrives, or immediately after birth. It will set a pattern not only for better sleep, but also for a healthy, nurturing relationship with your children for a lifetime to come.

—**Nancy Peplinsky, Ph.D.**
Founder, Holistic Moms Network
http://www.holisticmoms.org/

When parents ask about sleep training, I'm happy that I can recommend an alternative: a book that allows everyone to get the sleep they need without resorting to potentially harmful cry-it-out methods. Thank you, Elizabeth Pantley, for *The No-Cry Sleep Solution for Newborns.* It's just what we need.

—**Kathleen Kendall-Tackett, Ph.D., IBCLC, FAPA**
Author, The Science of Mother-Infant Sleep
Clinical Professor, School of Nursing,
University of Hawai'i, Manoa
Editor-in-Chief, Psychological Trauma*;*
Editor-in-Chief, Clinical Lactation

The No-Cry Sleep Solution for Newborns is a brilliant guide for parents of infants. If you feel strongly, as I do, that human newborns should be treated gently, their needs respected, and their parents supported, you will find much to like in this book. It contains helpful strategies for supporting your baby's natural sleep behaviour and coping with the sleeplessness that goes with the territory of having a new baby. This book will be a key resource for parents of new babies, and for those who seek to support them.

Professor Helen L Ball, Ph.D.
Head of Anthropology & Director, Parent-Infant Sleep Lab,
Durham University
Co-Founder of the Infant Sleep Information Source
Chair-elect, Scientific Committee, Lullaby Trust
www.dur.ac.uk/sleep.lab | www.isisonline.org.uk

the no-cry sleep solution for newborns

Amazing Sleep from Day One—
for Baby and You

Elizabeth Pantley

Mc Graw Hill Education

New York Chicago San Francisco Athens London Madrid
Mexico City Milan New Delhi Singapore Sydney Toronto

1 2 3 4 5 6 7 8 9   QFR   21 20 19 18 17 16

ISBN   978-1-259-64117-6
MHID   1-259-64117-1

e-ISBN   978-1-259-64118-3
e-MHID   1-259-64118-X

This book provides a variety of ideas and suggestions. It is sold with the understanding that the publisher and author are not rendering psychological, medical, or professional services. The author is not a doctor or psychologist, and the information in this book is based on the author's opinion unless otherwise stated. Questions and comments attributed to parents may represent a compilation and adaptation of reader letters and test parent surveys. Names are changed to protect the privacy of the parents and children.

This material is presented without any warranty or guarantee of any kind, express or implied, including but not limited to the implied warranties of merchantability or fitness for a particular purpose. It is not possible to cover every eventuality in any book, and the reader should consult a professional for individual needs.

Information and suggestions regarding co-sleeping, bed-sharing, swaddling, white noise, pacifiers, bedding, and all other topics covered are included for your review, consideration, and personal decision on whether you use each idea or not. You must determine which ideas are safe and practical for your baby and your family. Please do your own research when making these choices for your family.

Readers should bring their baby to a medical care provider for regular checkups and bring questions they have to a medical professional. This book is not a substitute for competent professional healthcare or professional counseling.

McGraw-Hill Education books are available at special quantity discounts to use as premiums and sales promotions or for use in corporate training programs. To contact a representative, please visit the Contact Us pages at www.mhprofessional.com.

This book is dedicated to Hunter Augustus, my precious grand-baby, for gracing my world with his smiles, giggles, and cuddles. I always thought that having my own four babies was the ultimate experience of loving, but the tender feelings for the first child of my first child bring an explosion of emotions rushing to the surface. He reawakened in me my intense desire to protect those most precious people in our world—newborn babies—and to help those who are entrusted with their care. Hunter, you are my sunshine, I find myself enchanted in even the simplest of moments we share together and I treasure our very special relationship.

Elizabeth and newborn Hunter

Contents

Acknowledgments

I would like to express my heartfelt appreciation to the many people who provide me with their support every day, in so many ways:

Meredith Bernstein, of The Meredith Bernstein Literary Agency: counselor, friend, and an extraordinary literary agent.

The entire team of people at McGraw-Hill who help me to create all of the *No-Cry Solution* books.

Patti Hughes: my incredible, indispensable assistant and a valued friend.

My husband, Robert: my partner, my friend, my love, my soul mate, and my sanctuary.

My family; my ultimate source of daily joy and inspiration: Mom, Vanessa, David, Coleton, Angela, Greg, and Hunter. And all my family who are long-distance in location, but close in my heart.

All the readers who have written to me about their precious children: I feel a special friendship with each and every person who writes to me, and warm affection for their children.

The photographers who shared their beautiful photos: Elizabeth and Hunter by Carmen Emmi, Jesse by Cassandra Parshall, Billy by Courtney Holmes Photography, Ireland by Perry Vaile Photography, Paxton by Doula Tiffany Wilson, and Amari and Azari by Apple Dapples Photography.

The test mommies, test daddies, and test babies, for sharing this piece of their lives with me: Abel Alexander, Abigail, Alejandra, Adam, Adelaide, Ahmed, Aimee, Airie, AJ, Akasha, Alana, Alex, Alexander, Alexis, Allison, Altu, Alvin, Amanda, Amari, Amie, Amity, Amy, Andrea, Andrew, Angela, Anke, Anna, Annabelle, Annie, Annika, Anthea, Arielle, Arlene, Arum, Aryan, Ashlene, Augustyn, Ava, Azari, Balin, Becky, Billy, Brad, Bradey, Brandi, Brandy, Brantley, Breanna, Brenna, Brentley, Brian, Brock,

Brooklyn, Bruce, Caleb, Casey, Catherine, Cecelia, Celeste, Chanda, Charlotte, Chris, Christi, Christina, Christine, Christy, Claire, Clara Grace, Clemente, Conall, Corlia, Daisy, Daniel, David, Deaan, Debbie, Declan, Denise, Diana, Dixie, Donna, Dwain, Edie, Edward, Eleanor, Eleni, Eli, Elisa, Eliza, Elizabeth, Emilio, Emma, Erin, Eva, Evan, Evi, Evie, Ezra, Felicity, Fraser, Gabriel, Gabriella, Grace, Grady, Greg, Hannah, Harper, Hayden, Hayley, Heath, Helene, Holly, Hope, Hugo, Hunter, Ian, Ireland, Isabelle, Isla, Ivory, Jack, Jackson, Jaco, Jacob, Jacyln, Jahsim, Jalisa, Janet, Janieva, Jannah, Jason, Jay, Jaya, Jayde, Jayleen, Jen, Jenna, Jenny, Jesse, Jessica, Jianna, Jo, Joanne, Joe, Joel, John, Johnathan, Jonathan, Jonelle, Joshua, Juan, Judah, Julian, Julie, Justin, Justine, Kalen, Kate, Katharine, Katherine, Katy, Keith, Kellie, Kelly, Kerbie, Kim, Laura, Leigh, Lexi, Liesl, Ligori, Lili, Liliana, Lily, Li-Ming, Lisa, Louis, Lucia, Lucy, Luke, Lynda, Mackenzie, Maddison, Madeline, Maeve, Mandy, Marceline, Marcello, Maria, Marina, Marissa, Mark, Marnie, Martin, Mary, Mason, Matais, Matt, Matteo, Matthew, Maxwell, Meagan, Megan, Meilee, Melinda, Melisa, Meredith, Michael, Michelle, Miguel, Mike, Mitchell, Mohammed, Morgan, Nadia, Natacha, Natalia, Nate, Neema, Neil, Nicola, Noa, Noah, Nolan, Olga, Olive, Oliver, Owen, Patti, Pattie, Paul, Paxton, Pedro, Perry, Pete, Quyen, Rachel, Rebecca, Renee, Reuben, Richard, Rodney, Rory, Rosa, Rose, Rosemary, Rosie, Ross, Roy, Ruby, Russell, Ryan, Samantha, Samuel, Sara, Sarah, Sarina, Sean, Selawe, Shalom, Shandi, Shari, Shawn, Shreya, Silas, Sitara, Simon, Siobhán, Sofia, Sol, Somaila, Sophia, Sophie, Soren, Steve, Stella Jade, Stellina, Stephen, Stormi, Sún, Susannah, Suzie, Tess, Thea, Theodore, Thiana, Thomas, Tiffani, Tom, Trang, Trillian, Trina, Trish, Tristan, Ty, Tyler, Valexia, Vanessa, Veronique, Victor, Victoria, Vince, Violet, Vivienne, Whitney, William, Xiomara, Yen, Zaara, Zack, Zoe.

About the Test Parents

During the creation of this book, I received input, ideas, questions, and adorable photos from an incredible group of test parents. These families worked with me throughout their babies' newborn months to provide insight and valuable ideas to help others find amazing sleep with their new babies.

The No-Cry Test Parents live all over the world, and they represent all different kinds of families: married, single, unmarried partners, from one child up to six children, twins, adopted children, young parents, older parents, at-home moms, at-home dads, working parents, interracial families, multicultural families, and gay-parent families. The Test Mommies and Daddies, as I affectionately call them, became my friends during this long and complicated process, and I believe I learned as much from them as they learned from me. They are a varied and interesting group; each family contributed something valuable to the material for this book, and I am grateful for their participation.

Introduction

A newborn baby changes your life in monumental ways. No matter how prepared you think you are, I guarantee you'll discover that this tiny little person finds ways to take you by surprise. The love you feel for your newborn is an indescribable emotion. When your sweet new baby falls asleep in your arms, you look down at your child and the sensation of fierce protectiveness rises to the surface as subtle as a tsunami. The utter bone-deep desire to keep this miniature person safe and well cared for is overpowering and unlike anything else you've experienced in life.

But the sleeplessness! Oh, my goodness, the sleeplessness! You have likely never before experienced the level of fatigue that you feel with a newborn in your life. And, possibly, you've never before faced a problem that seems this insurmountable because of the delicate nature of the subject of your sleeplessness. Yet, if you are like me, one of your main goals is to take loving care of your baby, and to do everything you can to prevent your precious newborn from crying, or to respond to your baby's distress and fix whatever is causing the tears. Consequently, right from the very first day, deciphering the mystery of your baby's sleep becomes your biggest challenge.

Professional-Speak

"Making the decision to have a child—it is momentous. It is to decide forever to have your heart go walking around outside your body."

—Elizabeth Stone, Author, *A Boy I Once Knew: What a Teacher Learned from her Student*

Altu, eighteen days old, with Mommy

Why "No-Cry"?

When I had my very first baby, over twenty-five years ago, I immediately and irrevocably became a tender mother. I did not believe
that my baby—or any baby—should be left to cry it out to sleep—
ever. I thought it was a cruel and heartless way to treat the tiny
little love of your life, and I could not understand how anyone
could do it. However, I also believed that babies need their sleep—
and so do their parents.

Fast-forward—four children, one grandchild, thirteen parenting
books written (four of these about sleep), and much work with
many thousands of new parents—and guess what? I now fully
understand the critical importance of sleep for a baby's health and
well-being, and I *still* do not believe that babies should be left to
cry it out to sleep. Ever. I *still* think it is a cruel and heartless way

to treat the tiny little love of your life, and I *still* cannot understand how anyone can do it, particularly since more and more research tells us that it is not a healthy or appropriate approach to getting a baby to sleep better.

Professional-Speak

"If you ignore a baby's signal for help, you don't teach him independence . . . what you teach him is that no other human being will take care of his needs."

—Dr. Lee Salk, author and professor of psychiatry and pediatrics New York Hospital–Cornell Medical Center

Since I first wrote the original book *The No-Cry Sleep Solution*, I've been awestruck in knowing that I've helped millions of parents and babies get better sleep. I've been overwhelmed in knowing that parents have read my books in twenty-seven different languages. You see? Sleepless parents looking for gentle solutions live all over the world.

I have received tens of thousands of letters from tired parents. Parents who write long, desperate letters because they would never, ever let their babies cry it out, but they are extremely, frustratingly, and sometimes dangerously sleep-deprived. I've learned so much about sleep issues by helping these families uncover their stumbling blocks and helping their children (and them) to sleep better. I've helped babies and parents gently solve their sleep problems for over fifteen years.

And Then, Things Got Real

My daughter, Angela, had her first baby—my first grandchild! My daughter is a person who does not function well without sleep, so while she was passionately looking forward to her new baby, she was dreading the newborn stage, as she knew to expect many sleepless nights ahead. She talked to me in great detail about newborn sleep. Beginning several months before her baby was even born she began peppering me with questions! Angela asked hundreds of questions and took notes. She paid close attention to all that I taught her, and when her baby arrived she applied the sleep tips with gusto.

We were shocked and amazed at the results in the first four weeks after our precious little Hunter was born! Somehow Angela was able to understand her brand-new baby's unique brand of communication. She was able to tell when he was tired, when he was hungry, and when he just needed to be held. Things in the sleep department actually began to flow in an easy pattern from about a week after Hunter's birth. Angela followed her newborn's lead, which brought them to a beautiful place where Baby, Mommy, and Daddy were all getting fabulous sleep and spending happy, not-*too*-sleep-deprived days together!

From watching my daughter and my new grandbaby I realized that there are so many sleep tips that can improve an infant's sleep *right from the very first day after birth*. Tips that do not involve ignoring a baby's needs or making him cry. Ideas that respectfully honor a newborn's instincts and needs. Ideas that arrange the world around the baby so that he can sleep peacefully and adequately. And when a baby is sleeping better, the new parents are sleeping better, and the whole family can have a more peaceful, rested, enjoyable time during those exquisite, irreplaceable newborn months.

What I Believe About Babies and Sleep

So that you can understand my philosophy and determine if it aligns with yours, here are my main beliefs about babies and, specifically, babies and sleep:

I believe . . . that you cannot spoil a baby. That there is no such thing as holding a baby too often, cuddling a baby too much, kissing a baby too many times, singing too many lullabies, or breastfeeding a baby too often. When it comes to babies, there is definitely no such thing as too much love, and babies define love in very physical ways.

I believe . . . that a newborn baby has joined this world and wants to know what it's all about. I believe that with all our actions and words we should tell our babies that the world is about kindness, connectivity, and love, and that our babies, from day one, should know that we are there for them—all day and all night, now, tomorrow, and always.

I believe . . . that being a parent is a 24/7 job. I believe that our parenting job does not end at bedtime and begin in the morning. I believe that nighttime parenting is every bit as important as daytime parenting.

I believe . . . that right from birth babies have legitimate needs that go far beyond the basic needs for food and safety. I believe that their needs for comfort and human connection are equally important.

I believe . . . that all babies are born knowing how to sleep, and that they just need an observant, caring adult to help them to sleep when they need to.

I believe . . . that the things we do with our babies, the way we treat them, and how we communicate with them is the foundation of our lifelong relationship with them.

Professional-Speak

"Babies enter the world with only one power—the power to elicit the emotion of tenderness and a caring response to them from other humans."

—James Kimmel, PhD

The Nonsleeper Versus the Great Sleeper

Here are two very real sleep logs from two very real mothers—specifically, me and my daughter Angela.

The first log is from my fourth child and award-winning most horrific sleeper, Coleton, from seventeen years ago. I bed-shared with baby Coleton from the day he was born (following all the safety rules, of course). I breastfed him "on demand" and allowed him to nurse throughout the night whenever he wanted to. I was hypersensitive to his every noise and movement and breastfed him anytime he sniffed, snorted, or wiggled—which I interpreted as calls to nurse him (erroneously, as you will soon learn). Coleton also resisted napping, and I had no idea how to help him sleep, other than holding him through his naps or walking with him in a sling, or, as he got bigger, a stroller.

The following log is real. Oh, it is very real. It was logged on tiny bits of paper one sleepless night. I actually published this log in the original *No-Cry Sleep Solution*, and here it is—from *when my baby was twelve months old*. Yes, I actually lived like this for *twelve months*, with my *fourth child*, though I seriously can't imagine how I did it! You can very clearly see why I was supremely motivated to find the answers and write a gentle sleep solutions book! (Necessity is the mother of invention, or shall I say, a sleepless mother is the inventor of *The No-Cry Sleep Solution*!)

Coleton's Sleep Log

12 *months* old

8:45 Lie in bed and nurse, still awake

9:00 Up again to read with siblings

9:20 Back to bed, lie down and nurse to sleep

9:40 Finally! Asleep!

11:00 Up to nurse for 10 minutes

12:46 Nurse for 5 minutes

1:55 Nurse for 10 minutes

3:38 Change diaper, nurse for 25 minutes

4:50 Nurse for 10 minutes

5:27 Nurse for 15 minutes

6:31 Nurse for 15 minutes

7:02 Nurse for 20 minutes

7:48 Up. Nurse, then up for the day

Number of night wakings: 8

Longest sleep stretch: 1½ hours

Total hours of nighttime sleep: 8¼ hours

Daytime nap: One restless nap for ¾ hour

Total hours of sleep: 9 hours

The following log is from my firstborn daughter Angela's baby—my first grandchild, and award-winning amazing "No-Cry" sleeper, Hunter.

Angela used a combination of bed-sharing and bassinet sleeping. She breastfed him "on demand" and allowed him to nurse throughout the night *whenever he wanted to*. Just about the only time the little guy cried was when his diaper was being changed (*"Excuse me! Why isn't someone picking me up?"*) He was surrounded by loving family day and night.

The log is one sample night of his, but most of his nights and days were very similar in style:

Hunter's Sleep Log

4 *weeks* old

8:55 Sleep in bassinet (located at arm's length, adjacent to his parents' bed)

2:15 Diaper change, nurse, bed-share with Mommy

5:40 Diaper change, nurse, back to bed-share with Mommy

7:10 Up for the day—eyes open and happy, no crying

Number of night wakings: 2

Longest sleep stretch: 5 hours and 20 minutes*

Total hours of nighttime sleep: 10 hours and 20 minutes

Daytime naps: One bassinet nap for 3 hours
Three in-arms naps for about 3 hours total

Total hours of sleep: 16 hours

*Hunter was a healthy, full-term baby born at eight pounds, eleven ounces, and was at the time of this log almost ten pounds. He was growing and developing at a perfect rate as expected for a breastfed infant. His pediatrician and midwife both gave a thumbs-up for his long stretches of sleep.

Please understand that getting "long stretches of sleep" was not ever the goal, and, actually, never expected. Learning to read his cues and respond in the best ways to support his sleep needs—that was the goal. Not having him wake up every hour and a half on his first birthday like his Uncle Coleton—*that* was the second goal!

Hunter typically "cluster fed" in the hour or two before bed, and again in the first few hours of waking up in the morning. He breastfed "on demand" night and day, and he was never left lying awake in his bassinet.

I know, this log is hard to believe—but, yes, when I wrote this he was four weeks old and this log is real!

Hunter is not a special snowflake when it comes to sleep. We can tell because when we have a super busy day, when his naps are disrupted, when he gets up too early, when we are on outings and miss his tired cues, when there are other major disruptions in the day, or even minor disruptions to his preferred napping routine, he will then tend to have a less than stellar night's sleep and shorter naps. But when all the parts and pieces are working, then sleep is working too.

Daily, reader letters arrive in my inbox from parents with poorly sleeping babies and toddlers, and I believe that a huge percentage of them have problems that could have been avoided if they had handled the newborn stage differently. This book is about starting off on the right foot. It's about learning and understanding your new baby's sleep needs and how to effectively use that knowledge to help your baby get the sleep that he needs, while you get enough sleep to enjoy your days getting to know your brand-new baby.

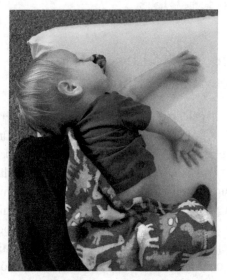

Hunter, thirteen months old

Just for fun, and to compare age-to-age with Coleton's log, I thought I'd update you on how Hunter slept last night. He is now thirteen months old:

Hunter's Sleep Log

13 months old

- 7:15 Asleep
- 3:20 Diaper change, nurse, bed-share with Mommy
- 7:05 Up for the day—eyes open and happy, no crying to sleep for this baby, ever!

Number of night wakings: 1
Longest sleep stretch: 8 hours
Total hours of nighttime sleep: Almost 12 hours!
Daytime naps: One nap in bed for 1½ hours
                  One in-sling snooze for about 45 minutes
Total hours of sleep: 14 hours

Why There Are No Logs or Forms to Complete in This Book

In all of my other sleep books (written for babies over four months old), I include logs to track your child's sleep, plus forms to create actual sleep plans to follow. However, when your baby is a newborn, none of this is necessary, and it can even be harmful, as it can set you up for unrealistic expectations. It can make you feel stressed over your baby's nap times or how many night-wakings occur. Newborns have very disjointed sleep, and each infant has a unique sleep pattern. So trying to keep track of all this would just distract your attention from what is absolutely most important: getting to know your baby.

During the writing of this book my group of test parents did complete sleep logs and check-in forms as a way for us to track the most helpful ideas. You will see their comments and questions throughout this book. They kept logs and completed forms to help us understand what's normal and how the sleep ideas worked in the real world. But there will be no homework for you!

Long-Term Rewards

What happens if you follow your baby's lead and learn to understand your child's sleep needs from the start? What happens when you ignore any advice from others that you are "spoiling your baby" or that you should "let your baby cry it out"? What happens when you treat your baby with respect and kindness right from the start? Does your baby get "spoiled" if you respond to every need? Will your baby grow to be clingy and demanding if you center your life around him when he's little?

These are all real questions that came up in the test group and that I've heard from parents over the years. Perhaps these concerns come from our society's call for children to be independent from the start, and the idea that nurturing our babies is somehow leading us down the road to demanding, clingy, dependent children. Whatever the reason for these concerns, I can tell you that, actually, the opposite happens when you baby your baby. Here's what two of my favorite experts have to say about this:

"Meeting an infant's needs quickly and tenderly during the early months makes him more poised, patient, and trusting. Nurturing your baby's confidence is one hundred times more important than pushing him to be independent."

—*Harvey Karp, MD, Author of The Happiest Baby on the Block and The Happiest Toddler on the Block*

"Telling the difference between needs and wants is not a problem that parents have to wrestle with during their early months of parenting. In the beginning, wants and needs are the same. During the first several months of life, a baby's wants *are* a baby's needs. Many scientific studies have shown that infants need a period of dependence so that they build a basis of trust in their caregivers."

—*William Sears, MD, Author of The Baby Book*
and many other parenting books

My personal experience has proven these statements to be true. As the mother of three adult children and one about to enter college, I am daily touched by the beautiful people they have become, and by the close relationships that we all share. They are all brilliantly independent and capable people, trusting and trustworthy, kind, thoughtful, and tightly bonded to family. They are four of my very best friends. I wish this immense gift of parenthood for you and hope to start you off by helping you and your baby achieve a bonded connection that will establish the tone of your lifetime relationship.

How This Book Can Help Your Newborn Have Amazing Sleep

Here's an exciting fact—just *reading* this book can help your baby sleep better. Yep, it's true! Once you've learned about how newborn babies sleep and become acquainted with the 15 Keys to Amazing Newborn Sleep, you'll easily make adjustments to how you treat your baby's sleep. You don't have to keep any logs, and you don't have to follow any schedules or specific rules. Just by being *aware* of these Keys you will do things that you wouldn't have known to do otherwise. And when baby sleeps better—so do you!

Summary of the 15 Keys to Amazing Newborn Sleep

As a mother of four, grandmother of one, and sleep advisor of many parents, I've been around the newborn block a few times! I understand that it can be very hard (and sometimes impossible) to find the time or the focus to read a book when you have a new baby taking up all the hours of your day and night. So, in this chapter, I have outlined the 15 Keys to Amazing Newborn Sleep. This chapter highlights the most important ideas, gives brief descriptions, and provides page numbers to easily reference the section that you need most in that particular moment.

If you and I had a cup of tea and an hour, and you asked me to outline this book for you, these are the things that I would say. You can use this chapter as a preview, a road map, a guideline, or a review. Or, if life is far too complicated for you to read this book now, then simply follow as many of these Keys as you feel comfortable with, and you will reap the sleep-filled rewards, even if you don't understand the reasoning behind each idea. Trust me now, and then, when time permits, or if a problem arises, you can read the referenced pages that will teach you more. (And please review the safe sleep checklists beginning on page 321.)

KEY 1: Your Top Priority: Get to Know Your New Baby

(PAGES 83 TO 100)

Your baby will tell you what he needs—but you need to watch, listen, and learn. Your baby is born with a unique personality, and you will soon become the best interpreter for your own baby. But it takes time to figure your baby out! You may feel more love than you've ever felt before in your life, but that doesn't mean you'll know how to interpret your baby's body language and noises right off the bat. The good news is that you will learn quickly. Don't let the outside world prevent you from taking the time you need to learn all you can about your brand-new baby. In the early weeks, avoid having too much company, too many outings, and too many distractions, as these can get in the way of focusing on your baby. Relax your housekeeping standards. Whittle down your to-do list. Remind yourself every day that your number one priority is getting to know your baby.

Your newborn will communicate to you with body language and sounds: hunger, tiredness, discomfort, or a need to be held. Beginning on page 91 you can review the typical signs babies show to tell you these things. Review the list, and then watch your own baby to learn his unique language. It will be fun when you can figure out what your infant is telling you! The more you accurately respond to your infant's cues, the happier he will be. If you can understand what your baby is trying to tell you, he will cry less, have more peaceful, alert moments, and enjoy amazing sleep.

KEY 2: Have Realistic Expectations

(PAGES 101 TO 115)

Newborns sleep a lot, but here's the challenge: their fifteen to eighteen hours of daily sleep are distributed over four to seven (or more!) brief periods—day and night. These sleep periods can be as short as twenty minutes or as long as five hours. At first, for your newborn, there is no difference between day and night, and no concept of hours, days, or weeks. Your baby simply exists in the moment, so don't expect your little one to grasp the concepts of nap time or bedtime.

Newborn babies have teaspoon-sized tummies, and they experience rapid growth. They need to be fed small amounts at a time, every two to four hours—and often more than that. This frequent feeding is necessary to fuel your newborn's amazing development.

Your new baby *will not sleep through the night*. Your newborn's naps will not adhere to any specific schedule. You cannot "sleep train" a newborn, and there are no shortcuts to sleep maturity—it takes time and patience. However, newborns *will* fall asleep easier and then sleep better and for longer stretches when you understand and respect their sleep needs. In addition, babies who are getting all the sleep they need, at the times they need it, are much happier and more peaceful.

KEY 3: Learn to Read Your Baby's Sleepy Signals

(PAGES 117 TO 130)

Your newborn will give you signs when she is tired. Reading these sleepy signals correctly is critically important, and will affect the results of every other Key. If you miss the window of tiredness, your baby will quickly become overtired. An overtired baby is cranky, cries more, and, ironically, won't fall asleep easily or for very long. On the flip side, a baby who is not yet tired will reject any efforts to get her to sleep and will fuss over your insistence! Dancing between just tired enough and too tired is a fine line, but, if you know what to look for, you can find the perfect moment with your baby.

A very common mistake is to misread a baby's signals and respond in just about the opposite way from how your baby wants you to. Many people interpret a baby's actions and sounds to mean "I need you to sing louder," or "shake the rattle more," or "bounce me more," or "try harder to get me to smile"—when what the baby is desperately trying to say is, "I am tired and I need to sleep—please put me to bed!" If you learn to speak your baby's language, you will enjoy the prize of clear communication and easier sleep.

Take time to review the list of typical signs of fatigue on page 92. Get familiar with your particular baby's unique sleepy signs, and put your baby down to sleep, rock her, or nurse or feed her to sleep right away the moment she seems tired. Your reward will be blissful, easy sleep.

KEY 4: Respect the Span of "Happily Awake Time"

(PAGES 131 TO 138)

Newborns can only stay happily awake for forty-five minutes to an hour or two at a time. At about three months some babies still need a nap every hour or two, but some can be awake as long as three hours if they are routinely sleeping well at night and getting good, long naps. By six months most babies can stay awake for two to three hours. However, most newborns—good sleepers and frequent wakers alike—do best with short awake spans interspersed with plenty of naps.

If your baby has stayed awake beyond this "happily awake time," you have likely missed some sleepy signals, and your newborn is overtired. An overtired baby will be fussy and find it hard to sleep, yet won't be able to stay happily awake, either. And the more overtired your baby gets the more he will cry, to the point of being unable to turn off his frustration long enough to fall asleep, until he eventually wears out. This becomes a pattern that can disrupt sleep, growth, and temperament.

If you want your baby to be peaceful, cry less, and sleep better, keep one eye on the clock. Perhaps even set your phone to buzz as a reminder that sleep time should be near—then watch for those tired signs. Don't let your newborn stay awake for too long at a time.

KEY 5: Differentiate Between Sleeping Noises and Awake Noises

(PAGES 139 TO 147)

Most newborns are not quiet sleepers. Many babies grunt, groan, coo, whimper, and sometimes even outright cry during sleep. These noises don't always signal awakening, and they don't always require any action on your part. These are what I call "sleeping noises," and your baby is nearly or even totally asleep during these episodes. These are not the cries that mean "I need you!" They are just normal sleeping sounds. Babies are also active sleepers. They move around, twitch, and shift position many times during sleep.

Billy, six days old, with Daddy

If you respond too quickly to every little peep or movement, you can actually teach your baby to wake up fully and frequently throughout the night, or in the middle of a nap, making it shorter than it should be. And that is the opposite of your goal of great sleep!

This Key is of primary importance to bed-sharing, breastfeeding mothers. It is instinct to put your baby to the breast anytime he wakes up. However, just because he is making noises or moving around *does not mean that he is awake*—so be patient, pretend to be asleep (that should be easy), and respond to your baby only if he really needs to nurse.

When your baby is making noises, and you're not sure if your little one is awake or not, but you are feeling ready to pounce—take a pause. If your baby is really awake and hungry, you will—*always, of course!*—want to feed her as quickly as possible, and you'll know right away if this is the case—newborns are built to be able to ask for food, and they can be very vocal about it. However, if your baby is just sleeping noisily, let her do it without your interference.

Watch closely and listen carefully when your baby moves about and makes noises during sleep. If Baby really is waking up and hungry, feed your newborn quickly. However, if Baby is just making sleeping noises and sleeping movements, let your newborn continue to sleep.

KEY 6: Use the Soothing Sounds of Pink-Hued White Noise

(PAGES 149 TO 162)

The environment that your baby enjoyed in the womb was filled with a constant symphony of sound; therefore, many newborns find a totally quiet room disconcerting. Because of this prenatal history, "white noise" sounds can be soothing to many babies and

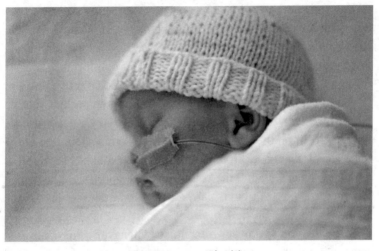

Hugo, one week old

help them to relax, fall asleep, and stay asleep. White noise is an indistinct background hum, such as the rumble of a motor, the drone of a fan, or the swish of ocean waves.

White noise is also helpful because it blocks out sharp noises (clinking dishes, dogs barking, television sounds, sibling squeals) that can wake your sleeping baby. It also creates a consistent sleep cue that tells your baby it is time to sleep.

Not all white noise is created equal! "Pink noise" is a variant of white noise that sounds full, deep, rich, and monotonous. Perfect examples of pink noise are the sounds of a heartbeat, a fan or humidifier, ocean waves, the patter of rainfall, or the rustling of leaves on a tree. In contrast, examples of pure white noise include things like a vacuum cleaner, the static between stations on a radio, and the squeal of a hair dryer, which are all made up of higher pitches and intensities. As you can see, there are subtle but important differences that make pink noise gentler on the ear and a better match for aiding sleep.

You can purchase white noise machines or apps, and most contain pink noise options, though they may not be labeled as such. It will be easy to pick out the right noise if you look for steady, lower-pitched sounds that feel relaxing and comfortable to your own ear. The noise must be loud enough to be effective, but not so loud as to harm your baby's hearing. Find the perfect volume by putting your own head near where your baby's head will be resting—turn on the noise and listen. The sound should be at the level of a pleasant background hum, about the volume of rainfall or a bathroom shower, and the source of the sound should be placed a distance away from your baby, such as on a dresser across the room, not right in his bed.

Turn on your baby's white noise whenever your little one is showing signs of tiredness and ready to sleep—for naps and nighttime sleep. It's perfectly fine to leave pink-hued white noise playing at a low volume during the entire nap and all night long if you would like. Turn the white noise off *as soon as your baby is awake* so that it retains its magical sleep-inducing powers.

KEY 7: Set Your Baby's Biological Clock

(PAGES 163 TO 178)

Human sleep is regulated by an internal body clock that primes us for wakefulness during the day and sleepiness at night. Babies are born with an undeveloped biological clock that takes many months to mature. While biology will largely dictate the maturity timeline of your baby's biological clock, there are a number of things that you can do to help the cause.

Daytime tips:
- Provide ample, frequent feedings during the day.
- Make your baby's awake times interesting, but avoid overstimulation.

- Have a bit of outside time daily, early in the day whenever possible.
- Try to enjoy a few minutes of sunshine (either outside or by a window) when possible.
- Aim for an early bedtime aligned with your baby's signs of tiredness.

Nighttime tips:
- Feed your baby at night whenever she's hungry.
- Keep night feedings dark, quiet, and toy free.
- Keep the house dimly lit and peaceful in the hour before bedtime.
- Maintain darkness throughout the night and use only a tiny nightlight for diaper changes.

KEY 8: Ensure Adequate Daily Naps

(PAGES 179 TO 193)

Before birth your baby slept twenty hours a day *or more*. Waking periods were random and for very short periods of time. (Much of what you felt during pregnancy was movement made during sleep.) After birth, newborns begin to consolidate their sleep into more defined sleep segments. They still need a lot of sleep and need to nap up to eight hours each day. (See the Sleep Chart on page 50.) These daytime nap hours are critically important to their health, growth, and happiness. And, in addition, ample, quality naps will actually help your baby sleep better at night. Sleep begets sleep, when it comes to babies.

Newborns want to sleep when they are tired, just like they did in the womb. But in the womb, the environment was always perfect for sleep. Your baby enjoyed a perfectly controlled temperature, gentle darkness, the soft white-noise thump-thump of your heartbeat, and a fluid cradle that gently rocked his floating body. And suddenly, one day, everything changed. The world outside the womb was an entirely different story. Since your baby cannot control his environment, he must rely on you to create a perfect napping situation for him when he is tired.

What happens when your baby's needs are not correctly interpreted, and he isn't given a cozy place to snooze? He cries. He fusses. He does not sleep.

You'll remember from the summary of Key 4 (page 16) that your newborn can only stay happily awake for a short period of time (forty-five minutes to three hours, depending on age) before needing to sleep again. Keep one eye on the clock and one eye on your baby (watching for signs of tiredness), and when it's time for sleep, create a cozy environment for your baby's nap.

Newborns aren't very flexible when it comes to their sleep. Missing a nap or pushing a bedtime past your infant's desired sleep times can interfere with sleep, not only for that particular sleep session but for the remainder of that day or even the next one. So, if your newborn is particularly fussy and not sleeping well, consider if yesterday's nap needs were compromised and pay closer attention to sleep today.

KEY 9: Understand and Respect Your Baby's Sucking Reflex

(PAGES 195 TO 203)

Babies are born with an incredibly strong sucking reflex that is possibly their most important instinct. Feeding frequently is the means to their survival, so the need to suck is an unstoppable instinct. In addition, your baby's sucking reflex is also a method of stress release and relaxation. Most babies need the soothing effect of sucking even in between feedings. If you are breastfeeding your baby, this sucking will be important for feeding, relaxing, bonding, and milk production, so you can't breastfeed your baby "too much." (And, in the early days, the more you nurse the easier it will become for both of you.)

Feeding requires your baby's complete and focused attention, so it's likely that your baby will fall asleep after expending the energy that feeding requires. It's nearly impossible to prevent your baby from becoming drowsy as she sucks. It's normal for your newborn to fall asleep while sucking.

When a baby gets past the newborn stage and continues to *always* fall asleep sucking, for every nap and every nighttime sleep, he comes to associate sucking with falling asleep; over time, there is a very good chance that she will not be able to fall asleep any other way.

Once breastfeeding is fully established, and your baby is past the early weeks and growing well, you can begin to separate the act of sucking from the act of falling asleep. Your baby will likely become very drowsy when sucking, and that's what you want, but you don't always have to keep your baby attached until she is so fully asleep that the nipple falls from her mouth. If you want your baby to be able to fall asleep without your help a few months from now, it is essential that you *sometimes* let your baby suck on the nipple until she is very sleepy, but not totally limp-asleep. After the first few weeks of life, about one-third or more of the time, remove your baby from your breast or the bottle when she is done feeding but before she begins the fluttery, on-off pacifying sucking that is nonnutritive but sleep-inducing.

This nonnutritive sucking does not have to be totally avoided, because it provides a lovely bonding opportunity between parent and baby, but it should not be an absolute necessity for sleep. So, some of the time, before your baby is totally limp-limbed and snoring, remove her from the breast or bottle so she can finish falling asleep without the nipple in her mouth.

AFTER 3 weeks can use Pacifier

Once breastfeeding is firmly established and going well for both of you (three to eight weeks, typically), or if your baby is exclusively bottle-fed, it is fine to offer your baby a pacifier to help her fall asleep, as it is a soothing nonfood sleep aid and might possibly help reduce the risk of SIDS (see page 79). Use pacifiers judiciously, though—this often means keeping them linked specifically to sleep times or colicky periods only. Don't replace the pacifier once it falls out after your baby is sleeping, and avoid having it become an all-day attachment or the first line of defense for fussiness.

KEY 10: Help Your Baby Make Friends with the Bassinet

(PAGES 205 TO 228)

It doesn't matter whether you plan to use a crib, cradle, or bassinet full-time or part-time or avoid it altogether in favor of a family bed—once your baby arrives she may have an entirely different plan, and she may be adamant about it! Many babies don't like sleeping alone in a bed, and many new parents give in to their basic instinct to hold their sleeping newborn for naps and then bed-share all night. This is a perfectly normal situation the world over and is much too lovely of an experience to pass up—as long as you do it carefully (please review the safety list on page 326). However, there are reasons to help your baby snooze happily in a bassinet or crib no matter your sleep plans—for at least part of the time.

As glorious as it is to hold a sleeping infant, and as wonderful as it is to sleep beside your baby, this is a decision you should make with the future in mind, since the newborn months pass in a speedy haze, and, before you know it, you can have a two-year-old who is still sleeping like a newborn with no desire to make a change. It's a rare parent who wants to hold a toddler for daily

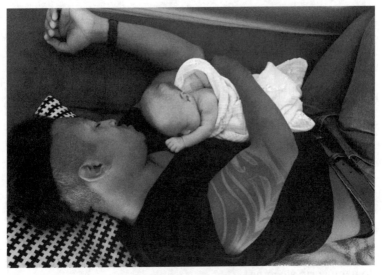

Janieva, one day old, with Daddy

SAFETY NOTE: This photo was taken in the birth center with plenty of supervision. Napping like this on a sofa is dangerous if there isn't an awake adult nearby to keep watch.

1x per day sleep NOT being held.

naps and go to bed with her little one at 7:00 p.m. because the child refuses to sleep alone.

So, as difficult as it may be, I recommend that when your baby is asleep, at least once every day, *put your sleeping baby down in a cradle, bassinet, or crib.* If you start this from the beginning, your baby will learn to enjoy independent sleep.

In addition to arranging at least one nap per day in the crib, it's helpful to have at least one nighttime sleep cycle in the crib. (If you've looked at the safe sleep lists, you know that your baby's crib or cradle should always be located in your room during the newborn months.) An easy way to make a crib-sleep session happen is to select the first sleep time of the night as the crib sleep. Feed your baby in a chair or on a sofa that is *not* in your sleeping room—and then move your baby to a cradle, crib, or bassinet for the first sleep

→ 1x night in crib/solo

segment of the night. (The first segment of the "night" happens any time after 5:00 to 6:00 p.m. when your baby is showing you clear signs of being tired, or when he normally has his first long sleep of the night.) An advantage of doing this for your baby's first sleep of the night is that you are less likely to fall asleep with your baby feeding in a chair, recliner, or sofa, which can happen during night feedings and is a very risky situation.

Once your baby falls asleep in the crib, even if it turns out to be a five-minute snooze, it can help to make it a familiar sleep place. Then, after this, when your baby wakes for feeding during the night, you can either return your baby to the crib or bring him into your safely arranged family bed.

If your baby is already avoiding any efforts for independent sleep, then check out this chapter for ideas to introduce your child to happy crib sleeping.

And remember—there are no absolute rules when it comes to these Keys. If you are a 100 percent bed-sharing family and comfortable with having your baby in your safely arranged family bed, then just skip this Key.

KEY 11: Swaddle Your Baby at the Right Times in the Right Way

(PAGES 229 TO 250)

After nine months of living in a snug body-hugging, pretzel-folded space, your newborn can find it very unsettling to be put on her back on a flat surface—yet this is the safest way for your newborn to sleep to protect against SIDS. To help make sleep more pleasant, many babies are comforted and sleep better and longer when parents create a womb-like experience for sleep by wrapping them securely in a receiving blanket—swaddling. When done correctly, swaddling can be an effective technique to help calm infants and promote sleep.

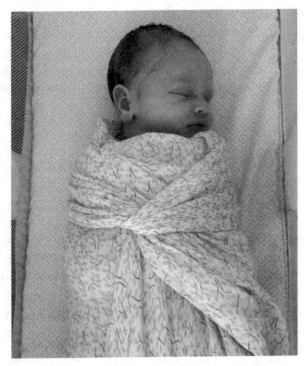

Hunter, six days old

Your pediatrician, nurse, midwife, doula, or lactation consultant can teach you how to swaddle your newborn. You can also find step-by-step instructions for swaddling your baby in a baby care book or a YouTube video. Check reputable sources for safe and proper swaddling techniques, such as the International Hip Dysplasia Institute.

If you decide to swaddle your baby, read this chapter for all the dos, don'ts and safety rules, such as not ever swaddling your baby when you bed-share and making sure your baby's legs can bend up and out when swaddled to protect hip development.

If your baby enjoys swaddling, and if it helps him sleep better, you can swaddle every day for naps and at nighttime, right from the day of birth, provided that you adhere to all the safety aspects of proper swaddling. If this idea resonates with you, I suggest you read the chapter and discuss it with your baby's healthcare provider.

Key 12: Give Your Baby Opportunities to Fall Asleep Unaided

(PAGES 251 TO 265)

Having a newborn fall asleep in your arms, at your breast, or in your sling is one of life's greatest pleasures and should be enjoyed fully. It's easy to keep these precious packages in your arms long after they have fallen asleep, and it is a joy you should treasure every time it happens. This Key is about understanding how this lovely routine can affect your baby's sleep rituals over time and suggests ways to enjoy a balance between holding your sleeping baby as she falls asleep and allowing her a chance to fall asleep on her own.

The reason this concept is important is not about today. It's about next month and the month after that, and the year after that. Babies love being nurtured to sleep; however, if you *always* hold or nurse your baby to sleep, your little one will very easily become accustomed to being held as she falls asleep and as she moves between most of her sleep cycles. Eventually she will be *unable* to fall asleep or maintain sleep on her own, and this is when night-time parenting often falls to pieces. Most parents cannot maintain the pace of being the sandman every hour or two all night long for the first year or two of their child's life, and it's wise to keep your eye on this factor as you move past the newborn phase.

You can avoid creating the almost inevitable scenario of a totally sleep-dependent child by placing your baby in her crib, cradle, hammock, or cradle-swing when she is comfortable and drowsy but not entirely asleep *at least some of the time*. Most newborns will accept this idea much more easily than an older baby who has come to learn that sleep only comes when Mommy, Daddy, or Nana is there to provide it. If you think you like the sound of this idea, there is no harm, no risk, and no tears involved in giving it a try.

It can help to set up a cozy sleep place to aid with falling asleep. Use soft bedding, such as fleece or flannel (always use sheets made to fit your baby's exact mattress size), and keep the room dark and quiet except for your baby's white noise. Then watch the clock for approximate sleep time and observe your baby for signs of tiredness. Make sure Baby is well fed and has a dry diaper, then place her in her bed.

If your baby is already hooked on being parented to sleep and resists any efforts to be put down unless in a deep sleep, then check this chapter for gentle ideas to help your baby fall asleep unaided.

KEY 13: Provide Motion for Peaceful Sleep

(PAGES 267 TO 292)

Prior to birth, 100 percent of your baby's sleep occurred in a cozy bed of fluid that sloshed and moved with your every step and motion. You walked, you bounced up stairs, and you may have even jogged or biked! Even during the typically disjointed sleep that pregnancy so kindly provides, you likely shifted and moved throughout the night. That's why lying on an unmoving, rigid crib surface can be unsettling to your new baby, and why babies are naturally attracted to motion for sleep.

In the womb, the fluid sway of movement was a constant, soothing sleep-inducer, and that is now missing. At birth, your baby is still the same motion-loving person from just a minute before—he doesn't magically transform into a different life form! That's the reason that the first three months of life are often referred to as the fourth trimester. It is a time of transition.

Babies often sleep better when we recreate some of the experiences from the womb. This explains why infants enjoy a sleeping place that is warm, closely held, filled with a rhythm of white noise, and gently moving. Being held in a parent's arms creates the perfect combination of these things—but most busy parents cannot possibly hold a napping baby for the many hours that a newborn sleeps every day. The next best solution is a swing, glider, hammock, or rocking cradle. These are very often a baby's favored location for napping over a stationary cradle, crib, or bed.

When used properly, these devices are not only safe and helpful—they can be sanity savers. The biggest risks are the temptation to overuse them and the possibility that your baby will become so accustomed to them that you'll be battling a set-in-concrete sleep association six months from now—which, for some parents of colicky infants, or for those who are desperate for a way to help their infant sleep better, can be a trade they are willing to make.

Clearly, having 100 percent of naps occur with motion can lead to dependence, but other than that, every baby benefits from a unique balance of the two—motion sleep and stationary sleep. After the first few weeks of your baby's life, I recommend that you intentionally balance motion naps with some stationary crib naps. If your baby can fall asleep in several different ways, this gives you more flexibility and will likely make it easier if you wish to modify sleep locations down the road.

For tips on what kind of motion device to purchase, the pros and cons, the safety rules, and weaning ideas, check out this chapter.

KEY 14: Develop a Hint of a Bedtime Routine

(PAGE 293 TO 301)

Newborn babies don't require much of a bedtime routine since they sleep and wake all through the day and night. But there are many simple things you can do to help the sleep process flow easier and to gradually build a good bedtime routine that will be helpful once your baby becomes a toddler. In addition, it can help you to pinpoint and strengthen your baby's ideal point of "tired but not overtired" by including factors that help your baby to be perfectly tired at bedtime.

The following bedtime routine factors are helpful to almost all babies:

- Help your baby "wind down" for ten to twenty minutes before sleep time by keeping the people around him quiet and relaxed. Turn down the music or TV and keep your voices hushed.
- Bright lights are an alerting factor in the biological clock process, whereas darkness brings relaxation and sleepiness. So dim the lights in the fifteen to thirty minutes before a nap or bedtime.
- Use white noise to mask harsh noises and create a soothing prebed mood. This also creates a powerful sleep cue.
- Warm touches are relaxing, so hold and rock your baby, feed her, or give her a massage.
- Your voice is your baby's favorite sound—so read a book (even a novel will do at this age!) or sing a lullaby or your favorite song.
- Create a short but peaceful presleep routine, possibly including a change into pajamas, a quiet diaper change, and taking the last feeding in a specific and relaxing location.

KEY 15: Live by the *No-Cry Philosophy* and Enjoy Your Happy Family

(PAGES 303 TO 317)

To be a kind, compassionate parent, view your actions through the eyes and the experiences of your child. Be a knowledgeable parent. Read, listen, and learn. Make thoughtful, purposeful decisions. Build a friendship with your child right from the start. Enjoy the moments and rise to the challenges. Don't be so focused on sleep issues or any other distraction that you miss the glorious loveliness of your new baby—this time passes in a blink of an eye. When your baby is (finally) asleep, take a few minutes to bask in the breathtaking beauty of his soft hair, tiny ears, smooth-as-silk skin, the gentle rise and fall of his breath, or those adorable baby snores. These are the moments when memories are built.

Tune out the outside advice or criticism that doesn't fit with your parenting style. There are no absolute rules about raising children and no guarantees for any parenting techniques. Raise your children how you choose to raise them and in ways that are right for you, and politely ignore those who feel they must provide their opinions. Don't create or imagine problems because someone else has a different lifestyle than you do. Be true to yourself.

Sleep is an ever-changing state of affairs. There will be many disruptions to your child's sleep during childhood, such as colic, teething, milestones, growth spurts, illness, vacations, separation anxiety, or starting daycare. When problems arise, take a deep breath, do your research, and make a plan. When sleep needs change over time, keep in mind that there are always gentle No-Cry sleep solutions to address them.

Understand that raising a child is a complicated lifelong event and that you are, and always should be, the best expert on your own child. This is only the beginning of a relationship that will blossom from what you plant today.

Part 1

Important Facts You Need to Know

Newborn Babies Are like the Princess and the Pea

Without a doubt, one of the top concerns among parents of newborns is *sleep*. New babies have a way of keeping their parents up all night long, and then refusing to nap during the day, and then being fussy because they aren't sleeping enough. Everyone has a story, and these typically revolve around the difficulties of sleep-deprived, blurry days with a new baby who won't easily sleep. Even though sleepless newborns are an exceptionally common theme, it's really somewhat of a mystery.

In the womb, newborn babies slept up to twenty hours per day. Twenty hours! Per day! That means that all these sleepless newborns we hear about were snoozing the day away, just mere days or weeks ago. How is that possible? Clearly newborns do not need to be "trained" how to sleep—they know how to sleep already, and they've had plenty of practice! Then why do so many parents have trouble with getting their new babies to sleep? Let's start with a story.

The Princess and the Pea

Did you ever hear the fairy tale *The Princess and the Pea* by Hans Christian Andersen? In case you haven't, or if you've forgotten it, here's a quick summary for you.

> Once upon a time there was a prince who was of the age to get married.
> The king decreed that he marry a genuine princess. The prince traveled
> all across the country to find a bride, and he found many willing girls,
> but it was difficult to know whether a girl was an authentic princess.

The queen told her son that she had a surefire method to determine if a girl was a true princess, and that he should invite the top contenders for an overnight visit at the castle. The queen prepared the guest room for the arriving contenders. The first thing she did was to remove the mattress and bedding from the guest bed. She laid one single hard, dried pea on the very, very bottom. Then she piled twenty mattresses and twenty thick blankets on top of that single pea. On this odd (and very high) bed, the princess in question had to lie all night. The queen knew that a true princess would be delicate and sensitive enough to feel the pea.

In the morning each girl was asked how she had slept, and most of them said they slept well, thank you very much. The queen knew immediately that they were impostors, gave them a cup of tea, and then sent them on their way.

Finally, one of the professed princesses woke in the morning to report that she had slept very badly, indeed! "I tossed and turned and was awake every hour. Heaven only knows what was in the bed, but I was lying on something very bumpy and hard. It was ghastly, and no matter how tired I got, it prevented me from sleeping!"

Now, the queen and prince knew that she was a real princess, because she had felt the pea under the twenty mattresses and twenty blankets. So the prince married her. Because nobody but a real princess could be as sensitive as that.

Well . . . nobody, except a newborn baby.

Your Newborn Princess or Prince

The problem with newborns who won't sleep—those very same newborns who were sleeping up to twenty hours per day in the womb—is that they are all little Princesses and little Princes, and their beds are strewn with peas that only they can detect. Because, even worse than this story, there is not just one "pea" in the bed

Michael, one day old

SAFETY NOTE: A basket and blanket make a great photo, but
don't leave your baby to sleep alone like this.

that prevents these babies from sleeping—there are dozens of
"peas" that disrupt their sleep, night and day.

Newborns want to sleep when they are tired, and they want to
wake up when they are ready to wake—just like they did in the
womb. But in the womb, the environment was always perfect for
sleep. Your baby enjoyed a perfectly controlled temperature, gentle darkness, the soft white-noise thump-thump of his mother's
heartbeat, and a fluid cradle that gently rocked his floating body.
There was no learning to attend to, no new experiences to process.
Nourishment was constant, so there were no feelings of hunger to
contend with. Wet diapers? Confining clothing? Gas pains? Nope!
Nope! And Nope!

And suddenly, one day, everything changed. The world outside
the womb is an entirely different story.

Your newborn now has to contend with feelings of hunger, wet diapers, bright lights, harsh noises, and a day filled with stimulation and hundreds of new experiences. Since he cannot feed himself or put himself to bed, someone else must decide when he should eat and when and where he should sleep. Since he cannot control his environment, or even his own body, he must accept whatever place, position, and situation he is placed into for sleep. It's overwhelming!

Even More Complications—a Foreign Language

Your little Prince or Princess is a human being and has very specific needs. But your baby does not speak in words. Baby talk is a foreign language spoken in body language, facial expressions, movement, and sounds. And to make matters even more complicated, each baby has her own secret language that even she does not know! It must be slowly uncovered, bit by bit, by Baby and those who care for her.

What happens when your baby's needs are not immediately and correctly communicated and interpreted? She cries. She fusses. She does not sleep. And neither do you.

Dealing with Those Pesky Peas

Many new parents do not understand their baby's natural sleep needs, and so they don't realize that many of the things that they do are like tossing "peas" into the path of their baby's natural rhythms and ability to sleep.

What's worse, new parents often misinterpret their baby's wishes, and they "fix the sleep problems" in ways that unknowingly create *more* sleep problems. And before they know it, their baby is six months old . . . ten months old . . . or even blowing out a candle on the first birthday cake and *still* having sleep problems!

Newborn babies want their sleep. They really do! They need a *lot* of sleep, and they love good sleep. When you learn how to apply the No-Cry Sleep Solution Keys you can help your newborn sleep well.

And guess what? When your baby sleeps well—you will, too!

Mother-Speak

"The effects of your ideas are less dramatic if you use them from the beginning—but less dramatic is a good thing when it comes to a baby's sleep!"

—Judith,* mother of two, including three-month-old Harry

*Judith was my publisher for the original No-Cry Sleep Solution book. Her second child, Harry, was born when NCSS was in the final stages of editing. She used the manuscript as a guideline for her own baby, and this quote came from an e-mail that she sent me when he was just three months old.

Why You Are So Lucky

You are very lucky to be reading this book *now*. The things that you do during the first few months will not only make the newborn months easier and more enjoyable, they can set a pattern for the next year or two or even more. You can set the stage for great sleep right from the very beginning, because you learn how to understand your newborn, which leads to understanding the changing needs of your baby or toddler or child. And the beauty of these ideas is that you do *not* ever have to force your baby to "self-soothe." You do *not* ever have to leave your baby to "cry it out."

(I don't believe in that, and I never will, so any idea that involves crying will never make it into one of my books!)

You can take many gentle, easy steps during the first few months of your baby's life that will help your baby sleep better. And, as a result, *you* will be sleeping much better too! You can do this in a kind, loving way that requires absolutely no crying, no stress, and no rigid schedules or rules.

The 15 Keys to Remove All the Peas

The Keys to Amazing Newborn Sleep that make up the heart of this book will provide you with the tools you need to protect your newborn's sleep. They will enable you to understand and respond to your baby's sleep needs, and to create the perfect environment for healthy newborn sleep. But first, let's review just a few facts about how newborns sleep to help you better understand why and how these keys will work.

How Do Newborn Babies Sleep?

"How's your baby sleeping?" It's a question asked by your pediatrician, your friends, and your mother-in-law. But you won't know how your baby is sleeping if you don't know what's *normal* for a newborn. Infants have very different sleep patterns than adults, children, and even older babies. If you have an accurate frame of reference by which to judge your baby's sleep, then you can relax and enjoy this newborn time without stressing over sleep issues that might be challenging for you—but are absolutely normal for your baby.

This section will help you understand your baby's developing sleep patterns as they are *now*. It will help you to differentiate between sleep problems and sleep realities.

The Primary Regulator of Newborn Sleep

There is one thing that affects your newborn's sleep more than anything else: the need for frequent nourishment.

Prior to birth your baby was fed via the umbilical cord *every single moment.* Hunger and the need to eat was not a factor of existence. Once Baby is born, even if you feed your baby every hour or two, it's a drastic reduction of incoming nourishment!

In addition to this, babies have very, very, *very* tiny tummies that don't hold much food at all. A one-day-old baby's stomach is only about the size of a *cherry.* A three-day-old baby's stomach is about the size of a walnut. By one month, it's still only about the size of an egg. As you can imagine, this itsy-bitsy stomach fills and empties quickly, and since new babies grow rapidly they require a near-constant influx of food.

Point to Remember

A newborn's wake/sleep pattern revolves mainly around his stomach: he's awake when he's hungry and asleep when he's full, with very small slivers of alert time in between to observe his new world. And with a stomach the size of a cherry, a liquid and easily digestible diet, and a tremendous amount of growth, your newborn must call on you for food frequently—day and night—twenty-four hours a day.

How Do Human Beings Sleep?

People have lots of opinions about babies and sleep. Even your childless friends with no facts whatsoever on this topic will be happy to enlighten you with their suggestions. So, let's offset that with information. Here we'll discuss a few basic sleep facts, so you will have the information to make good decisions about your newborn's sleep, and, maybe equally important, have the facts you need to avoid letting unwanted and incorrect opinions erode your confidence in parenting your child.

Let's start with a few sleep facts that apply to all humans (adults included!). Without this information you'll be prey to much nonsense that abounds in regard to the ever-popular goal among parents with babies: "sleeping through the night." *The shocking truth is this: no human being sleeps "through the night."*

During the night, we all move through a series of sleep cycles. We rotate many times through *light sleep* to *deep sleep* to *dreaming* all

Silas, four months old

night long. In between these stages, we briefly come to the surface, often without awakening fully. We may fluff a pillow, straighten a blanket, or roll over. Sometimes we'll even make a visit to the bathroom or get a drink of water, but generally we fade right back into sleep without memory of the episode. Waking during the night is a normal aspect of human sleep. Babies, however, are ahead of the pack on this because they have many more sleep cycles and often need help to get back to sleep between these cycles.

Sleep Stages and Cycles

While "sleeping through the night" is often a cited goal for parents of babies, you have now learned that no baby can do this. No adult can, either. You don't do it, and neither do I. It's impossible.

Sleep is actually a dynamic activity of sleep stages alternated with brief awakenings. It is a complex series of phases, and each phase contributes important aspects to our health and well-being. During sleep we pass through these various stages of sleep in cycles. A full and healthy night's sleep for an adult or older child allows an adequate number of these cycles, usually between four and six. Newborns, however, have a more varied and complex sleep pattern.

Infant Sleep Cycles

A newborn's sleep pattern consists of more brief awakenings and shorter sleep cycles than older children or adults have. An infant's sleep pattern looks something like this (a baby who is born early or who has special health needs may have even shorter cycles and more wake-ups than shown here):

Drowsy—falling asleep

Light sleep

Deep sleep for about an hour

Brief awakening

Deep sleep for one to two hours

Light sleep

Brief awakening

REM ("rapid eye movement"—dreaming sleep)

Brief awakening

Light sleep

Brief awakening

REM (dreaming sleep)

Brief awakening

Toward morning: another period of deep sleep

Brief awakening

REM (dreaming sleep)

Brief awakening

Light sleep

Awake for the day

As you can see, newborns have very short sleep cycles and lots of light sleep, and they wake easily between cycles. Understanding the *newborn sleep cycle sequence* is crucial to your acceptance of night-waking. We have no control over this. As your newborn matures, so does her sleep cycle sequence; attaining sleep maturity is a *biological* process, not a parenting issue.

The Human Biological Clock

Our sleep is regulated by an internal body clock scientists have dubbed the "biological clock" or "circadian rhythm." This body clock has specific times of day that are primed for sleep and other times for wakefulness. Our clock affects how alert or how sleepy we feel at various times of the day and night. During our lifetime the patterns controlled by our biological clock change: from newborn to baby to child to adolescent, and through the various stages of adulthood.

Babies are not born with an adult circadian rhythm. A newborn baby's sleep/wake cycles are spread throughout the day *and* throughout the night, just as it happened in the womb. This biological clock is responsible for consolidating a baby's many sleep stages and cycles until they gradually function more like an adult cycle—with a majority of sleep happening during the night in longer sleep segments.

Some babies have internal clocks that set easily and early in infancy, but many others have a system that takes many months to begin working. This isn't determined by birthweight, the sex of the baby, or even the actions of the parents, though we can nudge things in that direction. The setting of the clock can be affected by external cues: light that turns on after your baby falls asleep, noise from dishwashing in the kitchen, the beeping of a parent's alarm clock early in the morning. Missing baby's sleep cues, not creating a welcoming sleep environment, too much activity at bedtime, or not enough light in the morning—these are more things that can skew a baby's developing biological clock, disturbing his state of biochemical equilibrium and causing an inability to fall asleep, poor-quality sleep, or too-early waking. (Check Key 7, page 163, for more information on setting your baby's biological clock.)

How Much Sleep Does Your Newborn Baby Need?

Everyone knows that newborns sleep a lot, but since they sleep off and on all day and night you may not be aware of just how many hours those bits and pieces add up to. If you added up all the catnaps, long naps, and nighttime sleep, you'd likely see that in the first few weeks of life your baby is sleeping fifteen to eighteen hours per day. While that may seem like a large number of hours, it's nothing compared to being in the womb, where your baby slept up to twenty hours out of twenty-four! Even though the pokes and prods you felt during pregnancy made it seem like your baby was exercising all day long, much of the movement you felt was made during sleep. What this twenty-hour in utero sleep pattern tells us is that, no matter how many hours your newborn sleeps in a day, it's less than what your infant has been accustomed to.

Juan, seven days old, with Mommy

New babies don't require twenty hours of sleep after birth, but they do still need those fifteen to eighteen hours. The actual number of hours your newborn sleeps every day will impact his growth and health. An adequate number of overall sleep hours best supports his development.

Babies are amazing regulators of their own sleep—but only under the right conditions. A large percentage of babies do not get enough sleep, and their fussing and crying is a telltale sign. By learning to read your baby's sleepy signs, and helping him to sleep when he's tired, you'll be doing one of your most important jobs: protecting your baby's sleep. As you go through your days with your baby, it's helpful to know what typical sleep looks like at various ages, so that you can keep an eye on your little one's sleep health.

The following chart is only a guide, but if your baby is not getting *close to* the amount of sleep on this chart, does not fall asleep easily, doesn't nap well, and is not usually calm and peaceful, he may be "chronically overtired"—and this can affect his health, mood, and the quality and length of both his nap sleep and his nighttime sleep, since it's a spiral effect. Less sleep = more symptoms = less sleep.

Your baby may not *seem* tired, because overtired babies (and children) don't always *act* tired—at least not in the ways that we expect. Instead, they may be whiny, fussy, clingy, inattentive, hyperactive, or cry easily and more often. A surprising sign of sleep-short babies is that they may resist sleep! This is because they have no understanding that sleep is what they really need, so it is up to you to help your baby get plenty of sleep. This guide can be very helpful as you analyze your own baby's sleep and make decisions about naps and bedtime.

A sleep study completed by Dr. Avi Sadeh at Tel Aviv University demonstrated that even a *one-hour* shortage in appropriate sleep time can compromise a child's alertness and brain functioning and increase fatigue in the early evening, leading to more fussing and crying. That's an amazing finding—and it calls for us to look very closely at the total number of hours our babies are sleeping.

The Happily Awake Span

In addition to the number of sleep hours, the length of time that your baby is awake from one sleep period to the next will also have a powerful impact on her temperament and behavior, so it is an important consideration and earns a prominent place on the chart. You'll see that the span of awake time is very, *very* short for a newborn baby and gradually increases over time. Your brand-new baby will only be awake for an hour or two of "happily awake time" before needing to sleep again!

I call this the "happily awake span" because your baby *can* stay awake longer, but typically if she does she'll be unhappy—fussing and crying and working herself up so much that it's hard for her to fall asleep, yet hard for her to stay awake. It's an unpleasant situation for babies and their caregivers!

Studies show that young babies who typically have long stretches of awake time during the day (more than three consecutive hours) appear to have more disjointed sleep and shorter sleep stretches. So take a good look at that column in the sleep chart—and make sure your newborn isn't staying awake past the time when she demonstrates her unique signals of fatigue. (See Key 3, Learn to Read Your Baby's Sleepy Signals, page 117.)

Sleep Hours Chart

The following chart is an important guide to your child's sleep hours. All children are different, and a few truly do need less (or more) sleep than shown here, but the vast majority of children have sleep needs that fall within the range shown on this chart. This is a guide to help you sort out your own baby's sleep needs; it's not a rigid directive! Use these numbers as a starting point, and then watch your baby for signs of fatigue and overtiredness. A baby who is frequently fussy and cranky is often telling you that more sleep is needed. A happy, calm baby is likely getting the right amount of sleep hours, even if it's less than shown here. To let you see where sleep hours are headed (and to help if you have older children), I've included numbers up to the first birthday.

Sleep Chart—Average Hours of Daytime and Nighttime Sleep and Awake Spans

Age	Number of naps	Hours of naptime sleep	Endurable awake hours between sleep periods	Hours of nighttime sleep*	Total hours of nap and night sleep**
The first 4 weeks***			45 minutes–2 hours		
1 month old	3–4	6–7	1–3 hours	8½–10	15–16
3 months old	3–4	5–6	1–3 hours	10–11	15
6 months old	2–3	3–4	2–3 hours	10–11	14–15
9 months old	2	2½–4	2–4 hours	11–12	14
12 months old	1–2	2–3	3–5 hours	11½–12	13½–14

*These are averages, and they do not necessarily represent *unbroken* stretches of sleep, since a brief awakening between sleep cycles is normal.

**The hours shown don't always add up because when children take longer naps, they may sleep less at night and vice versa.

***In the first month, babies do not separate their sleep into separate day and night compartments. They sleep fifteen to eighteen hours out of every twenty-four, and these hours are distributed fairly evenly over four to seven (or more) sleep periods. (Babies who were born prematurely, or those born with special health needs, may need more hours, and might distribute those hours over more sleep periods.) This will gradually shift into more recognizable day/night sleep over the coming weeks.

Where Should My Baby Sleep?

"Imagine being hired as an airline pilot—with no training. 'Here's the cockpit. Good luck getting to Houston.' That's what it's like coming home with a newborn. And it's like that for everyone."

—Shawn Bean, author, Dadvice: The Ultimate Collection of Advice for Fathers

Shawn obviously had a newborn in the house when he wrote this piece of wisdom! I'd add one more aspect to this imaginary scenario—the passengers in the airplane are all calling out their opinions, many of which directly conflict with one another. And since they are discussing newborn babies, the voices are loud and passionate. Especially when it comes to this question of where to have your newborn sleep! So, if you think you are too confused when it comes to deciding where to have your baby sleep, you aren't. You are exactly the right amount of confused—because this is a topic that doesn't have a precisely perfect answer.

So, should you bring your baby into bed with you, or have your baby sleep in a crib (down the hall or in your room), or use a bedside cradle attached to your bed? This is a question that is difficult to answer before your baby arrives and becomes more challenging the more you research it. And then, it becomes far more perplexing once your little one moves into your home. No matter what your plan is in advance of baby's arrival, newborns have a tendency to shake up your life and everything in it. What you *thought* was the plan may not match your baby's plan—and, believe it or not, that seven-pound bundle often has a bigger vote than you do!

Where New Babies Commonly Sleep

Around the world, the most common locations for newborns to have their night's sleep fall into four main categories:

Bed-sharing (often referred to as co-sleeping or the family bed). Your baby sleeps in your bed with you.

Room-sharing (also called rooming-in or co-sleeping). Your baby sleeps in your room, but in a separate bed, such as a cradle or bassinet. Often the baby's bed is placed directly beside the parent's bed, sometimes in a bedside crib attached to the side of the adult's bed with one side open to the parent for ease of access and to provide the benefits of proximity. (*Co-sleeping* traditionally meant having your baby in your bed with you, but the definition is changing to mean room-sharing, but sleeping on separate surfaces. However, the terms *co-sleeping* and *bed-sharing* are often used interchangeably.)

Separate bedroom. Your baby sleeps in a crib in a separate room from you.

Combination of these. Baby spends part of the night in one location and part in another. This is a popular scenario during the newborn months when babies wake up often throughout the night.

Crib, Cradle, and Bassinet Sleep

Many parents choose to have their baby sleep mainly in a crib, cradle, or bassinet. There are four important safety factors regarding this type of sleeping arrangement:

- Always put your baby on his back for sleep (not on his tummy, unless your doctor tells you to).

- Make sure the crib is safe (see the safety list on page 324).
- Keep your baby's bed in your bedroom during these newborn months.
- Don't fall asleep while feeding your baby on a sofa, recliner, or rocking chair.

Nearly every professional group agrees that a newborn is safe when sharing a sleeping room with you, in a separate infant bed, about an arm's-reach distance from your bed. This way you can keep one eye and one ear on your baby all night long. After about six months of age, most healthy babies can move to their own bedroom, though many people believe it's better to wait until the first birthday. Part of this decision depends on how well your baby sleeps, how close his bedroom is to yours, and where he slept up to that point.

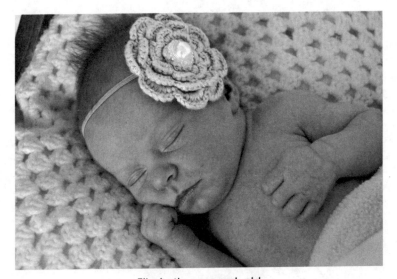

Elizabeth, one week old

SAFETY NOTE: While adorable for a photo, a hair ornament like this should be removed for sleep.

If you plan to use a crib or cradle exclusively, or if you start off with your newborn sleeping in her own bed, you may be tempted to skip the rest of this chapter. If you do, you might need to revisit this section later. Many new babies resist independent sleep, so while it may not be your plan to bed-share, it's possible you'll "accidentally" wind up with your baby in your bed from time to time, or even all the time. In addition, it can be very danger-ous to fall asleep while feeding your baby in a recliner, chair, or sofa—and this happens frequently during those drowsy middle-of-the-night feedings. Therefore, it's not a bad idea to skim this section so that you'll know the ways to create a safe family bed, if you find you need or want one.

Bed-Sharing: Should You Bring Your Newborn Baby into Your Bed?

If a full-time crib or cradle isn't your first choice, you may be wondering if it's safe to have your baby sleep in your bed with you. Many new parents or parents-to-be consider the idea of having a family bed, or find themselves sharing sleep with their baby by accident, and they want to know if it is safe to do so. If you are looking for an exact yes or no answer to this question, you won't find it here, and I'll explain why. After spending more than twenty years watching the news, scanning research reports, reading books on this topic, and having four babies of my own, I've learned that this is a complex question for which there is no simple answer.

My Personal Experience

I want you to know that I brought all four of my babies into bed with me. Over the years we've had a full-time family bed, part-time bed-sharing, a bedside cradle, bedroom hopping, a "sibling bed in the sleeping room," and possibly every other combination you can think of! We loved the closeness and convenience that a family bed provided. (Between you and me, I really miss those lovely times.)

My four children are now all young adults. They are all independent, successful people, and all of them are tightly bonded to us. Our home is rarely without at least one of them brightening my day. We sincerely believe that this bond began with our close connections to them from the day they were born, which included family sleep. Clearly my experience colors my opinions on this topic.

My primary focus is to provide you with the known information about bed-sharing so that you can make the best and safest choice for your own family.

The Impact on Night Waking

Studies tell us that babies who sleep beside their breastfeeding mothers wake up more often throughout the night. But here's the kicker—the mothers actually get *more overall sleep* than those whose babies are in cribs. This is partly because of the ease of waking beside your baby, flipping him over to the other side, and dozing right back off—sometimes so quickly you barely recall the wake-up. (Does it sound like I know what I'm talking about here?) You don't have to turn on a light, get out of bed, perhaps travel to the kitchen to prepare a bottle, remove Baby from the bed, then wait for Baby to finish his feeding, return him to the crib, and return to your bed. The difference results in more net sleep for baby and mother when neither has to leave their comfortable bed.

The reality is that newborn babies are designed to sleep next to their warm, cozy mothers, with full access to breast milk throughout the night. They are intended to wake up every few hours, likely as a protective device, and mothers of newborns have a heightened sensitivity to their child throughout the night, whether or not they are sleeping in the same bed.

The Debate over the Safety of Bed-Sharing

The safety of bringing a baby into an adult bed is a subject of ongoing debate. Many professional groups advise against it; however, there are other reputable groups that tout the many benefits of bed-sharing, some even believing that the baby/breastfeeding-mother dyad might protect against SIDS.

I would be remiss if I just conveyed my personal experience and gave you a big thumbs-up for bed-sharing without providing a summary of the information and recommendations that exist. There is much research yet to be done on this topic, and it's important that you do your own homework, watch for new science, and make the best decision for your unique family. To help get you started, I'll provide some information here, plus provide links to places for more information.

The Difference Between SIDS and Accidental Death

Far too many books and articles link SIDS and bed-sharing. Therefore, even if you are sure that bed-sharing is right for your family, and even if you've done your homework and created a 100 percent safe sleeping environment for your baby, there is still a tiny voice in the very back of your head that keeps reminding you that SIDS is out there and wondering if bed-sharing is increasing that risk. Let me first remind you that SIDS used to be called "crib death" because it happened to babies *asleep in their cribs*. SIDS is a medical condition. It can happen to babies *no matter where they sleep*. There is a difference between SIDS and accidental death that occurs during bed-sharing—and the majority of risks of accidental death while bed-sharing are controllable when you follow the safety rules.

What the Professionals Say

The American Academy of Pediatrics (AAP) recommends "the arrangement of room-sharing without bed-sharing, or having the infant sleep in the parents' room but on a separate sleep surface (crib or similar surface) close to the parents' bed." They state, "there is evidence that this arrangement decreases the risk of SIDS* by as much as 50%." (*As I noted previously, I believe this actually refers to accidental death, not SIDS.)

The Canadian Paediatric Society also recommends that your baby sleep in your room for at least the first six months, but in his own separate bed.

These groups, and others like them, have not done any research to ascertain that bed-sharing is safe, so they err on the side of extreme caution in their recommendations on this topic. In their book *The Science of Mother-Infant Sleep, Current Findings on Bedsharing, Breastfeeding, Sleep Training, and Normal Infant Sleep*, Dr. Wendy Middlemiss and Dr. Kathleen Kendall-Tackett say, "Breastfeeding cannot protect an infant from risks introduced by hazardous parental behavior, and so guidance that infants are safest sleeping in a crib next to their parents' bed is defensible as a general public health message; but this message must also acknowledge that not all parent-infant bedsharing is inherently dangerous, and that breastfeeding, bedsharing mothers and infants are a particularly low-risk group."

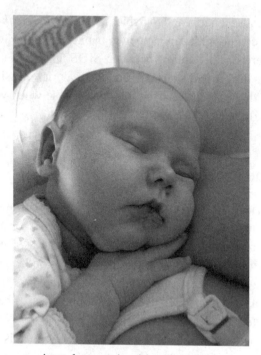

Lucy, four weeks old, with Mommy

Bed-sharing is a common practice worldwide. According to some sleep polls, over 50 percent of families follow some sort of bed-sharing arrangement in their home, and among breastfeeding mothers this number appears to be as high as 60 to 70 percent.

There are a number of groups who present arguments for the benefits of bed-sharing, such as these:

- **The Academy of Breastfeeding Medicine**, a worldwide organization of physicians dedicated to the promotion, protection, and support of breastfeeding, supports safe bed-sharing as a method to facilitate the success of breastfeeding. In their protocol report, they state that they believe research has been inconclusive on the topic of the risks of bed-sharing, as some studies use uncertified death certificates, lack information about unsafe sleep conditions, don't include data about intoxication of the co-sleeping adult (drugs, medication, or alcohol), and fail to consider the sleep position of the baby at time of death, even though prone sleep position appears to be one of the most significant risk factors for SIDS. In addition, they state: "There is no autopsy method to differentiate between death caused by SIDS versus death from accidental or intentional causes. Thus, infant deaths that occur in a crib are usually designated as SIDS, whereas deaths in a couch or adult bed are usually labeled as smothering." For more information, visit their website at http://www.bfmed.org.

This highlights a critical point: the cause of SIDS is *unknown*, and it is different from suffocation or other factors, yet they tend to be viewed together in many reports. We'll talk more about this later.

- **La Leche League International (LLL)**, a nonprofit organization that distributes information on and provides support for breastfeeding mothers, is in support of safe bed-sharing. La Leche League International says, "Exclusive breastfeeding for the first six months is recommended by virtually every health authority in the world. Breastfeeding mothers *will* bedshare. Failure to provide safe bedsharing information may result in more harm than good."

Studies show that if we give a blanket warning against bed-sharing, it will not stop the practice, but it can make parents hide the fact that they are bringing their baby into their bed. It makes much more sense to provide information about how to make bed-sharing safe for those parents who choose this practice.

Diana West, a leading lactation consultant writing for the LLL group, says, "Bed-sharing works so well because breastfeeding mothers and babies are hardwired to be together during vulnerable sleep periods. When they bed-share, the baby's happier and doesn't have to cry to get the mother's attention, and mother doesn't have to get out of bed—she just latches the baby on and maybe even falls back to sleep." West adds, "She automatically lies on her side facing the baby with her lower arm up and knee bent. This creates a protected 'cove' that keeps her from rolling toward the baby and prevents anyone else from rolling into that space. The baby stays oriented toward her breasts in that safe cove, away from pillows. Their sleep-wake cycles synchronize so that they both have low-stress, low-level arousals through the night."

- **Helen Ball, PhD, Head of Anthropology at Durham University**, UK, and a director of the Parent-Infant Sleep Lab, sums up the confusion about bed-sharing research and recommendations when she says: "The issues surrounding bed-sharing are not simple, and so many of the questions posed do not have simple answers. The research evidence is contradictory, and so is the guidance issued by different organizations. Most of the questions are also not easy to research, because bed-sharing is difficult to disentangle from many other aspects of parenting that contribute to various outcomes, and very little research into bed-sharing risks considers breastfed and non-breastfed infants separately. What we know, therefore, is incomplete, and guidance comes with a certain "spin" that reflects the remit or priorities of the organization providing the guidance."

Professional Views on Bed-Sharing

Most mainstream groups, such as the American Academy of Pediatrics, the Centers for Disease Control and Prevention (CDC), and the Canadian Paediatric Society, have made separate surface sleep a factor in their recommendations. You can read their viewpoints on this and other infant health issues on their websites:

American Academy of Pediatrics
https://www.aap.org/en-us/Pages/Default.aspx

Centers for Disease Control and Prevention (CDC)
http://www.cdc.gov/

Canadian Paediatric Society
http://www.cps.ca/en/

While the above-named groups recommend having your baby sleep on a separate surface, other groups question the policy of a directive advising all parents against bed-sharing, and a few even suggest that when done according to very specific safety guidelines bed-sharing might reduce the risk of unexpected death. In addition, creating a purposeful and safe bed-sharing situation is considerably safer than accidentally falling asleep with your baby in an unsafe environment, such as on a recliner, rocking chair or sofa.

Point to Remember
The Danger of Falling Asleep with Your Baby on a Sofa or Chair
Many parents of newborns are so frightened about the possibility of risk to their baby if they bed-share that they make a huge mistake—falling asleep with their baby while sitting or lying on a sofa, rocking chair, or recliner. Sleep-deprived new parents can easily fall asleep while feeding their baby, particularly in the middle of the night. This situation is far more dangerous for your baby than purposefully setting up a safe bed-sharing environment. (See the safety list on page 326.)

Parent-Speak

"With our first baby I often fell asleep nursing on the recliner. Once I was jolted awake because she wasn't on my lap—she had slipped down sideways—but she was still sound asleep. It was a terrifying close call. I had the illogical fear put into me about her sleeping in my bed, but I was so exhausted I couldn't always stay awake when I was nursing her. For our second baby, we carefully constructed the safest family bed possible and now I can doze off confidently."

—**Sarah, mother of two-year-old Charlotte and three-month-old Hayley**

Sources for Bed-Sharing Information

If you are bed-sharing already, or if you are considering bed-sharing with your baby, you will want to do it as safely as possible. You may want to check out some of the following sources of information for safe bed-sharing:

James J. McKenna, PhD, Mother-Baby Behavioral Sleep Laboratory, University of Notre Dame
http://cosleeping.nd.edu/

Professor McKenna is recognized as the world's leading authority on mother-infant sleep in relation to breastfeeding. He coined the term *breastsleeping* to define the practice of a breastfeeding mother sleeping beside her nursing baby. (See page 73.) His website contains many articles and plenty of information regarding bed-sharing.

The Academy of Breastfeeding Medicine
http://www.bfmed.org/Default.aspx

In their *Guideline on Co-Sleeping and Breastfeeding*, the Academy states: "There is currently not enough evidence to support routine recommendations against co-sleeping. Parents should be educated about risks and benefits of co-sleeping and unsafe co-sleeping practices and should be allowed to make their own informed decision."

La Leche League International (LLL)
http://www.llli.org/

In regard to bed-sharing, LLL says: "The latest research shows that breastfeeding mothers and babies who meet very clear criteria, which we call The Safe Sleep Seven, are low-risk and can bed-share with confidence. (1—No smoking. 2—Sober parents. 3—Breastfeeding mother. 4—Healthy baby. 5—Baby on back. 6—No sweat. 7—Safe surface.) And by bed-sharing with their babies, mothers are likely to breastfeed more easily and longer,

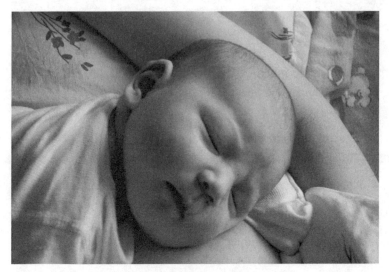

Isabelle, four hours old, with Mommy

Professional-Speak

"Breastfeeding and co-sleeping are huge parts of evolutionary parenting; they facilitate the bond between mother and infant via skin-to-skin contact, co-sleeping works to keep baby's temperature and breathing regulated, and it seems to provide parents and baby with better sleep, while breastfeeding offers vital immune protection to infants necessary for survival.

"While there is no direct evidence that breastfeeding *causes* a reduction in SIDS *for bedsharing babies*, there is ample circumstantial evidence to suggest this is the case.

"Most prominently, cross-cultural data shows that cultures in which bedsharing *and* breastfeeding are the norm have substantially lower SIDS rates than cultures in which they are not the norm."

—**Wendy Middlemiss and Kathleen Kendall-Tackett,**
The Science of Mother-Infant Sleep,
Current Findings on Bedsharing, Breastfeeding,
Sleep Training, and Normal Infant Sleep

and often have much easier nights." They add, "A tired mother may not plan to fall asleep with her baby. A prepared bed makes it safer if she does."

Attachment Parenting International

http://www.attachmentparenting.org/infantsleepsafety/

Attachment Parenting International (API) is a nonprofit organization that promotes parenting practices that create strong, healthy emotional bonds between children and their parents. They provide infant sleep safety guidance that includes information about co-sleeping and bed-sharing.

Professional-Speak

"We know that breastfeeding mothers and babies (including those who have previously breastfed) sleep next to one another in a very characteristic way involving the mother's body position, the infant's arousal patterns, responsiveness to one another's movements and sounds, with consequences for their sleep architecture (how much time spent in various sleep stages, and how and when they move between sleep stages) which appears to be different for mother-infant pairs who have never breastfed."

—Dr. Helen L. Ball, Durham University Parent-Infant Sleep Lab

Australian Breastfeeding Association

https://www.breastfeeding.asn.au/

The ABA's Position Statement on Safe Infant Sleeping states: "The Association aims to provide factual and up-to-date information on safe sleeping practices so that parents who choose to co-sleep with their baby can do so fully informed about the potential risks and benefits for their particular circumstances. Co-sleeping can benefit babies by supporting breastfeeding and therefore a baby's health. The challenge is to lower infant death rates without compromising breastfeeding thus avoiding exposing the baby to the nutritional, immunological and developmental risks of not breastfeeding, including an increased risk of SIDS. It is unlikely that co-sleeping per se is a risk factor for SUDI [Sudden Unexplained Death in Infancy] but rather the particular circumstances in which co-sleeping occurs. If a parent decides to co-sleep with their baby, they should be made aware of [safe-sleeping rules.]"

Professional-Speak

"In sum, overwhelmingly, bed-sharing deaths are associated with at least one independent risk factor. These include an infant being placed prone (on the stomach), placed in an adult bed without supervision, or absence of breastfeeding, or other children in the bed, or infants being placed in an adult bed on top of a pillow, or those who bed-shared even though the mothers smoked during the pregnancy therein compromising potentially the infant's ability to arouse. Drug use and alcohol have historically been associated with poor outcomes for bed-sharing babies, so if drugs and/or alcohol are present, please don't bedshare."

—Dr. James J. McKenna

The Very Safest Bed-Sharing Situation

Based on research and statistics from a wide variety of sources, when bed-sharing is a family's chosen location for their infant's sleep the very safest situation is this: *a nonsmoking, breastfeeding mother, who is sober and free from all drug use (prescription, over-the-counter, and recreational), sleeping beside her healthy, full-term baby, in a bed that has been purposefully set up for bed-sharing per the safety list on page 326.*

I appreciate that fathers, grandparents, and mothers who have never breastfed may wish to bed-share with their newborns; however, in the name of safety I suggest you wait on this experience until your baby is older, which is the recommendation of pro-bed-sharing organizations. The best alternative for you during the newborn months is to use a bed-side cradle, crib or bassinet so that your baby is safe and snug at arm's-length from where you sleep. This way you can attend to your baby's needs easily throughout the night.

The Benefits of Safe Bed-Sharing

Mothers who safely bed-share with their babies often list the following reasons for their choice:

- Having their baby close at their side all night makes nighttime breastfeeding easier, so it increases the chance of breastfeeding success.
- Sleeping with the baby by their side is easier than having to get up and down all night to tend to their baby's nighttime needs and is less disruptive to everyone's sleep.
- Cuddling quietly throughout the night is a peaceful balance to busy days and allows a special brand of bonding.

Those in favor of bed- sharing believe that it can be done safely, and millions of mothers do safely share sleep with their babies. I've researched a wide array of available information on this topic to compile the safety list on page 326. I recommend that if your baby sleeps with you, or any adult, either for naps or at nighttime, you should adhere to the listed safety guidelines. In addition, watch the news and visit the Infant Sleep Info website (www.isisonline.org.uk) for ongoing research on this subject.

Making Your Own Best Decision

You likely came into this chapter confused and indecisive, and I'm sorry that I didn't help that situation! This is just the first in a lifetime of parenting decisions that you have ahead of you. This is a very complex topic and requires diligence and thoughtfulness. My advice is to do your research, discuss the situation with your parenting partner or others who are involved in raising your baby, and then make the best decision for your unique baby and your family.

Sudden Infant Death Syndrome (SIDS)

I know that this is a difficult and uncomfortable topic to talk about, but it's one we need to discuss. For most parents, SIDS is the most terrifying fear of babyhood. SIDS (sudden infant death syndrome) labels the unexplained death, usually during sleep, of a seemingly healthy baby less than a year old. According to the American SIDS Institute, the rate of SIDS worldwide has decreased dramatically in the last thirty years, particularly since the 1990s when the emphasis on "back to sleep" was initiated; however, even the loss of one baby to SIDS is too many. In this chapter we'll cover what we know about SIDS and describe the things that may reduce your baby's risk.

SIDS Is Different from Accidental Death

Some professionals are using the terms "sudden unexpected death in infancy" (SUDI) or "sudden unexpected infant death" (SUID) for clarity. This would include any unexplained death including SIDS. SIDS itself is a medical condition, whereas accidental death is related to a specific risk factor. The death of a baby by suffocation or smothering is *not SIDS* but is a separate tragedy by a different cause. However, too much of what is written about these two issues lump them together in any discussion about baby sleep safety.

The CDC, in a paper about SIDS, says, "although the causes of death in many of these children can't be explained, *most occur while the infant is sleeping in an unsafe sleeping environment.*"

The fact here is that where and how the baby is sleeping can be a major risk factor. For example, when bed-sharing is not done according to safety protocol, it may increase the risk of overheating, airway obstruction, tummy-sleeping, head-covering, and exposure to tobacco smoke, which are all *risk factors for SIDS*. In addition, unsafe bed arrangements introduce the risk of entrapment, falls, smothering, and strangulation, which are often incorrectly labeled as SIDS—this is why these two conditions are frequently discussed together. (See page 326 for information regarding safe bed-sharing.)

The Triple-Risk Model and How It Relates to SIDS

There have been, and continue to be, many studies about what causes SIDS, yet we do not yet have definitive answers. However, research continues to uncover more information. The U.S. Department of Health and Human Services tells us this:

> More and more research evidence suggests that infants who die from SIDS are born with brain abnormalities or defects. These defects are typically found within a network of nerve cells that send signals to other nerve cells. The cells are located in the part of the brain that probably controls breathing, heart rate, blood pressure, temperature, and waking from sleep. At the present time, there is no way to identify babies who have these abnormalities, but researchers are working to develop specific screening tests.

Scientists believe that brain defects alone may not be enough to cause a SIDS death. Evidence suggests that other events must also occur for an infant to die from SIDS. Researchers use the triple-risk model to explain this concept:

The Triple-Risk Model

Vulnerable infant. An underlying defect or brain abnormality makes the baby vulnerable. In the triple-risk model, certain factors, such as defects in the parts of the brain that control respiration or heart rate, or genetic mutations, confer vulnerability.

Critical developmental period. During the infant's first six months of life, rapid growth and changes in homeostatic controls occur. These changes may be evident (e.g., sleeping and waking patterns), or they may be subtle (e.g., variations in breathing, heart rate, blood pressure, and body temperature). Some of these changes may temporarily or periodically destabilize the infant's internal systems.

Outside stressor(s). Most babies encounter and can survive environmental stressors, such as second-hand tobacco smoke, overheating, a stomach-sleep position, or an upper-respiratory infection. However, an already-vulnerable infant may not be able to overcome them. Although these stressors are not believed to single-handedly cause infant death, they may tip the balance against a vulnerable infant's chances of survival.

According to the triple-risk model, all three elements must be present for a sudden infant death to occur:

1. The baby's vulnerability is undetected;
2. The infant is in a critical developmental period that can temporarily destabilize his or her systems; and
3. The infant is exposed to one or more outside stressors that he or she cannot overcome because of the first two factors.

(continued)

If caregivers can remove one or more outside stressors, such as placing an infant to sleep on his or her back instead of on the stomach to sleep, they can reduce the risk of SIDS.

Source: The U.S. Department of Health and Human Services, *Safe to Sleep*, https://www.nichd.nih.gov/sts/campaign/science/Pages/causes.aspx#triple.

Things that Reduce the Risk of SIDS

Researchers have uncovered a variety of specific things that can *reduce the risk* of SIDS. Because so little is known about what causes SIDS, it cannot absolutely be prevented; however, it is wise to follow the known prevention factors that almost all major medical and scientific groups now agree upon:

1. Put Your Baby to Sleep on His or Her Back— for Naps and Night Sleep

There's no question that back-to-sleep is important. The incidence of SIDS has been reduced significantly in places where this recommendation is followed. It's critical that all caregivers know this fact since babies accustomed to sleeping on their backs who are suddenly put to sleep on their stomachs are at much higher risk. Even when you bed-share you can gently shift your baby to the back-lying position after feedings.

2. Have Your Baby Sleep on a Firm Surface with Snug, Secure Sheets

Soft surfaces pose a breathing risk to small babies who are not able to control their head, neck, and body muscles. Don't let your

> ### The American Academy of Pediatrics:
> ### Where We Stand on Breastfeeding
> "The American Academy of Pediatrics believes that breast-feeding is the optimal source of nutrition through the first year of life. We recommend exclusively breastfeeding for about the first six months of a baby's life, and then gradually adding solid foods while continuing breastfeeding until at least the baby's first birthday. Thereafter, breastfeeding can be continued for as long as both mother and baby desire it."
>
> **—American Academy of Pediatrics (AAP)**
> **Policy statement regarding breastfeeding**

newborn sleep on sofas, recliners, cushions, pillows, nursing cushions, waterbeds, or soft pillow-top mattresses.

3. Breastfeed Your Baby, if at All Possible

The American Academy of Pediatrics Task Force on Sudden Infant Death Syndrome concluded that many factors associated with breastfeeding combine to result in a significantly lower incidence of SIDS compared to formula feeding.

> ### "Breastsleeping"
> Dr. James J. McKenna, one of the world's leading experts on mother-baby sleep and director of the Mother-Baby Behavioral Sleep Laboratory at the University of Notre Dame, along with along with Dr. Lee T. Gettler of the Hormones, Health and Human Behavior Laboratory at the University of Notre Dame,

(continued)

have coined a new term to define the bed-sharing/breast-feeding dyad that defines the close relationship between breastfeeding and sleeping: *breastsleeping*. They say, "There is no such thing as infant sleep, there is no such thing as breast-feeding, there is only breastsleeping." In an interview with *Kindred* magazine, Dr. McKenna explains:

> Well, you probably wonder why such a peculiar title. Cer-tainly, it does catch your attention, but it actually is making a very important point, and the point is that models of how [human infants breastfeed and sleep] are generally studied quite distinctly from each other, and I am trying to make an important biological point, that is to say, based on empirical data there really is no way to measure normal human infant sleep nor any way to measure what constitutes normative patterns of breastfeeding, that is numbers of times per night and sleep architecture that goes along with it, unless you have the two conjoined together because in fact it is a biological and behavioral system that coevolved and is indeed simply one system. . . . We are now a breastfeeding-normal culture, and the point of the word *breastsleeping* is to indicate that where you find one you find the other, and it is because of the biological interdependence of the two. They are functionally interdependent systems.

He continues, explaining why it is safer for a breastfed baby to bed-share with the mother than for a bottle-fed baby:

> The baby and the mother on a physiological and behavioral level are enormously differentially situated compared with what happens when bottle feeding and bed sharing. Let me explain. A breastfeeding mother who places her baby on a surface next to her, places that baby underneath her triceps

at mid-chest level, the baby is always put on its back even without instruction, and the baby turns toward the mother and for most of the night as our laboratory work [has] documented the baby is looking right at the mother and is really very, very immobile. The baby is able to get to the breast and away from the breast. Now, as they engage with each other the whole sleep architecture of the baby and the feeding patterns change too. With the baby being so close to the mother the baby detects the arousals [of the] mom that keeps the baby sleeping more lightly but it also puts the baby in position to process the smells of her milk, which also keeps the baby more aroused and more likely to suckle. So, the amount of feeds that this breastfeeding baby will have immediately does go up. In so far as the mother is concerned, she too is changed by the presence of her baby. She is very much alerted to the baby's sounds and movements and touches, and we in our laboratory here have documented how mothers increasingly become even more sensitive to the arousals of their babies and their movements and sensory stimuli. I can tell you that [in] one of our papers we calculated by observation and polysomnography that 60% of the mother's arousals are explained by the baby having aroused plus or minus two seconds before her, and 40% of the baby's arousals can be explained by the mother having aroused plus or minus two seconds before the baby did, meaning *these arousals are induced by the partner and are synchronized and that is telling us that mothers maintain a great sensitivity to what the baby is doing and likewise the baby too[,] that is[,] breastsleeping maintains quite a sensitivity to the mother.*

You do not find that degree of arousal overlap or partner-inducing-arousal in the bottle feeding bed sharing dyad. . . .

(continued)

> We similarly know that the breastfeeding baby is more sensitive and aware of and interested in what the mother is doing and thus is aware of where he is sleeping in relationship to her too and is able to manage the protection of its own breathing much better by virtue of this awareness. So, you get in addition to all of that, the progression of sleep staging of each that is related to the sleep staging of the other.
>
> http://kindredmedia.org/2015/10/breastsleeping-what-is-it-can-the-new-science
> -insight-create-cultural-support-and-resources-for-parents/

I love this concept, and I found it to be extremely helpful as a busy, working mother of four children. "Breastsleeping" allowed me to get my sleep without having to roam the halls all night tending to a baby, or trying to stay awake during many night feedings. I became highly in tune with my baby and woke at the slightest noise or movement. It almost seemed that I would wake up just before my baby awoke and easily shift position for feeding, and apparently this is common. This easily arousable state of sleep is safer for babies and bed-sharing mothers, which is why things like alcohol, medications, or even having dad or a sibling sleeping next to the baby can be dangerous because these things can impact that extreme level of awareness between breastfeeding mother and baby.

4. Remove Blankets, Pillows, and Toys from Baby's Sleep Area

Any item that could present a risk of suffocation, strangulation, or entrapment has no place in your newborn's bed. This includes things such as pillows, blankets, comforters, bumper pads, and stuffed animals. (You can add child-sized versions of blankets and pillows and child-safe stuffed animals once your baby is past infancy.)

5. Take Your Baby for Regular Well-Baby Checkups

Keep your baby healthy by sticking to your healthcare provider's suggested newborn visit schedule, and discuss and research recommended vaccinations. Proper healthcare has shown to have a definite effect in protecting your baby.

6. Don't Permit Anyone to Smoke Near Your Baby or Where Your Baby Sleeps or Plays

Secondhand smoke affects a baby's developing heart and brain, including the brain center area that controls breathing, which greatly increases the risk of SIDS. Your baby's sleeping areas, play areas, and the cars he travels in should be free of smoke and smoke residue. (Due to the effect of smoke on a baby's developing system, babies whose mothers smoked during pregnancy have a higher risk of SIDS, which warrants a separate sleeping surface for these newborns.)

According to the U.S. Department of Health, Office on Smoking and Health, secondhand smoke can cause these serious health problems in children:

- Studies show that older children whose parents smoke get sick more often. Their lungs grow less than children who do not breathe secondhand smoke, and they get more bronchitis and pneumonia.
- Wheezing and coughing are more common in children who breathe secondhand smoke.
- Secondhand smoke can trigger an asthma attack in a child. Children with asthma who are around secondhand smoke have more severe and frequent asthma attacks.
- Children whose parents smoke around them get more ear infections. They also have fluid in their ears more often and have more operations to put in ear tubes for drainage.

Vaccinations and Your Baby: Do Your Research

Vaccination is another of those confusing baby care topics rife with passionate emotions and filled with false information, so let's stop a minute and discuss. When you are making decisions about your baby's vaccinations, and healthcare in general, *do your homework*, and keep in mind these points:

- Social media is not the best source for accurate, up-to-date information. Keep in mind this popular quote: "The problem with information on the Internet is that it is hard to verify its authenticity." —Abraham Lincoln.
- Opinions from your friends and family may not reflect the most recent scientific knowledge on any topic, and it will be heavily weighted by their personal experience and opinions.
- Scientific research is on-going and changes with new information. Check the date of material you read. If it is more than a year or two old, it may be outdated, and new research might provide different outcomes.
- Check multiple, reputable sources, and consider personal agendas that may be behind the information. You must gather all the facts in order to make the best decision for your own baby's health and welfare.

7. Make Sure Your Baby Doesn't Get Overheated

Studies show that overheating inhibits a baby's ability to arouse from a risky sleep condition. Most babies should be dressed in no more than one extra layer over what you are comfortable wearing. Don't cover your newborn's head for sleep unless your doctor advises you to. (Premature babies or cold environments might warrant head-covering, but check with a doctor.) At the other extreme, your baby should not be chilled. Your baby's chest, neck, back, and stomach should feel warm and dry, and hands and feet should be pink and warm. Sweating is a sign that your baby is too warm. It's a natural desire to bundle up babies to make them cozy and to get them to sleep longer stretches, but in infancy it is a biologically protective device for them to stir and wake up regularly.

8. Offer Your Baby a Pacifier for Sleep

Once breastfeeding is established, or if your baby is bottle-fed, it is fine to offer your baby a pacifier to help him fall asleep. There is no evidence that using a pacifier creates any health or developmental problems for young babies, unless they are overused and used in place of feeding. Some studies show that pacifier use may actually reduce the risk of SIDS, although it is unclear why the connection exists. At this time, medical organizations no longer discourage the use of pacifiers for naps and nighttime sleep for babies up to one year of age. They do not make a recommendation of pacifier use for all babies, but if your baby benefits from having a pacifier for sleep you can rest assured that it is fine to use one.

Scientists and breastfeeding groups feel that more research needs to be done before a blanket recommendation of pacifier use should be made, since pacifier use might interfere with the quantity or length of breastfeeding, so watch the news and talk this over with your lactation consultant or healthcare professional.

9. Do Not Use Commercial Products Marketed as SIDS Protection

As of this writing, there are no products known to protect a baby from SIDS. There are no sleep positioners, special mattresses, wedges, or monitors that are deemed safe for use with babies, and some can pose dangerous risks. Just because something is sold does not ensure that it is safe. Watch the news and do your homework, as new products could become available over time.

10. Create a Safe Sleeping Environment for Your Baby

As we've already discussed, there is one recommendation for safe sleep that is often mentioned by professional groups: *Have your baby sleep in your bedroom, but in a separate, safe sleep area, such as a crib, cradle, or bassinet.*

While all the experts agree that your newborn should sleep in *your bedroom*, there is much conflicting information about bed-sharing versus separate-surface sleep. However, professionals and groups who do approve of bed-sharing agree that there are safe-sleep parameters to be followed. These safety factors are outlined in detail for you in the chapter Where Should My Baby Sleep?, page 51, and in the Sleeping Safety Checklists, page 321. If you bed-share with your baby, please scrutinize this information and pay close attention to creating a safe situation for your newborn— every single night, and for every single nap.

Part 2

The 15 Keys to Amazing Newborn Sleep

KEY 1

Your Top Priority: Get to Know Your New Baby

It's remarkable, but true—your baby is born with a distinct personality that exists from the moment of birth, and it will be your privilege and joy to get to know this new little person. Babies are similar in their actions and needs, but they are *not* all exactly alike. Even two children born to the same parents on the same day—twins!—can be very different from each other. Your newborn baby is a unique person with likes and dislikes, emotions and distinct character traits. Your most important job in these early months is to get to know your unique and precious baby.

Listen to Your Instincts and to Your Baby

This new little person relies on you for every single thing. He cannot exist without you, and you are the key to his happiness. Yet he cannot even tell you what he needs in words. Even though it may not feel like it quite yet, you have some pretty whopping significant instincts when it comes to caring for your very own baby. You have within you the ability to tune in to your child and understand your baby's special brand of communication, and, from that, you can fulfill your newborn's specific needs and have a happier, more peaceful baby.

As a brand-new parent, you have a brand-new job. Your baby doesn't arrive with an owner's manual—it's completely on-the-job training. It's easy to become confused because there are so many people, books, articles, and "experts" throwing their advice your way. There is a lot of good advice out there, of course, but there is also plenty of hogwash. If you listen to everyone else's opinions, you can easily drown out your own inner voice and those powerful instincts. It can be incredibly helpful for you to quiet the outside storms, take a deep breath, and listen to your gut instincts. The material in this chapter will help you learn how to cue in to the special and personal connection you already have with your baby in a way that will allow you to understand and meet his needs.

Allow Time for Adjustment

There will be nothing in your life that parallels your first few months with your newborn. This is a unique and delightful time

Jesse, one hour old, with Papa

for you, but also a time of recovery, fatigue, and confusion. Even if this is your fourth baby, this is a novel experience with a brand-new human being. It is time to learn about this little person who just joined your life. Even if you've already raised a houseful of children, you don't know anything about this particular baby to start with! Be open to letting your baby tell you all about herself.

Parent-Speak

"Your book gave us a lot of good things to try with our fourth baby, Hannah, and it has really helped her to become an awesome sleeper. She's taught us that, even if you have other kids, every new baby is a new experience capable of making you feel like a bumbling first-time parent all over again."

—**Edward, father to four-month-old Hannah**

Don't try too hard to make your child fit into any preconceived image that you have about babies, or that others have created for you about babies. Relax, enjoy, and follow your baby's lead. Listen to ideas and suggestions from others, but then think them through and temper them with your intuition. Take things one day at a time, or, even better, one moment at a time, and allow this relationship to bloom.

When Your Baby Cries

It's hard to hear your newborn cry! But newborns will cry as part of their array of communication devices. Just because your baby happens to cry for five minutes while you finish on the toilet and run to pick her up doesn't mean she's scarred for life. Often, babies

> **Mega-Important Point to Remember**
>
> Your newborn is crying. Your instinct says *pick up the baby.* Don't confuse the issue by evaluating the neighborhood consensus on the right response to a crying child. Don't take the time to look through a few books to find instructions on how to interpret or respond to a baby's cries. Don't analyze how long to wait, or what to do when you get to him. The answer is within you—and it is loud and clear. Do what your instincts tell you to do: *Pick up your baby.* Of course you won't have all the answers! You're new at this, and your baby is new to the world. But your fabulous gift of instinct can direct you even when you don't know exactly what to do. It almost always starts with this: *Pick up your baby.*

will quickly move from a fuss and a whimper to a full-out hold-your-breath cry. When this happens, new parents frequently panic. It's hard to think clearly when your precious child is displaying such intense unhappiness. Take five seconds for a deep breath and then pick up your baby. You will both figure it out from that starting point.

Much of the time, a new baby has a meltdown because her previous more subtle signals have been missed. For example, it's often recommended that you feed your newborn whenever your baby cries to be fed. But crying is actually considered a *late indicator of hunger.* So missing your baby's early signals of hunger might quickly bring her to total loss of control. She rapidly escalates from "Hmm. I think I might be hungry." to "Yep. Definitely hungry." to "Oh, my God! I'm starving here; someone needs to feed me right *now!*"

It's obviously better to feed your little one *before* she gets so hungry that her tears escalate, because then she *can't feed* through

Parent-Speak

"I remember this feeling of panic so clearly with my first son. It would make me physically ill to hear him cry. I had a need to take him from anyone who was holding him (even my husband!) and give him whatever he needed to calm down. Luckily, I was more attuned to those subtle signals with my second son so that we rarely reached that level of panic."

—Shari, mother of Matteo and Julian

her intense emotions, and it becomes difficult to calm her down. This occasionally happens because newborns sometimes have clustered feeding frenzies—you may be thinking, "I just fed her! She can't possibility be hungry again!" But oh, yes. She is!

Your Baby's Unique Brand of Communication

You might love your newborn with every cell in your being, but when you first meet you don't know anything about this brand-new person, and your baby doesn't know you. The first few weeks are about meeting each other and learning how to connect and communicate.

How do you learn to understand your baby? First, by staring at your newborn! Yep, just what you are craving to do—stare at your baby. A lot! I know you want to do this—and I just gave you the reason you should. Spend plenty of quiet time just observing your baby. Watch your little one's facial expressions and body language and listen to her sounds. After a while you will begin to see patterns. You'll notice that a certain expression proceeds crying. That a particular noise means "I'm hungry!" and those special movements, sounds, and posture signal tiredness.

The World Can Wait

You cannot learn to read your baby if you are focused on your many visitors, or on being a great hostess to your company. You can't make the most of this time if you are spending hours folding laundry or making meals. You can't be staring at your baby if you're busy updating all your social media accounts. Of course, you still have plenty to do, and some things, like tending to older children and paying the bills, won't wait—but learn how to prioritize. Learn when to say yes and when to say, "Sorry, I can't right now." (This skill will be an important way to maintain your happiness and peace throughout your many future child-rearing years, so you might as well start now!)

Don't let the outside world prevent you from taking the time you need to learn all about your brand-new baby. Can you tell when he's wet his diaper? Can you tell when he wants to eat? When he is tired? When he just wants to be quietly held in your arms? These are the things you should be learning in the early months, and having too much company, too many outings, and too much distraction can get in the way of what you are learning.

How Do I Learn My Baby's Language?

At first, you will feel like you don't know anything! And, of course, you don't! Even if you've been around many other babies, even your own older children, this new little person has a language that is entirely his own. It's natural to feel confused and often overwhelmed. This will pass with time.

If you took a foreign language class, you would accept that there was no way you would walk into the class the first week and already know the language, but you would expect to learn. And so it is with your baby. Believe me, over the next few weeks and months you will become a true expert in understanding your newborn! It just takes a little time.

The most important things you'll want to learn are how your baby signals that she is:

- Hungry
- Full
- Tired
- Uncomfortable (wet or soiled diaper, tight clothing, body position, too hot or cold)
- Overstimulated (too much noise, toys, people)
- Understimulated (bored)
- Hurting or in pain (pinched stroller strap, gas pain, ear infection, sickness, string wound around finger or toe)
- Needing to be held or comforted

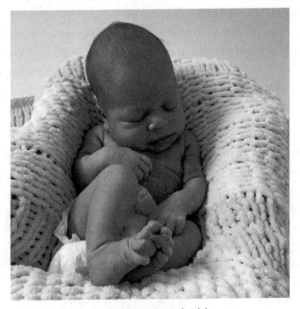

Janieva, one week old

Typically, people will advise that you run through the list of possibilities to figure out what is bothering your baby: change a diaper, burp her, check a chart to see when she has last eaten, and so on. However, most of the time I believe that's backward and way too technical! That's like telling someone you're hungry and having him or her say, "Really? Then let's take a walk, go to the store, and have a coffee."

There is a better way. And that is watching your baby closely those early days and weeks and cueing in to what your little one is trying to communicate to you. And communicate she will! At first, you might not understand. But babies are clever and persistent. They will keep trying until you figure it out. Your baby may signal that she's hungry, but you'll think she's tired. As you put her into bed, she'll let you know loud and clear that you've misunderstood! As soon as you begin to feed her, you'll notice that her entire body melts into you, her breathing slows, and she contentedly gulps. "You got it, Mommy—I was hungry!"

This is one of the reasons I adamantly discourage parents from using any kind of cry-it-out method of sleep training. When you ignore your baby's communication, you are missing important cues to what your child needs, and your baby loses trust in being

Point to Remember

When your baby cries, no matter where you are, no matter who you are with, ignore everything and everyone except your baby. Take a few minutes to quietly listen to your child's communication. ("Excuse me a minute people; I need to find out what's bothering the little guy.") It's easier to figure out what he's trying to tell you when you block out everything in the world but him.

understood by you, which is heartbreaking. Babies are not capable of intentionally crying to manipulate you. Babies cry because they cannot talk. They are saying, "Please hear me and understand me."

Typical Infant Communication Signals

While your baby is unique and will present you with a very individualized language, there are many similarities among babies. So let's talk about some common signals to give you a guideline as you begin the process of learning your own baby's language. Once you get through the first few weeks or months, you won't need a list of any kind, as you will learn how to read your baby better than anyone else in the world. But, in the meantime, knowing what things to be looking out for can speed the translation process.

Signs that your baby may be hungry:
- Opening mouth
- Sticking out tongue
- Sucking on hands (unless directly after feeding, then it's likely sucking for soothing)
- Intense pacifier sucking, as if trying to get food
- Moving mouth and lips in a sucking motion
- Nuzzling against mother's breasts or father's chest
- Sucking on anyone's face or arm or other places when placed close to skin
- Displaying the rooting reflex (opening his mouth in the direction of something touching his cheek)
- Rapid breathing that is a prelude to crying

Signs that your baby may be *very hungry*:
- Crying that doesn't stop when you pick him up
- Moving head restlessly from side to side

Nurse ≈ 1-3 hrs

Time from the last feeding can give you a clue to hunger:

- Breastfed newborns will nurse every one to three hours (at least eight times in twenty-four hours, but typically ten to twelve times).
- Bottle-fed babies will need to be fed every two to four hours, depending on their age, amount at each feeding, and personal needs.

Signs that your baby may be full:

- Slow, intermittent sucking, with long rests in between
- Uninterested, weak sucking
- Leaving nipple resting in her mouth, but making no movements
- Pushing the nipple out of her mouth
- Turning away from the breast or bottle
- Resisting and fussing when you try to offer the nipple
- Showing more interest in the surroundings than the food

Signs that your baby may be tired:

- A lull in movement or activity; calm, slower movements
- Quieting down, making fewer or simpler sounds
- Losing interest in people and toys
- Looking away from you
- Appearing glazed or unfocused; staring off in the distance
- Limp, relaxed face and jaw
- Fussing or whining
- Eyes open wide and unblinking
- Rubbing eyes, ears, or face
- Not settling down in your arms, squirming
- Yawning
- Being awake for one to three hours
- Last sleep session was disrupted, and your baby woke up before she was ready

Signs that your baby might be *overtired*:
- Fretful crying (which can also indicate hunger)
- Arching backward or going rigid
- Flailing, jerky, uncoordinated movements of arms and legs
- Chin down, head nodding loosely
- Drooping eyelids, slow blinking, eyelid fluttering
- Dark circles appearing under the eyes; eyes appearing red or bloodshot
- Being awake for more than three hours

Signs that your baby may be uncomfortable:
- Squirming
- Straining to change position
- Arching back
- Sweating on the back of the neck or head
- Whimpering
- Torso feels cool or overly warm to the touch (Cold hands or feet aren't typically a good way to check temperature as Baby might just need socks or mittens.)
- Red marks on arms or legs from tight elastic or waistband
- Being positioned in a seat, swing, or carrier for too long

Signs that your baby may be overstimulated:
- Looking away from people or toys
- Breathing rate becomes more rapid
- Jerky movements
- Eyes shut, but not sleepy
- Staring into space rather than looking at the person or toy in front of her, but not appearing tired
- Becomes more upset if you add noise—even if it's shushing, singing, or talking
- Inconsolable crying after a period of happy playtime engagement with people
- It has been a busy day and Baby is being generally fussy

Point to Remember

When your newborn wants something, it's best to meet the need as quickly as possible. New babies have a way of increasing their passionate plea the longer you wait. This is a survival mechanism. Like a fire alarm, they are hardwired to get your attention and keep your attention until the matter is resolved.

Signs that your baby may be understimulated (bored):

- Whiny fussing and low-level crying after a period of sitting quietly
- Struggling to get out of car seat, stroller, or chair
- Tossing toys out and away
- Awake and alert, but staring dreamlike off into space
- Awake and sitting in one place for a long period of time (such as in a car seat on a long drive, or in a seat or carrier while in a restaurant)
- Being indoors or at home all day, or too many days in a row

Signs that your baby may be hurting:

- A sudden sharp cry
- Loud cry that doesn't lessen when you pick her up
- Intense cry that includes some breath-holding (This can also mean extreme hunger or that you waited too long to pick up on more subtle cues.)
- Intense crying that continues even during feeding and while being held
- A cry that makes your hair stand on end and makes you want to run to your child

Signs that your baby may need to be held or comforted:

- Not tired, not hungry, not wet or messy, but nothing else seems to make your baby happy. It's time for quiet holding in arms or a soft baby carrier. Physical closeness is as critical a need as food and sleep.

When You Can't Figure Out Why Your Baby Is Crying

Even if you become a master of reading your baby's signals, there will still be times when your newborn's communication isn't clear. There will be times when your baby's cry will be a mystery, and a difficult one to solve at that. When this happens, it's easy to get flustered and lose your confidence. You may feel like you are failing at the job of taking care of your newborn. But you're not! Babies are complicated—and your little one is as new to the world as you are new to being a parent.

At these times, try to take a few deep breaths and calm yourself down. Your baby will be paying close attention to you, and it is best that you try to convey a relaxed presence, as your baby could mirror your emotions. Calm yourself first, and then use those techniques that experience has shown to soothe your newborn. Often this means time at the breast (in our home we call it "The Secret Weapon"), time in the soft carrier, or a skin-to-skin cuddle with Daddy's big, warm chest. Your baby might not even know himself why he is crying, so a little tender loving care is what's needed. You cannot spoil your baby with love—so cuddle your baby gently and soothe him with soft words or a lullaby.

Rested Parents Are Better Students

Keep in mind that for the most part you are the student here, and your baby is the teacher. Babies make great teachers because, if you're slow to learn at first, they will keep trying and trying until

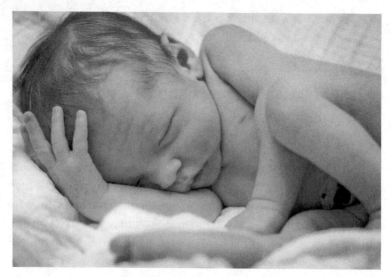

Abel Alexander, eight days old

you catch on. And they will reward you with a smile, coo, snuggle, or giggle no matter how well you've done on your work!

It is *simple* to learn to read your baby—but it's not *easy*. It takes the power of concentration and the ability to decipher the subtle differences between your baby's various sounds and motions. This can be very hard to do when you are overwhelmed with all that is involved with taking care of a newborn—not to mention the all-night waking and the extreme fatigue. An exhausted parent can find it harder to focus on anything.

One piece of advice you will hear over and over is "Sleep while Baby sleeps." In this case, common advice is great advice! New parents are tired. New babies are a lot of work. Adding a new person to your family is complicated. So please, nap whenever you can.

When people you trust ask if they can do anything to help you, suggest that they cuddle the little one while you take a nap. Seriously, most people will jump at the chance to do this delightful job! Even short naps can help you to be rested enough to care for your baby, and to be clearheaded enough to do the right things to help your baby sleep safely and sleep better.

Naps are a great idea, but as a busy mother of four, there were times when the last thing I could do was sleep when Baby sleeps! And I'm willing to bet your days are just as full as mine were. So, sometimes, long, blissful naps are out of the question. But . . . during the day, there is a secret to getting more rest. Your baby will be feeding frequently, right? View these sessions as relaxing time-outs. You can *rest* while you feed your baby.

If you are breastfeeding, and new to this experience, you many not yet be able to rest during feedings, but very soon you will be, and then feedings can become peaceful pauses in your day. In the meantime, take all the time you need to master nursing your baby. If you and your partner have agreed that bed-sharing works for your family, and you've set up a safe family bed, learn how to nurse lying down and once or twice a day have an in-bed nursing session so that you can nod off for a bit.

Your baby will require many, many feedings these first few months. It is your *job* to relax and feed your baby. Don't try to multitask with a baby on one side and your computer on the other, and don't sit there and fret about all those things that you *should* be doing instead. *This* is what you should be doing during these first few months of your baby's life.

Follow these steps each time you sit down to feed your new baby:

- Relax.
- Breathe slowly.
- Push your shoulders down, and relax them. (Mothers tend to tense and raise their shoulders during feeding, especially

during the first few months. When your shoulders are up around your ears somewhere, this creates muscle tension in your arms, shoulders, and neck that can lead to stress and headaches.)

- Circle your head to work out the stress.
- Enjoy a few minutes of peaceful baby time; take advantage of this opportunity to gaze at your precious little one. Start making memories.
- Call a friend or family member and provide an update of baby news.
- Read, if you enjoy it. It's time to catch up on all those novels you've been waiting to read!
- Watch television or a movie, or listen to music, if any of those things relax you.

Simplify Your Life

Simplify your life as much as you can during these early months of your baby's life. Relax your housekeeping standards. Graciously accept any help that anyone offers to you. (Repeat after me: "Yes, thank you, that would be nice.") Your first priority right now is to take care of your new baby. And to take care of yourself, so that you *can* take care of your baby. All those recipes and decluttering ideas you've learned from Pinterest can wait.

Tune Out Other People's Bad Advice— Even When It's Well Intentioned

Many people have very strong opinions about babies and sleep— even people who don't *have* babies have opinions about babies and sleep! Much of this opinion and advice is inaccurate, misguided, or downright dangerous. Inoculate yourself against bad advice. Do your own research and know the facts so that you can minimize its effects on you.

As an example, some people will try to tell you that letting your baby cry it out will solve all your sleep problems. Not only is this dangerous advice when applied to a newborn, it is rarely a simple one-time solution. Even with older babies, crying it out must be done over and over again at the expense of both Baby's and parents' emotions.

Professional-Speak

"When it comes to sleeping, whatever your baby does is normal. If one thing has damaged parents' enjoyment of their babies, it's rigid expectations about how and when the baby should sleep."

—**James McKenna, Director, Mother-Baby Behavioral Sleep Laboratory, University of Notre Dame**

As another example, older generations will tell you that *their* babies slept better and longer, and it's possible that they really did. In days past, babies slept anywhere their parents could coax them to sleep; this included soft surfaces, thick blankets, fluffy pillows, and while lying on their tummies. These practices often led to longer sleep periods, so older adults or grandparents might coax you to try these methods. However, be educated and perhaps educate them as well (particularly if they will be babysitting your newborn): placing babies to sleep on their backs on a safe mattress can cut the risk of SIDS in half, a result well worth losing a few minutes of sleep.

Professional-Speak

"New parents sometimes try to put their baby on what they view as a reasonable schedule. From the baby's point of view, that's not reasonable at all. The best solution, sleep specialists say, is a compromise, letting the baby call the shots while providing a stable, predictable home environment. A baby given this freedom likely will eat and sleep better, and cry less than if you try to make the baby conform to your schedule from the start."

—**Michael Smolensky, PhD, and Lynne Lamberg,**
The Body Clock Guide to Better Health

Relax and Be Flexible

It is a fact that your newborn baby *will* be waking you up at night and *will* be napping on an unpredictable, ever-changing schedule, so you may as well make yourself as flexible as possible about sleep issues right now. Being frustrated about your newborn baby's sleep patterns won't change a thing, and, in fact, it can make things worse as your frustration can lead you away from productive goals. Getting uptight about night wakings won't help your baby's biology mature any faster, and it will distract you from your most important and fascinating job right now—getting to know your new baby, and letting your new baby get to know you.

Gradually, your newborn will consolidate her sleeping and begin to sleep for longer spells during the night and combine those many short daytime sleeps into actual naps: by one month of age an infant will typically take three or four naps, and by six months most babies will shift to two daily naps.

KEY 2

Have Realistic Expectations

A baby fresh to this world needs milk, love, and cuddles—and lots of them. A new baby has these simple basic needs, and you cannot provide too much of them. It is completely impossible to spoil your baby by fulfilling these primal needs.

New babies cannot manipulate people, and they can't be stubborn. Their needs are controlled by instincts. They require pampering, and they deserve as much holding, cuddling, nursing, rocking, singing, and cooing as we can give. As a matter of fact, studies tell us that babies who are carried and cuddled throughout the day are happier—they will fuss and cry less than those left too often to their own devices in a crib, seat, swing, or stroller.

These newborn months pass by in a hypersonic blur, and one morning you'll be shocked to find that the sleep-deprived newborn stage is well behind you. But the ways that you respond to your newborn and the care that you provide will leave a lasting imprint on your baby's life. Take a deep breath, Mommas and Daddies—this is barely the beginning of a lifetime of joy. So please put the world on hold for just a little while and enjoy babying your baby as much as you want!

Expectations and Reality

When you're expecting a baby, one of the things you know for sure is that infants wake up at night, so you expect your baby will, too. It's normal, right? But once you have a real, live newborn in

Charlotte, two weeks old, with Mommy

the house you can be floored by how totally disrupted your sleep becomes. You may have had no idea that lots of newborns wake up every hour or two . . . all night long, every single night. To make things even more of a challenge, they then only nap in twenty-minute segments during the day. Only when you are actually living with a newborn do you really know what it means to be kept awake night after night after night, without any time during the day to recover your lost sleep.

New parents stress about their babies' sleep, and for good reason—it's a baffling time, and you feel so confused. You are unable to actually *do* anything that results in your baby sleeping on a schedule that's anywhere near what you need yourself, and so you stumble through your days in a blurry, half-asleep state, stressing about your baby's constant waking. Much of this stress is because many brand-new parents don't understand what a newborn's actual sleep needs are, nor how to help their baby achieve that sleep. And even parents who have already gone down this path with a first baby somehow forget exactly how difficult this time is (perhaps the sleeplessness carries a bit of amnesia with it?).

Your Newborn *Will Not* and *Cannot* Sleep Through the Night

Believing that something is wrong with you or your baby because your little one isn't sleeping all night and isn't taking long, blissful naps is illogical. Your newborn baby *will not* and *cannot* sleep through the night. Your newborn's naps will not adhere to any specific schedule. As we've discussed previously, babies need to eat every few hours day and night. And their biological clocks are undeveloped. There are no shortcuts to sleep maturity. These early months will unfold in their own unique way.

I cannot possibly promise you that your new baby will magically sleep through the night if you follow my suggestions, because, let me say it again: *Newborn babies do not, cannot, and should not sleep through the night.*

However, I can promise that if you understand, respect, and protect your baby's sleep needs, your infant will sleep as well as nature intended her to sleep. You can protect your baby's sleep from outside influences that would disturb her natural inclinations, and you can help her to meet her own exact needs for sleep. It won't be "through the night" (you got that, right?), but it can be good enough so that your own sleep deprivation is only blurring your life a little bit around the edges, and leaving you plenty of energy to enjoy these early months of your baby's life.

Your Expectations Have a Powerful Effect on Your Sleep Situation

Meet three of the test moms who recently filled out check-in forms about their one-month-old babies. These are their answers to the question, *How are things going?*

Mom A said, "OK, but not as good as I hoped."

Mom B said, "Very good. I'm happy with how sleep is going."

Mom C said, "Wonderful! Much better than I expected."

Now, let's take a look at their actual sleep situations. This is what I found:

All three babies were waking up three or four times a night

All three babies had a longest sleep stretch of four to five hours.

All three babies slept sometimes in the cradle, and sometimes in-arms or in bed with Mommy.

In case you didn't catch my point in your sleep-deprived state—*all three babies* were sleeping pretty much the same! But all the mothers interpreted their situations differently. They were having the *exact same results*, but their expectations defined how they felt about their sleep situation.

Modify Your Expectations Based on Your Efforts

If you eat healthy foods and exercise daily, you can expect that you will weigh less and be healthier than someone who eats junk foods and never gets off the sofa. In the same way, your knowledge of baby sleep patterns and the actions you take in this regard can rightfully change the expected outcome. The more you know, and the more of this knowledge that you apply, the higher you can raise the bar of your expectations.

Let's compare two other test mothers and their results. One of the test moms was struggling with her baby's sleep and said sleep wasn't going very well. I had her complete a check-in form, and she checked these boxes:

Did you read the booklet?	**Once before baby was born**
Can you read your baby's tired signs?	**No**
Are you consistently gauging the "happily awake time"?	**No**
Do you darken the room at bedtime?	**No**
Do you use white noise?	**No**
Do you swaddle your baby?	**No**
Have you tried to remove Baby from the nipple when done eating?	**No**

Another test mom reported exciting results and said her baby's sleep was wonderful, and she was having better than expected results. She marked these boxes on her check-in form:

Did you read the booklet?	**Many times**
Can you read your baby's tired signs?	**Yes**
Are you consistently gauging the "happily awake time"?	**Yes**
Do you darken the room at bedtime?	**Yes**
Do you use white noise?	**Yes**
Do you swaddle your baby?	**Yes**
Have you tried to remove Baby from the nipple when done eating?	**About half the time**

This comparison demonstrates another aspect of expectations. If you read, understand, and consistently apply the 15 Keys, you can modify your expectations, since it's likely that your baby will sleep better as a result of your efforts.

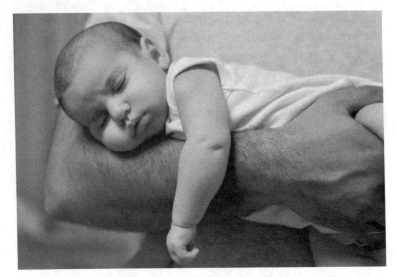

Stellina, one month old, with Daddy

Babies Are Unpredictable

When we talk about babies, there are always a few who make their own rules. If you happen to have a very sleepy newborn, you might think that other people must be exaggerating the number of times their babies wake up in the night. (They're not! You just lucked out!) Some babies will respond so well to the 15 Keys that they will sleep four or five hours straight, leaving their parents to worry if they should wake them for a feeding. The answer to this is an unequivocal maybe.

If your baby happens to fall into a pattern of long sleep stretches, you'll need to talk to your baby's doctor and find out if it's okay for your particular baby to stretch the time between feedings. (The Test Parents in this situation were blissfully happy to be in a position to ask that question!) The answer will depend on your baby's size, health, how much feeding occurs during waking hours, and possibly other factors as well.

The first week or so can be super-sleepy times for some babies. It can lull us into thinking we have been blessed with one of these prize-winning sleepers—until that fresh-from-the-womb sleepiness wears off and lo and behold—we have a normal newborn sleeper! Babies. They are unpredictable!

> "Dear Society:
>
> "Can we please stop asking new parents if their child is a 'good baby' and a 'good sleeper'? The answer to the first is a resounding *yes* because all babies are precious, and the answer to the second is a big fat *no* because newborns wake up a lot. Great, thanks."
>
> **—Halley Watson Kim**
> **Mother and blogger at**
> **https://peaceloveandspitup.wordpress.com**

When Will My Baby Sleep Through the Night?

The medical definition of "sleeping through the night" for a newborn is a five-hour stretch. That's five hours—*not* the eight, ten, or twelve hours that we may wish for! *Most* babies awaken two to three times a night up to six months, and once or twice a night up to one year old. A baby is considered to be "sleeping through the night" when he sleeps five consecutive hours without waking to feed. While this may not be *your* definition of sleeping through the night, it is the reasonable yardstick by which we measure a young baby's sleep. Yes—some newborns achieve this stretch much sooner than others, but they all get there eventually.

5 hrs = newborn sleeping Thagh night

My Friend's Newborn Sleeps So Much Better Than Mine!

All you have to do is bring up the topic of sleep around new parents, and you can see the defensive confusion on their faces. Our society is inundated with dictates that tell us our baby should be sleeping all night, and if he's not it is our fault somehow. There is so much pressure to prove that we are good parents and doing the right thing by having a sleeping baby that many parents hide their real truth from their friends and family members or even their doctors. The parenting website Netmums questioned almost 11,000 parents about sleep issues. The findings showed that the pressure to be a perfect parent is so great that around one-third admitted to lying about their child's sleeping habits. (And how many more lied but didn't admit it?)

Understanding the Science of Sleep

If you know what to expect in the sleep department, you can relax and enjoy your newborn fully. Having realistic expectations right up front can take a lot of pressure off of you and your new baby, and help you combat any bad advice thrown your way. So, erase all the opinions and theories that you've heard about newborn babies up to now, and let's go over a summary of a few important facts:

- Brand-new babies sleep fifteen to eighteen hours (or more!) out of every twenty-four-hour day. A three-month-old needs about fifteen hours of sleep per day. By six months a baby still needs fourteen to fifteen hours of sleep each day.
- A newborn's many sleep hours are distributed evenly over four to seven (or more!) brief periods—day and night.

Through those first few weeks of life, many newborns will sleep eight to nine hours throughout the day and another eight hours throughout the night—broken up into pieces, remember.

- Babies who are premature, sick, or have special needs may sleep even more hours each day, but they tend to break their sleep up into even shorter spans.
- Newborn sleep period lengths are inconsistent and range in length from twenty minutes to five or more hours, gradually working their way toward longer periods of time over the early months.
- At first, for your newborn, there is no difference between day and night. It takes about six to nine weeks for an infant's biological clock to even *begin* maturing, and this internal sleep/wake clock doesn't work smoothly until about four to five months of age.
- Newborns awaken very easily because they spend much of their time in the lightest stage of sleep.
- Remember, five consecutive hours is considered "sleeping through the night" for a young baby.
- Newborn babies have very tiny tummies (about the size of a cherry at birth, and by one month, it's still only the size of an egg), and they experience rapid growth. They need to be fed every two to four hours—and oftentimes more than that.

The more facts you know about infant sleep, the more realistic your expectations can be. You can read additional detailed information about this topic in the section beginning on page 41, "How Do Newborns Sleep?"

6-9 weeks for the biological clock to start.

Understanding Newborn Feeding Needs

Newborn babies cannot and should not be put on a sleep and feeding schedule, and it can be dangerous to your infant's well-being to even try. During the first weeks of your baby's life, she should sleep when she's tired and eat when she's hungry—it's that simple.

Keep in mind that all newborn babies need to be fed often, and according to their own unique needs. Breastfed babies will nurse about every one to three hours; at least eight times in twenty-four hours; but typically more like ten to twelve times. (As long as your baby is healthy and growing and has plenty of wet diapers, you don't need to count feedings.) Follow your baby's lead here. Keep in mind that milk does not "pour" out of the breast as you feed your newborn. It is more like a drip system, so each feeding takes time and can last from twenty minutes to an hour.

Formula-fed babies need to eat every two to four hours, depending on their age and personal needs, so you should talk to your healthcare provider about your baby.

Test Mom Question

Sometimes my newborn wants to breastfeed every hour during the day! And each session is twenty to forty-five minutes long. Is that normal? Can I overfeed her?

Yep, it's normal! And no, you can't over-breastfeed your baby.

Please talk to a lactation consultant if you have breastfeeding questions—these consultants are very happy to help you. Find one through your birth center, doctor, midwife, doula, or hospital. Or check La Leche League online for support at http://www.llli.org/webus.html.

A full-term, healthy baby might stretch the feeding schedule at times, but you should get the okay from your baby's healthcare provider for these longer spans. Check with your baby's doctor or healthcare provider about how often your unique baby should be fed. And remember, you know your baby best.

Night-Waking Serves a Purpose

No expert, chart, or book knows what your baby needs more than your baby knows what she needs. When your little one is hungry she wants to eat, when she is tired she wants to sleep. Encouraging a baby to sleep through the night too soon may be possible—but it's not in the best interest of the baby. This is why you should not feel pressured to get your baby to sleep longer by ignoring her needs at night.

Mother-Speak

"I remember when Rachael was a newborn, she would suck away happily for most of the day for a week or two at a time during one of her growth spurts. Had I not known that this sometimes happens, and that it is necessary for the wild growth babies sometimes experience, I might have tried to enforce a schedule. Instead, I simply accepted my role in life then: a binky with legs."

—Vanessa, mother of two-year-old Rachael

Newborns Have "Growth Spurts" That Affect Sleep

New babies grow rapidly, but they don't do it in one straight line of growth. Some days or weeks they grow faster than others. During these "spurts" your baby seems constantly hungry and doesn't sleep for long periods. He just wants to snooze and feed, snooze and feed, snooze and feed!

How do you know if it is a growth spurt or a sleep problem? If this is a "spurt," as the name implies, it's a sudden and unusual burst of behavior that's different from recent patterns—such as a baby who is suddenly taking shorter naps with lots of feedings in between, or who is suddenly extra fussy at bedtime and waking up more often through the night.

These "growth spurts" can last a few days or a week or more. When this happens, you'll want to follow your infant's lead and

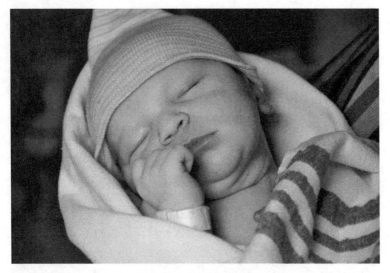

Matteo, a few hours old

reduce outside stimulation. And get some extra rest yourself! If you're breastfeeding, make sure you are staying hydrated and eating plenty of good nutritious foods.

New milestones can also affect sleep: once your baby starts to roll over and sit up, these newfound physical abilities may keep him up in the night. He'll wake up and want to practice his new skills! The best thing to do about this is to give him lots of supervised tummy time play during the day so that he can master his ability to control his body. This doesn't take long, and once your baby learns how to control his body and move around he will find it easier to get a comfortable sleeping position.

Point to Remember

It will work. Except when it doesn't . . .

Babies cannot be programmed. Babies are human beings. They are unique and complex. Their temperament and behavior can vary day to day. You can do everything outlined in the 15 Keys—and still have a baby who wakes up every two hours all night and will only nap for an hour at a time. However, things are improving, even if you don't immediately see it. Stay in tune with your baby. Keep following the Keys, and soon enough your little one will be sleeping well day and night.

The Road to Sleep Is More like a Dance

You will likely find that the road to all-night sleep and great naps is a long and winding one with many detours. It's almost like a dance—two steps forward, one step back, and plenty of side-sashaying in between.

It's very common to see things gradually moving into place over a period of a month or two—naps are getting longer, night sleep is settling into a pattern with your baby sleeping four hours in a stretch, then five hours, then six hours . . . and each time feeding and falling back to sleep easily. You are ready to brag to the world about your fantastic little sleeper—and then, suddenly, everything goes backward! There's a night or two or seven in a row when he's up every two or three hours fussing, crying, and wanting to feed, and he will only take catnaps during the day! That's when you need to pause, reread the Keys, and apply whichever ones seem right to you—since, of course, you know your baby best. With a little adjustment to what you've been doing and an added dose of love and patience, your baby will begin to settle into a more pleasant sleep routine. You'll take a deep breath and enjoy the quiet nights.

Mother-Speak

"Some days we wanted to give up, it got so frustrating trying to figure this all out. We kept following the Keys and persisted in learning to read our baby. We had our ups and downs. But we kept on track. Now I'm so glad that we did—our baby is sleeping so peacefully every night! We all are!"

—Amanda, mom to five-month-old Johnathan

What Does "Amazing" Sleep Look Like?

Every baby is unique, and, just like adults, they sleep differently from one another. There are so many different factors that affect how a baby sleeps, it's almost impossible to compare one to another—and I encourage you to not even try.

Many times a family finds a rhythm that works for them. They've arranged sleeping places and routines that feel right to them, and they are happy. Then a friend, neighbor, book, or Internet post pulls the rug out from under them, and they realize that what they are doing is all wrong! They become frustrated, and they try new things. Instead of seeing improvement, though, sleep deteriorates.

But wait a minute! I just said they were *happy* and things *worked for them*. What happened? Their change of perception came from an outside source that created confusion and disillusionment. It forced them into doing things that were not right for them at all. It took a good situation and completely destroyed it. Do not let this happen to you.

Here's how you should define amazing sleep during the newborn months:

- All the places where your baby sleeps are safe.
- Your baby is feeding well, growing well, and healthy.
- You are reading and responding to your baby's cues (day and night).
- You are happy with the way things are working, or the progress you are making.

If this describes your newborn's sleep situation, then nothing needs to be changed, regardless of what anyone else has to say. Whenever anyone asks you, "How's your baby's sleep?" you can honestly answer: "Amazing!"

KEY 3

Learn to Read Your Baby's Sleepy Signals

Your newborn needs a great amount of sleep—up to eighteen hours a day—but your baby doesn't know that! He exists in each moment and responds to his body's needs and his environment. Even if he's tired, your baby might only sleep when the situation is exactly right for slumber. Your baby doesn't understand anything about his own sleep needs but is instead driven by instinct. When your infant is tired, he'll sleep—or he will fuss and cry about not sleeping.

The good news is that when your baby is tired, he will show you this in many different ways. The not-so-good news is that it may take you some time and a lot of practice to learn how to understand the signals. The best news is that once you learn to read your baby's signals and respond to them, sleep will be blissful.

Your baby speaks a language that is unique, complex, and often confusing, and some of his communication is very subtle. If you don't pick up on your baby's sleepy cues when they first appear, your newborn can quickly dissolve into fussing and tears. Babies can become overtired very quickly, and when that happens they find it hard to fall asleep, but hard to stay awake, too. So they are stuck in the middle where they fuss and cry. For that reason, one of the most important keys to obtaining awesome newborn sleep is to learn how to read your baby's sleepy signals correctly: when to put your baby down to sleep, when to help him fall asleep by nursing, feeding, or rocking him, and how to identify when he is too overtired to be able to put himself to sleep and requires your assistance.

A baby cannot put himself to bed, nor can he understand his own sleep needs. Yet a baby who is encouraged to stay awake when his body is craving sleep is typically a very unhappy baby. Over time, this pattern develops into sleep deprivation, which creates more disjointed sleep and further complicates your baby's developing sleep maturity.

Parent-Speak

"Learning about sleepy signals and how much sleep babies need has been very important. A funny thing to illustrate this happened the other night when my husband was doing bedtime. The babies had been fed and changed, and he was singing to them and rocking them, but they wouldn't stop crying. He said he finally put them down in their cradles—and they fell right asleep! We laughed because in trying to figure out what was wrong at bedtime he said he forgot he needed to just let them sleep."

—**Elizabeth and Daniel, parents to Luke and Lily, twins, two months old**

How to Learn Your Baby's Language

The most natural way to learn about your baby is the simplest—spend time together. Time that is unrushed and undistracted is best, but all time in your baby's company counts.

During the newborn months, playtime with your baby is mainly about face-to-face engagement. For the most part, toys aren't necessary, since you are your newborn's most precious toy. The best way to learn about your baby is to spend lots of time in face-to-face conversation. Talk, sing, or hum to your little one. And watch her tiny face. Her smiles, grimaces, and eye contact will teach you so much about her. Watch her body: flailing about, stiffening her limbs, or curling softly into you are some of the ways your baby's body language conveys her needs.

During these early weeks, I suggest that you simplify your life. Cook easy meals, forget about folding towels, and live with a little more dust than you normally do. You may want to limit visits to your innermost circle of people. Of course, your closest family and friends will want to get to know this little person, too, but make sure that visiting isn't your primary activity these days—except for those truly helpful people who can make a meal, run a load of laundry, or hold the baby while you nap!

The more time you spend engaged with your baby, the sooner you will master your child's unique language and the signals that demonstrate a need to sleep. So, if your home has a revolving door of people coming in and out every day, and you're struggling to visit with them and cook complex meals or keep up your usual housekeeping routine, this can prevent you from gaining the hours of quiet concentration needed to get to know your little one.

Point to Remember

This is baby time. Your most important job is learning all about your baby. As you relax and enjoy your little one, you will soon be able to interpret all the subtle signals that your baby sends you. Let the world wait while you accomplish this important feat.

Jianna, six weeks old

Newborn Signs of Tiredness

There are a variety of typical signs of tiredness that babies show us—your little one may demonstrate only one or two of these, or a whole assortment of these signs. Some days your baby may show one particular sign, but, later that day, she may demonstrate tiredness in a different way.

Although babies are each unique in their communication, there are some typical ways that newborns show their fatigue. The list of the most common things that say "I'm tired!" can be found on pages 92 through 93 in Key 1, Get to Know Your Baby. Familiarize

yourself with this list, and add those signs that y
your own. This will help you to learn to read you
sleepy signs.

When You See Signs of Tiredness

When your baby shows signs of fatigue, it's not time to launch into a long presleep ritual. It's time to put your baby to bed—immediately—when those signs show up. When your baby signals tiredness, there is a window of opportunity for quickly falling asleep. When you identify and respond to that window of opportunity, you will enable your baby to fall asleep much, much more easily.

If you miss your baby's signs of tiredness, he can quickly move into an overtired phase. The problem with this is that an overtired baby doesn't fall asleep easily—instead he gets a second wind. He becomes ramped up, fussy, and anxious, and those feelings can prevent the sleep that he craves.

Don't worry—by watching your child carefully you'll get to know your own baby better than anyone else in the whole world. And soon, even if your baby doesn't show *any* of the signs on the list, your intuition will let you know when Baby needs to sleep.

Parent-Speak

"My friend is following a theory of rigidly set hours for her baby's naps and bedtime. Her baby fusses and cries sometimes for an hour or even more before she finally puts him to bed. My baby is the same age, but I have been paying attention to her tired signs. When she's been up for at least two hours and begins to look tired I get her settled for bed and she falls asleep easily and never cries at all."

—Catherine, mother of three-month-old Rose

Reading Tiredness Accurately Means Better Sleep Overall

In the test parent group, I discovered a direct correlation between parents who said that they could clearly read their baby's sleepy signals and those babies having better sleep overall. Those who said they could not tell when their baby was tired reported shorter naps, skipped naps, and a fussier prebedtime hour.

This seems to spiral into a cycle, either good or bad. Parents who were more in tune with their babies had babies who slept better, so they themselves slept better. As they were well rested, they seemed to be more able to read their babies. This helps a parent be more calm and confident, which can improve the entire parenting experience. Everyone is happier, so you are able to tackle new problems or setbacks with the same confidence. It's about building self-confidence as a mother or father, and about your baby feeling confident in your responses to his needs as well.

Parent-Speak

"It's been so much better now that I'm picking up on my daughter's tired cues. The yawns and grunts signal bedtime, and I change her and wrap her in a sleeping sack, take her immediately to her bassinet, and put on white noise. It usually takes about ten to fifteen minutes and she's out like a light. It may be my imagination, but now that I'm reading her sleep needs more accurately I just seem to get a bigger smile from her when I come get her in the morning."

—Sofia, mother of three-month-old Xiomara

What If You Can't Seem to Read Your Baby's Signs of Tiredness?

There are some babies who send very subtle signs of tiredness, and some parents who have a harder time deciphering the signs.

Test Parent Question

I have been carefully watching for sleepy signs in my five-week-old son. When I see the signs I put him down in his bed. He will often lie there for ages, calm and awake, but he eventually falls asleep. I feel guilty about leaving him in bed when he is awake. I feel confused about whether I'm doing the right thing.

Congratulations, new mommy! You are paying attention to your baby's "language," and that is most important. As far as leaving him awake in his bed—you say he "lies there for ages," but does he, really? In this case, your anticipation might make the time seem longer—seven or eight minutes could easily feel like "ages"! So I would suggest you watch the clock and see how long he actually lies in bed.

If your baby is relaxed and not crying, and just falling asleep in his own time, then there is nothing wrong with letting him rest for even ten to fifteen minutes. However, if he's in there for much longer, then I'd be reluctant to leave him, as quiet babies may have needs that they may not be communicating. Not all babies scream when they need something!

You can help by making sure it's an appropriate time for sleep (has he been awake an hour or two?) and that he's showing clear signs of tiredness, and then keeping the room slightly darkened and adding rumbly white noise to help him gently go to sleep. Refer to page 293 for more ideas to help your baby fall asleep calmly and quickly.

If you and your baby fall into one of these groups, it will take a little more concentration and may take a little longer, but you will get there. Use the clock as a guideline, and check out the span of happily awake times on the sleep chart on page 50. Review the typical signs of tiredness on pages 92–93. When it gets close to the average span of "happily awake time," start observing your baby closely. If you spot some indications of tiredness, do those things that seem to help your baby fall asleep—such as breastfeeding, rocking, or sling-carrying. If your baby falls asleep quickly, you'll know you've caught on!

Ignore Advice to Schedule Your Newborn

When your baby gets older, it can be helpful to have routine times for naps and bedtime, but your newborn is nowhere near ready for that! As an example, some people will suggest separating sleep and feeding by putting playtime in between. The problem here is that feeding is a natural sleep-inducer for a newborn, and trying to interfere with that connection can cause your baby distress and cause you unnecessary stress. This isn't the time to create an artificial schedule for your baby—it's time to let your newborn lead the way.

When Baby Sends Mixed Messages

There will be many times in the early months when your baby is displaying fussy behavior that is intended to tell you something—but you'll be totally confused about what that might be. Newborns can exhibit the same types of signals for various needs, such as tiredness, hunger, discomfort, or overstimulation.

Test Parent Question

What should I do when I suddenly realize I missed her signals completely and she is overtired? When this happens I struggle to get her to nap at all and get an overtired, fractious baby.

You and your baby are both new to this game, and life in your household is filled with activity, so there will absolutely be times that you miss the signals. That's perfectly normal. And sometimes your baby forgets to give you signals and bypasses normal tiredness by launching into total overtiredness. Once you figure out that your baby is overtired, resort to the methods that have proven to be helpful in days past. Typically, this can include walking with your baby in a sling, soft carrier, or stroller, or partaking in a gentle ride in the cradle-swing. The use of swaddling and white noise can also help settle an overtired baby into sleep.

When you aren't sure what your baby is saying, you can use the process of elimination to help decipher the message. Rather than instant action that could be off target, hold your baby in your arms or a soft carrier while you consider the main checkpoints to give clues to your little one's needs:

- When is the last time your baby ate? Was it a full meal? Could Baby be hungry?
- How long since your baby last slept? If awake more than an hour, your baby could be tired.
- Has Baby been having a lot of active play? Is it time for quiet cuddles?
- When was the last diaper change? Many babies dislike a wet or messy diaper.

By reviewing your baby's situation, you can often figure out what is causing fussiness.

Point to Remember

When your baby cries, it can feel like a smoke alarm going off. Your own heart begins to race, and you can feel a slight panic rising in you. As your baby cries harder, your own emotions can fall to pieces. Here's what I want you to remember: it takes time to learn your baby, but you will.

Take a deep breath. Center yourself. Look at your newborn and ask in a soothing voice, "What's the matter, baby? Why are you crying? How can Mommy help you?" Then think about the clues previously listed. When you are calm and thoughtful, you can help your baby stop crying and provide him what he needs. As you begin to practice this, it will become second nature. Pretty soon you will not feel panic set in when your little baby alarm begins to sound off.

What to Do When You Don't Understand the Message

Sometimes even the top soothing strategies—carrying, rocking, swaddling, or providing a pacifier—don't work to settle a crying baby, and Baby still cries. If you've exhausted all ideas and your baby won't sleep but is still crying or fussing, don't lose hope. As your baby gets a little older, when she moves past the disjointed sleep patterns of newbornship, and when you get more experienced, you'll be able to figure out what your baby needs even before she does based on patterns and experience.

In the meantime, if your newborn is unhappy, try some of the following activities to help her feel better and watch her closely for clues about which things get her to relax, since they might be helpful today and over the coming weeks. Stick with any method for ten minutes or more to determine if it's working, as your baby may take a few minutes to calm down. Here are some ideas for

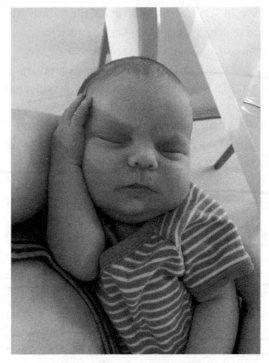

Mackenzie, three months old

things to do when your baby's fussing doesn't seem to mean tiredness, but otherwise you can't figure it out:

- ⭐ Breastfeed as a first and last resort—you can't use this Secret Weapon too much.
- Go for a walk outside with your baby in a soft carrier or sling.
- Step outside in your yard, sit on your deck, or pace around the yard. You can do this even if it is cold out (bundle up!).
- Lie on the floor with your baby for some tummy time play.

BABY Fussing c bf as 1st and last resort!

- Put some of your favorite music on, put your baby in a carrier and dance around, or let her sit in her swing and watch you being silly.
- Go up and down the stairs (slowly and carefully, and hold the handrail). It's a great workout for you and a relaxing, bouncy movement for your baby.
- Use a yoga ball, hold baby tightly to your chest or in a soft carrier, and bounce very gently while humming or talking softly to your baby. Or bounce quietly and watch a movie that is primarily talking (nothing loud or noisy).
- Introduce something new—a new texture, a new smell, or a new sound.
- Take a bath together. Don't worry about actually bathing; just enjoy the warm water and some gentle swimming.
- Go into a warm room, and strip baby down to a diaper. Place a towel over your lap and give your baby a gentle massage while you talk or sing to her.
- Take your baby to a playground or schoolyard and let him watch the kids run around. Older kids are mesmerizing to a baby, and you both might make some new friends.

Point to Remember

You cannot spoil a newborn baby! Even if you cater to every single whim, even if you jump at every peep and carry your baby every waking moment, and even if you nurse on demand every single hour—you cannot spoil a newborn baby! Anyone who tries to tell you that is following a very outdated line of reasoning. When you respond to all needs in babyhood, you build the foundation for a happier child.

- Pop your baby in a soft carrier and do what you need to do on your to-do list around the house and let Baby be your sidekick. You may feel less stressed once you load up the dishwasher—even if you have to do it with Baby strapped to your chest.

It's About So Much More Than Food and Sleep

Of course it's important to read your baby's tired signs so that you know when your little one is tired, as well as signs that she is hungry or stressed. But cueing in to your infant is about more than food and rest—it's actually building your relationship with this little person. You are creating a stability that will last for the rest of her life.

New babies are making connections with the human beings around them. They are learning who they can trust and who they can count on for care, security, and love. They are learning about the world and their place in it, and what it means to be a human being.

When you spend the early months focusing on making this connection with your baby, you will have easier days and nights, but, even more, you will reap the reward of a bonded, connected relationship. The pattern you set in babyhood is one that you will both build on throughout childhood and even into adulthood. Start on this path of connection, and you can enjoy a magical, treasured lifelong bond with your child.

The Joy of Learning to Read Your Baby's Tired Signs

In summary, take a close look at the list of typical sleepy signs and watch your baby carefully to learn your little one's unique combination of tired signs. If you put your baby down for a nap or to bed when you catch that perfectly tired moment, she'll fall asleep more easily—and stay asleep. If your baby isn't tired, it can take her a long time to fall asleep—and if she's overtired she'll be too wound up to sleep. But when you find that perfectly sleepy moment? Ahhhh, Zzzzzz.

KEY 4

Respect the Span of "Happily Awake Time"

Your new baby arrived not too long ago fresh from the womb, a place of quiet, darkness, peace, and sleep. Once brought into this world your baby is surrounded by sounds, smells, sights, and touch experiences every waking moment. Your baby has a lot to learn about the world and an amazing desire and capacity to do so—but only in short batches of time. If we push too much alert learning time all at once, newborns tend to shut down—by fussing, crying, or zoning out. It's in their best interest to respect their needs for short awake spans so that they can make the best use of their amazing learning abilities and enjoy connecting with the big, wide world.

Benefits of Refreshing Short Awake Spans With Plenty of Naps

Newborns need a slow and steady diet of sleep throughout the day to refresh, rehearse, and take a break from their busy world. Even those who are great nighttime sleepers require frequent daytime naps to rejuvenate in between lifetime learning segments of time. Each and every time that your baby sleeps, he is gifted with an amazing array of benefits, including these:

Oliver and Luke, seven weeks old, with Mommy

Brain Development and Information Organization

Nearly everything your newborn baby sees, touches, feels, and experiences is *new*. That little brain works overtime to take it all in, make sense of it, and compartmentalize it for future reference. His little brain fills up quickly and requires frequent sleep sessions to transfer all the new information into a permanent place in memory and free up new space for the remainder of the day's learning. Studies show that sufficient sleep helps young brains organize information and develop the ability to achieve high levels of abstract thinking.

Your baby's brain is like a miniature computer that opens a new file for every bit of information, whether it is a sound, a smell, a sight, or an emotion. Eventually, your little one's screen is so filled up with files that they become a disorganized mess that creates confusion, stress, and fatigue. After an hour or two of awake time, their screens are full of information. Your baby cannot catalog all this information while awake, because new sensations continue to arrive at a record pace. During sleep your baby's brain catalogs and files all the new information in its proper places. After a nap your baby's desktop is clean and organized and ready to take on more new information.

An Increased Capacity for Learning

A tired baby cannot learn because her primal focus becomes the need to sleep. Tired babies are less likely to enjoy exploring the world around them. They may be awake, but their fatigue prevents them from absorbing any new information, so they try to shut down. Parents then get frustrated by the baby's disinterest, fussiness, and clinginess, and even their relationship is impacted because both baby and parent are feeling overwhelmed and pushed past their limits.

Babies who have the perfect amount of awake time, interspersed with adequate rest and naps, spend more of their waking hours in a relaxed, alert condition. They learn more, they enjoy life more, and their parents are provided with added time for engaging, teaching, and bonding with their babies.

Calmness and Lower Stress

When your baby's awake periods are portioned out with sufficient sleep time in between, it reduces the amount of fussiness and tears each day. Every time your baby sleeps, it enables the body to release cortisol and other hormones that combat stress and tension. Without the release of these hormones every few hours, they build to uncontrollable levels, which creates inner pressure that erupts as fussiness and crying. Babies who stay awake for too long can dissolve into tears much more easily than those who get sufficient rest breaks.

Oliver, five months old, with Mommy

Infants with more intense personalities can have an exaggerated effect from being awake for too long. So an exceptionally alert and attentive baby might fight sleep while at the same time desperately needing it.

The Happily Awake Span

As shown on the sleep hours chart on page 50, as children age, the length of time that they can stay happily awake increases. In the first few weeks, most newborns can only handle *one to two hours of wakefulness*—and at times even less than that. By three months of age, many babies can stay happily awake one to three hours, but it isn't until about seven to nine months that some babies begin to stay awake for four hours without a meltdown, though some don't make that happy four-hour mark until eighteen months of age.

When babies are pushed beyond their biological awake time span without a break, that's when they become fatigued and unhappy. As the minutes pass and the sleep pressure builds, a baby becomes fussier, whinier, and less flexible, and he has more crying spells. He loses concentration and the ability to take in new information.

As always when talking about children, these hours are a guideline, and a few babies make up their own rules about their best "happily awake span"—but trust me, they all have one! Don't push your baby into fitting any particular time pattern if her cues do not match, but do always go back to Key 1 and read your unique baby's telltale signs and respond by providing adequate rest breaks and naps.

Parent-Speak

"This baby in general is easier than my now three-year-old was. She is a lot less fussy, has more quiet alert times, and naps more often. I think it's because I didn't understand the "happily awake concept" with my first. I had no idea that her long periods of being awake were the cause of her crabbiness. Paying attention to how long this baby has been awake has been super helpful, so I've referenced the chart often. She is generally content, since if I'm aware that she's been awake for about an hour I can start watching for sleepy signs more carefully, and start preparing to help her get back to sleep *before* she starts to get fussy. It has made an amazing difference."

—Megan, mother of three-year-old Anna and two-month-old Felicity

Squeezing or Stretching the Awake Span

Your baby might typically have two full hours of happily awake time under normal circumstances. However, if a nap is cut short by a dog's bark, a sibling's squeal, or a full diaper, it might reduce the awake span that follows. In the same vein, a nice long nap might have benefits that last a little longer, providing your baby with an extra-long alert time. In addition, your baby might shorten that span and need some extra naps around the time of developmental or growth spurts or to fend off illnesses that may be floating around.

The Volcano Effect

From the moment your baby wakes in the morning or after a nap, he is slowly using up the many benefits of the previous sleep session. He wakes up totally refreshed and ready to take on the day, but as the time passes, little by little, the benefits of his sleep time are used up, and an urge to return to sleep begins to build. When we catch a baby at in-between stages and provide naps, we build up his reservoir of sleep-related benefits, allowing him a "fresh start" after each sleep period.

The scientific term for the process we've been discussing is "homeostatic sleep pressure" or "homeostatic sleep drive"—I call it the *Volcano Effect*. We've all seen the effects of this on a baby or child, as it is often as clear as watching a volcano erupt; nearly everyone has observed a fussy, crying child and thought or said, *"It's time for a nap!"*

As a baby progresses through his day, his biology demands these sleep breaks to regroup and refresh. If a baby does not get these breaks, the problem intensifies: the rumblings and tremors become an outright explosion. Without nap breaks, the homeostatic pressure continues building and building until the end of the day, growing in intensity—like a volcano—so that a baby becomes overtired, wired, and unable to stop the explosion. The result is a cranky, fussy, overtired baby who won't fall asleep no matter how tired he is. The problem grows because once the volcano erupts and a baby is melting down, it is much harder to bring her back to center, calm her down, and help her to fall asleep. Overtired babies find it much harder to settle and go to sleep. Even more, a child whose signs are missed day after day builds a sleep deprivation that launches her into the volcano stage much more easily and quickly.

Point to Remember

Do not let your baby stay awake for too long at a time. Newborns can only stay happily awake for an hour or two at a time, and sometimes less than that. After a few weeks, some babies can be awake as long as three hours, if they are routinely sleeping well at night and getting good, long naps. By three months of age many babies routinely enjoy a two- to three-hour awake span, although some still can barely make it an hour without getting tired.

If your baby has been awake for too long, you have likely missed his sleepy signals, and he is overtired. An overtired baby will find it hard to sleep yet hard to stay happily awake. This becomes a pattern that can disrupt both sleep and temperament. So, keep one eye on your baby (watch for tired signs) and one eye on the clock.

Naps Trump Night Sleep in the Volcano Department

This concept brings to light one more important point: frequent quality naps can make up for lost night sleep, but extra nighttime sleep does *not* make up for missed naps, due to the Volcano Effect—the homeostatic sleep pressure concept. Therefore, no matter how your baby sleeps at night—great sleeper or poor sleeper—daily naps are critically important to release the rising sleep pressure that occurs throughout the day.

KEY 5

Differentiate Between Sleeping Noises and Awake Noises

'm excited to be able to share this next idea with you now, because it can be life-changing. Surprisingly, many new parents don't have this information; it's a hidden treasure! Yet, when you learn and apply it during these early months, your baby will absolutely sleep longer stretches during the night. If you don't, you could accidentally reinforce night-waking behaviors and be dealing with excessive, unnecessary night waking throughout babyhood. Here is the critically important fact that you must know:

> BABIES MAKE SOUNDS IN THEIR SLEEP.

The majority of newborns are not quiet sleepers. Babies grunt, groan, coo, whimper, and sometimes even outright cry out during sleep. These noises don't always signal awakening, and they don't require any action on your part. These are what I call "sleeping noises," because your baby is nearly or even totally asleep during these episodes. These are not the cries that mean, "I need you!" They are just normal sleeping sounds.

Many new parents are awakened throughout the night by their newborns, and they immediately jump to action at every peep.

While an admirable intention is at the heart of this, many times, their newborns are fully asleep, and the parent's actions actually wake them up! In their desire to be caring parents and respond to Baby's every need, they actually disrupt their baby's sleep (and their own!)—and they can actually teach their babies to wake up more often!

Babies Are Not Just Noisy Sleepers— They're Active Sleepers, Too

Most newborns are not calm, still sleepers. They move, squirm, wiggle, stretch, and have sudden jerky limb movements. They

Stella Jade, two months old

can do this quite often throughout the night. These are *sleeping actions*, and your baby is sound asleep, or nearly asleep, during these episodes.

Babies can be almost as active in their sleep as they are when awake! If you'll recall, babies in the womb sleep up to twenty hours per day—yet during pregnancy you felt many pokes and prods throughout the day. Those movements were often sleeping activities.

During sleep, your baby's little fingers and toes will twitch, his legs and arms will stretch and move, and his facial expressions will change. He may make sucking or chewing motions, and, amazingly, he could even open his eyes briefly. He'll change his entire body's position, often squirming or fidgeting. All of this activity is normal and it is done during sleep, so it doesn't require any intervention from you. In fact, if you intervene during these sleeping activities, you will actually wake your baby up when he's not ready to be awake, so very often that means a tired, fussy baby.

Deciphering Newborn Waking Cues

It takes time and practice to decipher your newborn's cues and to be able to clearly identify when your baby is actually waking up and needing your care, versus when he is just noisily sleeping. You will learn to interpret your baby's sounds and actions with practice over time by listening and watching your baby carefully, and then patiently applying what you observe night by night as you improve your translation skills.

By observing your newborn's behaviors, you can learn to differentiate between these sleeping sounds and actions versus awake and hungry sounds, and the result is better sleep for your baby (and you).

Test Parent Question

My six-week-old baby is healthy, feeding well, and growing beautifully. In the middle of the night last night he woke up and made a lot of noise, moved around and opened his eyes. He never cried, but he did this for at least ten minutes then just fell back to sleep. Then I felt bad. Should I have fed him?

Sounds like your little guy was transitioning through sleep cycles—and bravo to you for letting him! Believe me—if your healthy, full-term, fed-on-demand newborn is hungry: He. Will. Let. You. Know. He won't peacefully fall back to sleep if he's hungry!

This is a situation that gets lots of parents of newborns in a pickle—they actually create a sleep-cycle-changing routine of picking up, holding, and feeding. So keep doing what you're doing!

Since your baby is healthy and growing well, and you're responding to feeding cues day and night, you are doing the right thing, so keep it up!

Sleeping? Awake? . . . Take a Pause

When your baby is making noises, and you're not sure if your little one is awake or not, but you are feeling ready to pounce—take a pause. Sometimes it's hard to be patient since your instinct is to pick your baby up—which is an instinct you should pay close attention to, of course—but sometimes your response should be to just watch and listen. Responding with action could be a little too quick.

What if you realize you are always responding too quickly, so consequently you and your baby are awake together every hour? Try this: when your baby begins to stir, get yourself up, go to the

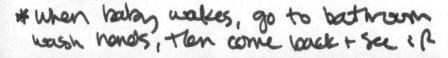

bathroom, wash your hands (quietly!), and by the time you come back Baby will either be ready for you or . . . sound asleep! Your pause may have allowed Baby to resettle into sleep.

I suggest that you start doing this from the beginning, because reacting too quickly from the start creates a pattern that is very hard to break later on since you will actually be teaching your baby to fully wake between sleep cycles and expect your help to fall back to sleep again.

Master the Skill of Reading Your Baby's Sounds

I found that test parents who said that their baby "frequently" makes nighttime noises and then falls back to sleep with no help had babies who sleep longer stretches at night and for naps than those who said their baby "rarely" made sleeping noises. Hmmm. Based on what you have just learned about newborns being noisy sleepers, you can see that new parents sometimes interfere with their babies' sleep cycles by not understanding this important concept.

So if your baby only "sometimes" makes noises and goes back to sleep without help, maybe you should pause a little longer and see if your baby is just changing sleep cycles and not really awake and needing you. (Of course, if it's time to eat, it's time to eat, no matter how long it's been!)

Special Advice for Breastfeeding/ Bed-sharing Moms

Not understanding this concept of sleeping noises is what created the bulk of my sleep issues with my challenging nonsleeper, my fourth baby, Coleton, who inspired my first sleep book, *The No-Cry Sleep Solution*. I slept with my baby beside me, and, like most

awake or asleep!

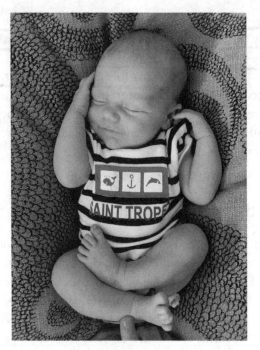

Alexis, three weeks old

mothers, when you breastfeed and bed-share with your baby, I found it to be very true that your sleep cycles become synchronized. This means that you will both experience sleep-cycle brief awakenings at the same time. When this happens, it is a beautiful sign that you and your baby have found perfect sleep harmony, and it will make your night waking job easier, since when your baby wakes you won't be roused from a state of deep sleep. It is easy for you, in your partially awake state, to attach your baby to your breast, and then, when your baby easily falls back to sleep, so do you.

During the night, when both you and your baby are in your brief awakening periods, he may simply breathe noisily or shift position, and you'll automatically attach him to the breast; the two of you will both drift back off to sleep. This is a wonderful, peaceful experience when you have a newborn lying beside you, and it can be a new mother's best solution for much-craved sleep.

But beneath the surface of this peaceful scenario lies a potentially massive problem: While your baby has a cycle change every hour or two, he does not necessarily need to be fed every hour or two. However, your baby will come to expect a nursing at every brief awakening. While you may find this arrangement tolerable for the early newborn months, it's a very rare mother who will still find it endurable eight or ten or twelve months later. I know because that is exactly what happened to me! Every time my baby *sniffed loudly*, I automatically switched him to the other side and nursed him back to sleep . . . but I later learned that many of these times he was not really awake—I roused him for feeding! Even worse, sometimes these babies can breastfeed while almost fully asleep.

You may agree with me that the goal is to help your co-sleeping baby to feel comfortable sleeping next to you without having to order from Mommy's all-night snack bar every hour! A breast-feeding/bed-sharing mother's best long-term sleep enhancer is to learn how to pretend to be asleep while listening to Baby's sounds. And to pause a minute and do nothing. (Isn't that a wonderful set of instructions?) Your baby may fall back to sleep without your help. If your newborn needs to breastfeed, trust me, you'll know that soon enough.

Test Parent Question

My eight-week-old baby sometimes wakes up halfway through a nap, or in the middle of the night, and makes a bunch of noise and moves around. I find it hard to tell when he is transitioning sleep cycles versus if he needs to be fed. Can you explain in more detail what I should look for?

The answer to this is different for every baby. But keep in mind that it's not unusual for a baby for grunt, groan, squeak, move, and even open his eyes and then settle back to sleep on his own.

Part of your investigation process should include your baby's age, size, health, and how long he can typically go without feeding. Consider also how much your baby fed the previous session, since a short session won't hold your baby for as long a period of time. Also, consider the establishment of breastfeeding and how that is going. Some babies are working really hard to master feeding and tire themselves out after only half a feeding, while other expert breastfeeders are fine to go for long sleep stretches at night up to six, seven, or even eight hours!

So take a peek at the clock, and if you are not concerned about the length of the time since the last feeding, then it's perfectly fine to sit it out a bit. Wait. Watch. Listen. If your baby is just settling—let him settle. He will clearly let you know if he is hungry or needs your help!

> **Point to Remember**
> Watch closely and listen carefully when your baby moves and makes noises during sleep.
>   If Baby really is waking up and hungry—feed your newborn quickly.
>   If Baby is making sleeping noises and sleeping movements—let your newborn sleep!

If Baby Really Is Awake

If your baby is really awake and hungry, you will—*always, of course!*—want to feed her as quickly as possible. If you do respond immediately when she is hungry, she will most likely go back to sleep quickly and calmly. However, if you let her cry escalate, she will wake herself up totally, and it will be harder and take longer for her to go back to sleep. Not to mention that *you* will then be wide awake, too! Remember that your newborn will wake up for nighttime feedings, and it's important for growth.

However, if it's only been an hour or two since her last feeding and your baby is just grunting her way through a sleep-cycle change—let her do it without your interference. Keep in mind that these sleeping noises can last five minutes or longer, so be patient! If you watch your baby, you'll be able to see that she is actually noisily sleeping.

To learn more about this, take a look at Key 3, Learn to Read Your Baby's Sleepy Signals (page 117). A hungry cry is much different than a noise made during sleep, and you will quickly learn the difference.

KEY 6

Use the Soothing Sounds of Pink-Hued White Noise

Many people tiptoe around sleeping babies thinking that any noise will wake them up. This isn't exactly the case. There are many noises that wake a sleeping baby, but there are many that actually soothe them to sleep.

The prenatal environment that your baby enjoyed in the womb was not a quiet one. In fact, it was exactly the opposite! There was a constant loud symphony of sounds, from the muffled noises of the world outside to the sounds from inside your body. If you have a dog or older children in the house, if you work in a busy environment, or if you frequently listen to music or the TV, your baby heard all of these sounds through the walls of the uterus. In addition, there was a continuous background of the whoosh-whoosh of your heartbeat and the thunderous rush of blood through your arteries, along with the rumbles of your digestive system. Because of this prenatal history, "white noise" sounds can help many babies to relax and fall asleep—and stay asleep—much more easily than a totally quiet room. This is partly because these sounds create an environment more familiar to your baby than a silent room.

White noise is sound that contains many frequencies of equal intensities so that the individual sounds are not heard and a blended hum of sound results, serving as indistinct background noise. Examples are the drone of a fan, the back-and-forth whooshing of waves on a beach, the rumble of an airplane engine, or the muffled hum of voices at a large gathering of people.

It's common for human beings to find the sounds of white noise soothing. Even adults can find these sounds helpful in aiding sleep. For many people it's relaxing to nod off to the hum of a fan or the steady tranquil lapping of ocean waves. This is because white noise reduces the audio clutter surrounding you, distracting you with an almost hypnotic beat and helping you to tune out other sounds and thoughts that can keep you awake.

Don't Noises Wake a Sleeping Baby?

You may be thinking that this all makes sense, but noises *do* wake babies up! The clink of a fork on a plate or the ding of the doorbell, and your peacefully sleeping baby is awake and crying. That's why everyone always says, "Shhh, be quiet! The baby's sleeping!" So, then, it's confusing: noise or no noise?

As we discussed, the womb was a very noisy place, and the rumbles and ka-thump, ka-thump of your heart and blood flow were continuous twenty-four hours a day. So the sounds were constant and actually quite loud. The defining fact to keep in mind, though, is that your baby was floating in a pool of water, and her ears were also filled with fluid, so every sound was cushioned to a soft blur. Did you ever play "tea party" in a swimming pool? It's a game when you dive under the water and say something to your friend, who tries to guess what you said. It's a hard game, because sounds are very muffled and softened under the water. This is how your baby heard the world while in the womb. So, while the hum of family household noise, such as voices quietly talking, is soothing, a sharp, sudden, or harsh noise breaks through your baby's sleep and jars her awake. When we create an environment of proper white noise, we can prevent having those abrupt noises disturb Baby's sleep.

Four Ways White Noise Works Its Magic

The right kind of background noise is a perfect sleep aid for most babies because it is effective in a variety of ways. Whether your baby is an easy sleeper or a more challenged sleeper, white noise can be helpful to your little one in four different ways:

The Gentle, Consistent Sound Can Soothe Your Baby to Sleep

From the beginning of time, adults have used the sounds of "Shhh shhh" or similar utterances to help calm a baby. It's an instinctual sound that mimics a mother's heartbeat, and it works. When a baby hears these types of sounds, it allows him to focus on those, and then he can center himself and relax or fall asleep.

The Sound Can Mask Harsh Noises That Can Startle Your Baby Awake

A steady hum of background noise can help to block out sharp sudden sounds. Typically, it's not the noise itself that wakes your baby, but the sudden change in sound that jars your baby from sleep. White noise, played just loud enough, conceals these sharp sounds. You don't want to have to always tiptoe around a sleeping baby, and the sounds of the house, like talking or soft footsteps, are actually soothing, as babies love to hear the sounds of the village as they sleep. However, sharp sounds like dishes clinking, a doorbell or phone ringing, dogs barking, or older siblings shouting can be intrusive sounds that wake your sleeping newborn. Having white noise playing can mask any of these baby-waking noises.

White Noise Can Act as a Bridge Between Sleep Cycles

Daytime in your house is likely noisier than nighttime, both inside your home and outside, containing many abrupt baby-waking noises. Yet nighttime can contain sounds, such as car horns, dogs barking, or a television playing in another room. White noise can cover many of those disruptive sounds that happen during naps or in the middle of the night. When your baby is having a brief awakening between sleep cycles and hears these noises, they can gain his attention and bring him fully awake. White noise can help your baby move seamlessly through sleep cycles (when hunger doesn't interfere) so that your baby has a longer nap or fewer night wakings.

A Sound Used Frequently for Sleep Times Creates a Consistent Cue

When your baby hears this specific sound, she knows it's time to sleep. When you routinely use the sounds as soon as you notice signs of tiredness, your baby comes to recognize it as sleeping music. Add some warm milk and a cuddle to easily lull your baby to sleep.

Your baby will become accustomed to these sounds for falling asleep, so it becomes an easy-to-use sleep cue, at home or away. If you purchase a small white noise machine, it is easy to travel with. In a pinch you can buy a white noise app on your phone or other device. This isn't the best first choice because the small speakers can give the sounds a tinny edge, but when other options are not available this fits the bill. Check out the various apps and find one that provides a steady, relaxing sound, described in detail for you on page 153.

White noise can be a magic answer for improved sleep for babies, children, and even adults! You can leave it on for an entire nap and even all night long. These peaceful sounds are just one more piece in the puzzle that helps you to help your baby sleep better—gently, without any stress or crying at all.

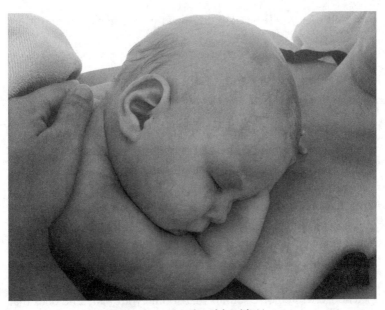

Augustyn, four months old, with Mommy

What Kind of White Noise Is Best?

The sounds that help a baby to fall asleep and stay asleep are steady and repetitive, without any major changes in volume or pitch, and don't contain any sudden sharp sounds. For newborns, a great option is the actual sound from the womb. You can now purchase a variety of toys or CDs that provide the sounds of the womb for your newborn. While the sounds may seem slightly odd to you, these are familiar to your newborn and often are very effective at helping a baby sleep better. The only problem with these womb sounds is that you also have to listen to them, and many adults don't care for the sound. Luckily, there are many similar sounds, such as the whoosh of ocean waves, that work just as well and that you'll be happy to listen to for naps and nighttime every day.

Finding the Right White Noise

As white noise has become more popular as a sleep aid, choices abound. There are machines, stuffed animals, CDs, MP3 tracks, digital music, and apps. I've found that when using this idea for a newborn the best option may be the white noise machines or CDs that play various white noise options such as rainfall, a babbling brook, forest sounds, or ocean waves. Look for a white noise machine that can operate all night long. Some have automatic turn-offs, and they shut off just as Baby is falling asleep and can wake him up with a click or sudden silence.

Choose white noise sounds that soothe your baby and ones that you will be happy to listen to, as well. Once your baby is familiar with these sounds as his sleep-time cue, they can be used effectively for years to come.

Using Music as White Noise

A few babies don't take to womb sounds or white noise and prefer actual music. If you opt for music for your baby, choose carefully. You'll want to find relaxing music, such as classical or soft jazz music, without any harsh or jarring sounds or sudden tempo changes. There are a wide variety of recordings available that have been created specifically for relaxation, yoga, meditation, or sleep that make great options for your baby. Check your favorite bookstore for these.

The level and type of noise that disrupts sleep is different for each baby. Some children can sleep through a fire alarm siren, but some are awakened by the slightest noise, so you may have to try a few different options to find your best match.

Make Your White Noise the Pink-Hued Variety

When it comes to the soothing nature of white noise, various studies show that "pink noise" is an even better choice for sleeping.

Pink noise is a variant of white noise that is filtered to reduce the intensity as the frequency increases. It sounds fuller, deeper, or richer than white noise. This more refined type of white noise seems to do an even better job of improving sleep because of its subdued quality. It's no surprise that a heartbeat falls into the category of pink noise.

Most white noise machines, CDs, and apps contain pink noise options, though they often aren't labeled as such, since "white noise" is the more commonly used term. To stay in the pink spectrum, choose sounds that are repetitive and use a lower, deeper sound and a slower pace. Perfect examples of pink noise in addition to a heartbeat are the hum of many quietly talking voices, a fan or humidifier, ocean waves, the pitter-patter of rainfall, the deep whoosh of a waterfall, the sound of rain falling on pavement, a car engine when driving on a freeway, or the rustling of leaves on a tree. In contrast, examples of nonpink white noise include things like a vacuum cleaner, the static between stations on a radio, and the squeal of a hair dryer, which are all a higher pitch and intensity, with a slightly harsh or tinny edge. As you can see, there are subtle differences that make pink noise gentler on the ear and a better match for aiding sleep.

While most white noise serves the purpose of masking sharp background sounds, pink noise adds a layer of relaxation and peacefulness. Pink noise might help you sleep better too. A study conducted at China's Peking University found that 75 percent of adults reported that they slept better, deeper, and longer when listening to pink noise as compared to having no sound in the bedroom. Another study, in Germany, found that pink noise improves brain wave activity during prolonged deep sleep—this represents enhanced memory retention. This is another reason to consider the use of white noise.

Parent-Speak

"White noise is a miracle! We got a machine that plays ocean waves all night (as opposed to our first try that ran for only forty-five minutes and shut off, so the baby slept forty-five minutes and woke up), and it really helps our baby stay asleep through the night. The bonus is that is also helps with our older daughter's sleep! And I love it because it reminds me of our vacation in Hawaii, so I sleep peacefully, too! Who would have guessed?"

—Brandi, mother of four-month-old Cecelia

Negative Aspects of Using White Noise

As long as you use white noise properly (such as keeping the volume controlled and turning it off when your baby is awake), I've not discovered any dangers or side effects. Likely the only negative would be that your baby can become very used to the sound for sleep, and you'll need to be sure you can accommodate this. That means finding a portable sound that can travel with you on vacation or to Grandma and Grandpa's house. You'll also need to find out if your daycare supports the use of white noise for napping, if your little one naps away from home.

Test Parent Question

I just read about a study that says white noise can be danger-ous to a newborn's hearing. We used it for our first child, and definitely found it helpful. Is it safe to use for our new baby?

That news did make the rounds! If you read the actual study, it says that the researchers tested fourteen sleep machines at *maximum volume*—which on many machines is uncomfortably loud. I always advise parents to put their head down to where the baby's head will be resting to test the volume. Maximum volume is shockingly loud on some machines, so it's unlikely you would ever have it turned up that high! However, until the manufacturers of white noise machines and white noise apps put a limit on the volume for use with babies, use your com-mon sense. Is the sound at a pleasant and relaxing background hum, or does it sound like an airplane is flying over the room?

Watch for new research about the use of white noise for babies. In the meantime, it makes sense to follow the rec-ommendation of the American Academy of Pediatrics. They recommend a maximum safe noise level of 45 decibels, or follow the current recommendation for infants in hospital nurs-eries of 50 decibels—which is about the level of conversation in an office environment.

In addition, it has been found to be better to place the actual device away from the baby. So, instead of having it at your child's bedside, place it farther away on a dresser or table across the room.

Remember that the womb is a very, very noisy place—mother's heartbeat, blood rushing, digestive system rumbling along with the filtered sounds of anything outside that can be detected by the fetus. My daughter has two large dogs, and their barks are deep and loud—yet my grandson never flinched even when he was just a few days old! He was used to hearing them from being in Mommy's womb, so it was a familiar sound. Your baby heard all the rumbly noises that you hear around you every day. So, for a newborn, a quiet room can be disconcerting. White noise is very helpful in aiding sleep—but be wise about the use and volume.

How to Use White and Pink Noise Safely for Your Baby

The use of white or pink noise is helpful to almost all newborns. But it's not as simple as finding some noise online and playing it

Stellina, one month old, with Mommy

randomly. Here are some test parent questions and answers that will refine this idea even further for you.

How Do I Know What Volume to Play the White Noise?

There is a magical volume for white noise that makes it beneficial but not a problem for your baby's developing hearing. You don't want any noise that is too loud for your newborn's delicate ears. The easiest way to test volume is to put your own head where your baby's head will be resting—turn on the noise and listen. Is the sound too quiet to have an effect, thus allowing outside noises to disturb sleep? Or is it loud and uncomfortable? Aim for a pleasant background hum, about the level of a fan, rainfall, or bathroom shower. It does not need to be so loud that you can't hear the other noises around the house, just loud enough to blunt them and serve as a constant, consistent, soothing sound.

How Do I Choose Which Sound to Use, or Should I Alternate Between Sounds?

Based on what we've discussed, choose a sound that fits the pink noise range. Select a sound that soothes your baby and that you like to hear. No need to play sounds that annoy you, since you'll probably hear hours and hours of them over the next year or more!

Find something that is relaxing for both of you, and stick to one particular noise to reap the benefits of a specific sleep-time cue. If you find one perfect sound and use it exclusively, it will disappear into the background as a familiar melody. Changing it up will require your baby to identify and analyze it each time, rather than accepting its quiet, almost hypnotic rhythm.

Like so many baby sleep ideas (and parenting in general), keep in mind that things change! What is the right answer today can be different a month from now. So keep your antenna tuned in to your baby's needs.

When Should I Play White Noise? Every Time I Want My Baby to Sleep, or Just at Bedtime?

White noise is helpful, but it isn't magic sandman dust! If you turn on the sounds when your baby isn't tired and it's too soon for sleep, you might dilute their effectiveness over time. Use the sounds when your baby shows you specific tired signs.

There is no harm is playing white noise for every nap and all night long. However, rather than just leaving it to run constantly, you should experiment with this. If you leave it on, does your baby sleep better? If you turn it off, does she wake up soon afterward? Does it work to reduce the volume after your baby has fallen asleep? How loud is just enough sound to cover sharp outside noises in your baby's sleeping environment, but not so loud as to be annoying or pose a hearing risk? If you have dogs, other children, or a noisy home, you may have to use a louder volume, but don't assume this—remember my grandbaby and his big barking dogs.

The white noise will quickly become a sleep cue—so don't turn it on if your baby is wide awake and alert, hoping to force him to be tired. This can backfire and cause the sound to lose its relaxing properties if it's aligned with more active times. Wind your baby down first, hold/rock/feed—and when he is relaxed, *then* turn on the white noise.

Turn on your baby's white noise when your little one is showing signs of tiredness and appears ready to sleep. For a slightly older baby who has a regular bedtime, you can turn the sounds on during the prebedtime routine (diaper change, pajamas, rocking, feeding). It's perfectly fine then to leave the white noise playing at a low volume during the entire nap and all night long if you would like.

Turn White Noise Off When Baby Is Awake

Turn the white noise off *as soon as your baby is awake*. This keeps the sound exclusive to sleep. In addition, your infant needs to hear the sounds of the world when she is awake and alert, and you don't want to mask the sounds that teach her the things she needs to learn.

The exception here is that you can use the sounds to help calm a colicky baby during peak crying times. The soothing sounds can help calm both your unhappy baby and you.

Parent-Speak

"I would use white noise to help calm my colicky firstborn when he would get so worked up that he wouldn't even nurse. There were times when the only thing that would calm him was when I would go into the darkened bedroom, close the door, turn on the white noise, and then he would nurse."

—Sophia, mother to seven-month-old Matais

Just like All Ideas: It Doesn't Work for Every Baby

Babies are individuals, and just like most aspects of parenting, every idea doesn't work for every baby. The only way you can tell if the use of white noise works for your infant is to test it out. Does your baby fall asleep faster or stay asleep longer when you play the white noise? Experiment a bit so you can find the right answer for you. It may be that your baby prefers the quiet, or it could be that you need to select a different type of sound for when you are using it. Watch your baby for cues.

Keep in mind, though, that you shouldn't have to tiptoe around the house in fear of waking the baby during those precious sleeping hours. Having a noise machine could mean that you and your partner don't have to whisper or worry about watching a movie or listening to music after your baby goes to bed. It could mean that you can get some dishes or laundry done while your baby naps. And it can come in handy when you have visitors or other unusual noise disruptions.

Parent-Speak

"Our first attempt at white noise, strangely enough, seemed to disrupt our baby's sleep. I kept using her white-noise stuffed animal until my husband pointed out that it seemed to take her longer to fall asleep with it turned on. However, we found that if one of us was showering in the bathroom near our bedroom, it calmed her right down. So we actually found a noise app with a 'shower' setting! That did the trick."

—Melinda, mother to three-month-old Eliza

KEY 7

Set Your Baby's
Biological Clock

Many new parents don't believe me when I tell them that a
newborn sleeps fifteen to eighteen hours per day. That's a
lot of sleep—but for most parents it feels like your baby is only
sleeping half that much. The reason that it doesn't feel like that
much sleep is because a newborn's sleep is distributed over four to
seven (or more) sleep periods—day and night, oftentimes in small
chunks. In addition, new parents are exhausted by day's end and
looking forward to a good night's sleep, so a baby's waking every
few hours can make it seem you're not getting any sleep at all! All
this waking up is perfectly normal, I'm afraid, and part of the way
that babies are made. The good news is that you can help consolidate those many sleeping periods into longer stretches by helping
to set their biological clocks.

Guess What—Your Baby Doesn't Have
Her Days and Nights Mixed Up!

If your baby is sleeping a lot during the day, including a three- to
five-hour stretch, and then getting up frequently at night, it's common for people to note that she "has her days and nights mixed
up." From an adult perspective that makes sense. However, from a
baby's viewpoint everything is as it should be. In the womb your
baby knew no difference between day and night—before birth

your baby floated through the relative darkness of fetal life without time. So for her, nothing is "mixed up" at all! Or perhaps your baby thinks *you* are the one who is mixed up and trying to disturb her equilibrium by imposing this rigid day/night routine! But for the grown-ups in the house the world functions on a very specific day/night cycle, and it takes a baby a while to get in sync with that cycle.

Many infants get a large percentage of their long sleeps during the day and then wake up frequently throughout the night. There are a number of possible reasons that this might happen. When in the womb, the rumble of soothing voices (yours and others') and your daytime movements created a gentle rhythm that rocked your baby to sleep, while your quiet stillness at night may have kept him more awake—so perhaps he is just following his "normal" pattern of sleep.

Parent-Speak

As an active mother of three young ones I never realized that I was being so much more relaxed during night feedings—since I was half asleep anyway! Daytime feeds tended to be disrupted and noisy. So it makes sense that my new little one gravitated towards those night feeds!

—**Andrea, mother of Marissa, Emma, and Gabriella**

Newborns need to eat frequently—day and night. It's easier for parents to handle these around-the-clock feedings during the day when we are awake and alert, but a challenge to wake up every few hours in the middle of the night, so night waking is more disruptive to us and looms larger than life. In addition, a busy

Annabelle, two and a half months old

and distracted parent during the day often transforms into a calm, unrushed parent in the middle of the night, so a baby might gravitate toward those peaceful, undisturbed night feedings.

Human sleep is regulated by an internal body clock that primes us for wakefulness during the day and sleepiness at night. Babies are born with an undeveloped biological clock—this takes six to nine weeks before it kicks in, and nine to ten months before it becomes the primary regulator of a baby's daily sleep and wakefulness pattern. Newborn babies are simply not built to sleep the same way that adults or older children do.

It May Be a Challenge—But It's Not a "Problem"

This day/night reversal of sleep may be a challenge for the adults in the house, but it isn't a problem or a health concern for a newborn, particularly if Baby gets plenty of sleep under this arrangement. I realize this isn't good news for the parents who struggle to deal with this! Part of the solution here is simply patience and time—your baby's sleep cycle will become more in sync with day and night over the next few weeks. However, if your newborn is one of these reversal babies, you are probably already struggling with your own lack of sleep, so here are a few ideas that will gently nudge your baby's sleep maturity so that it is more aligned to yours.

Help Your Baby Distinguish Day from Night

While biology will largely dictate the maturity of your baby's body clock, there are a number of things that you can do to help the cause, since some things will aid this process and others hinder it. There are many environmental and social cues that can promote the development of your baby's personal clock and move it in the direction of your own. It helps to be aware of these ideas, since they are easy to put into action.

Keep Your Baby Close—Day and Night

Your baby is created to be very in sync with you right from birth. The closer you are in proximity, especially at night, the easier it will be for your baby to mirror your body clock cycles. All professional groups recommend that you keep your newborn in your room and close by at night for safety reasons, and this is another benefit of that arrangement.

Even during sleep, if your baby is arm's length from you, he will be subconsciously aware of your presence. Studies even show that breastfeeding/co-sleeping mothers and their babies wake up within a few *seconds* of each other during the night, which sleep expert Dr. James McKenna calls "interconnected, mutually dependent, synchronous arousals." In essence, you are helping to nudge your baby's body clock development by keeping him close to you at night.

Provide Activity During the Day

We've been talking a lot about sleep, because, of course, this is a sleep book! But adequate active awake time fits our topic because it will improve your baby's sleep. When your baby's peepers are wide open and she's calm and relaxed, it's time to enjoy her slowly budding personality.

Newborns do have times when they are wide awake for an hour or two, so make those times interesting. Talk to your new little friend. It really doesn't matter what you say. Tell him how adorable his is, narrate the process as you're making dinner, and share all the fun things that await him in life. Ask him lots of questions, because your voice automatically takes on a baby-friendly sing-song quality when asking questions.

Life shouldn't be all baby-tending chores. Have fun with your little one! Show your baby all those exciting new toys, clothes, and gadgets that you received as gifts. Read some baby board books out loud. Sing to your newborn. Carry your baby in a soft carrier or sling and allow her to watch all your daily tasks close-up. Take your baby to the park or the store or for a walk around your neighborhood.

Make sure your baby has a bit of tummy time every day on a safe, flat surface with your constant supervision. This is a fun daily activity that helps your little one develop the muscles that will lead to pushing up, crawling, and walking.

Your wide-awake newborn does not want to lie bored in an infant seat or cradle, so limit the use of seats, beds, and carriers during these awake times. If those little eyes are open, they need something to look at—so provide your baby lots of new things to see and do. This becomes a self-fulfilling cycle—the more alert your baby is during awake times, the better he sleeps, and then he's more alert when awake, and so the better he can sleep after that, and so on through the cycle of alert times alternated with healthy sleep. (Don't get to having so much fun that you forget to watch those "happily awake" time spans—keeping your baby up past his tired moments will only make him grumpy and unable to sleep.)

Research has uncovered that when mothers include their newborns in their daily activities, babies adapt more rapidly to the twenty-four-hour day/night sequence, and they more quickly adapt to their mother's awake and asleep times. So enjoy everyday life with your new little partner by your side.

Avoid Overstimulation and Understimulation

Your newborn's life in the womb was a perfect balance of sound and quiet, sensory stimulation and cozy surroundings, with the peacefulness of a consistent, perfect environment. Your baby was curled into the comfortable pretzel-like fetal position, slept, and was nourished without thought or effort. This peaceful hypnotizing bliss all changes the moment your baby enters the world.

A newborn must contend with an overwhelming array of sights, sounds, and tactile experiences. A baby is created to handle this, of course, and even relish it—but only in short doses with plenty of rest and recovery in between. So watch your baby's body language and listen to those preverbal noises so that you provide exactly the right amount of stimulus. (Check out the typical signs of over- and understimulation in Key 1, on pages 93 and 94.)

Understimulation can also affect your baby's developing clock since she needs to enjoy the world when she is awake. If she's bored (yes, newborns can get bored!) and lying in a gently moving swing, for example, she may be in a semi-sleepy stupor instead of actively learning about her world. So find the right balance of stimulation linked to your baby's natural awake and asleep pattern.

Locate Naps in the Middle of Family Life

If your baby is having excessively long naps, then shorting herself on night sleep, start having your baby take her daytime naps in a room where she can hear the noises of the day, perhaps in a bassinet or cradle located in the main area of your home.

Don't tiptoe around the house during naps! Keep up with your normal sounds of the day. These are sounds that your baby is used to from listening while in the womb.

If your baby is regularly taking long, blissful naps in a sling or soft carrier, consider having some daytime naps in her cradle, since sling naps can keep her sleeping for much longer periods of time. Or start out the nap in the sling and gently move her to the cradle when she's had adequate nap time.

Don't shush people from normal conversation and household noises, though it's wise to prevent loud, harsh alerting sounds (such as clinking dishes or noisy electronic toys) that can wake any baby, unless your baby is accustomed to these sounds and unbothered by them.

Most newborns can sleep through moderate household noise, but there are a few babies who wake up if you so much as drop a marshmallow! If your baby is one of those who wake up too easily using this plan, yet sleeps excessively long in a quiet room, you can allow a couple hours of quiet nap time, and then gradually introduce some normal daytime household noises.

Provide Ample, Frequent Feedings During the Day

Babies require many calories to fuel their rapid growth during the early months. Just look at the remarkable difference between a one-day-old newborn and a one-year-old walking-talking toddler! So much growth happens, and it is fueled by the tiny amount of food that a baby's stomach holds. This means frequent, small meals are best. Babies who are a bit short on calories during the day will take in more calories at night.

La Leche League explains another aspect of the breastfeeding process that affects your baby's feeding patterns: "During the early months, many babies do what is called 'cluster feeding': spacing feedings closer together at certain times of the day (typically during the evening) and going longer between feedings at other times." So be sure that you are responding to all of your baby's hunger cues, even if they are subtle, during the day, because if feedings are shortened during the day they will be made up during the night. Keep in mind that all newborn babies need to be fed often, but it's according to their own unique needs.

. . . *and* Provide Ample, Frequent Feedings During the Night

Night sleep provides your baby with an amazing array of special benefits that are all fueled by nighttime feedings. Growth hormones are released during the deepest sleep that occurs in larger quantities at night. And, in between those sessions of deep sleep, your baby will need to be fed. Waking up during the night to feed is normal and necessary. I know I've said this before, but in case you missed that important point, it bears repeating: waking up during the night to feed is *normal and necessary*!

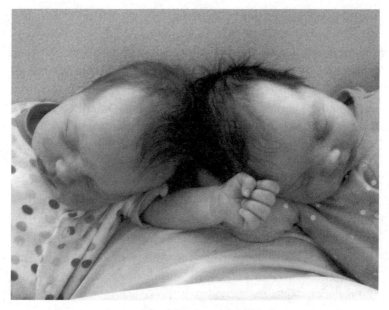

Ava and Sophie, six-week-old twins

Studies on breast milk show that nighttime milk is different from daytime breast milk. It's higher in substances that can help your baby's own biological clock develop. So those night feedings have more than one important purpose.

If you have a baby who is up for an excessive amount of times through the night, it is possible that hunger is the reason. If you are feeding your baby every hour or so, it's possible your baby is getting a series of nighttime mini-meals and falling asleep before a feeding is fully finished. This half-a-meal means your baby will be up again in an hour or less. Pay attention to see if your baby is falling asleep at the start of nighttime feedings, and when you see this happening shift his position and coax your little one to have a full meal before falling back to sleep.

Use the Power of Daylight

A simple way to cue your baby toward a regular day/night sleep schedule is by taking advantage of the effect that daylight has on your baby's maturing sleep patterns. There is a powerful structure wired into the human brain right from birth that interprets daylight as active and alert time. Within the first few months of life your baby will take in these light and darkness cues to help consolidate sleep patterns. You can help your baby's system along by using light and dark at the right times.

The most effective light for signaling alert time is natural daylight and sunshine. Make an effort to expose your baby to daylight first thing in the morning. You might create a routine where your baby's first feeding happens near a window that lets in morning light. Or schedule a morning walk outside or playtime in the yard. If it is dark outside, the second-best choice is bright artificial light.

> **Point to Remember**
> The human body clock interprets light as time to be awake and dark as time to sleep.

It can be helpful to have your baby take naps in a room that is lit with normal daytime light. Unless your baby is a finicky sleeper affected by the amount of light in a room, keep your normal daytime lights on during naps. Even with his eyes closed, he will detect the light of day. This helps to distinguished nap time versus nighttime when it is quiet and dark.

You can then also play with your baby in bright daylight several times throughout the early part of the day, furthering the announcement that daytime is awake time. By doing this consistently you can help your baby organize his day and night sleeping pattern.

Try to get outside a little every day, particularly early in the day. Even a walk to the mailbox or hanging out in your yard looking at the birds can have an effect on your baby's developing rhythm.

Beyond the body clock benefits, it's good for both of you to get out and do things, even if your baby is just a few weeks old. The sooner you get out of the house with your new baby, the sooner it will become easy and natural. So start with short, easy trips and work your way up to longer events.

Encourage Sleepiness with Darkness Cues

The second half of the light-affected sleep cue equation is that darkness signals to the brain that it is time to sleep. Darkness encourages release of the body's natural sleep hormone, melatonin. This is a very powerful natural phenomenon that allows your baby to be tired and fall asleep easily at bedtime. But it can be disrupted by exposure to bright light at bedtime.

Once past the initial newborn stage, when babies have an actual bedtime, it will tend to be early, around 6:00 to 7:30 p.m. Since this is hours away from the parents' bedtime, the house can be lit up as bright as daytime. So, even though your baby is feeling tired, the bright light signals to your baby's brain that it is time to be alert and active—and this often confuses the system so your baby becomes very fussy and cries easily in the evening. You can protect the natural melatonin creation process and the draw toward an early bedtime by keeping the lights dimmed in the hour or so before your baby's bedtime.

A second aspect of this process involves maintaining the darkness throughout the night. Even a small night-light can disrupt sleepiness and begin the daytime alerting process—which you don't want happening at 2:00 in the morning! Use as little light as possible during the middle of the night when your baby is awake for feeding or diapering. Keep night-lights very small and away from your baby's face. Keep glowing clocks turned away from your baby's bed. Don't turn on the television, iPad, Kindle, or any other light-producing device during midnight feedings—unless you can set it at a very dim night-light level. Avoiding artificial light can keep your baby in a sleepy state, allowing him—and you—to fall back to sleep easily after a diaper change and feeding.

If you have an early bird who is up at the crack of dawn, morning light might be the culprit. Cover the windows any way you can—blinds, curtains, or even a piece of cardboard, a black plastic trash bag or aluminum foil can prevent early light from waking your baby.

Parent-Speak

"This is our second child and we are doing things differently this time. With our older daughter we watched TV while I nursed her to sleep, and we took her up to bed whenever we went up. She woke a lot and we had many sleep issues. With Nicola we dim the lights and mute the noise. I nurse her, then pass her to Daddy to be rocked while I do bedtime for Arielle. When she's tucked in I return and nurse Nicola again and put her to bed. The pre-bed hour has become so peaceful in our house. The new baby sleeps great and our family is transitioning SO well!"

—Celeste, mother of four-year-old Arielle and two-month-old Nicola

Make Prebedtime Quiet and Peaceful

An actual bedtime routine isn't necessary for newborns, since they sleep when tired all day and all night, so a particular "bedtime" doesn't really exist. However, over the months, as sleep consolidates, your baby will begin to gravitate toward a set bedtime after which her longest sleep stretches will occur. You can help your little one along this path by keeping the hour or so before bedtime a bit quieter, peaceful, and dimly lit.

From the beginning of baby's "night sleep" hours, at around 6:00 to 7:30 p.m., turn down the volume on the TV or stereo and avoid any loud, jarring sounds. The only sounds your baby should hear are the quiet hum of voices and your white noise or soft lullaby music.

Keep Night Feedings Hushed, Mellow, and Toy Free

As strong as the release of the melatonin hormone is, the process can be halted with enough movement and action, causing your baby to pull out of sleepiness and into alertness. A fun parent, an interesting toy, a familiar song—any of these can jar a baby out of his sleepy state and into active alertness. Once your baby has entered this alert condition, it can last for quite a while, and you'll now have to guide him into the descent of tiredness all over again.

By keeping nighttime activities as unobtrusive and quiet as possible, you encourage your baby to recognize these quiet, dark times as sleeping times, as opposed to the more active and bright daytime nap sleeps. You'll also keep him in a semi-sleepy state, from which it is much easier to return to deep sleep.

When your baby wakes during the night, make sure you don't act too awake. (That should be easy.) Don't talk, sing, or say

Jianna, two weeks old

anything other than, "Shhh. Night night." Avoid fast movement, avoid any lights, avoid unnecessary diaper changes; keep the mood very sleepy. *Even if your baby is acting wakeful!* That's an even more important time for you to be *very* boring! Show your baby that nighttime is not playtime.

Stay mellow during nighttime feedings and diaper changes. Use only a small night-light. There's no need to sing or play with your little one in the middle of the night; save all that for daytime.

Make Sure Your Baby Has Plenty of Naps

When your baby is awake frequently throughout the night, but very sleepy all day, it may be tempting to keep her awake more during the day in hopes that she'll then sleep better at night. This idea typically backfires, and you end up with a cranky baby all day—and then a night filled with many additional wake-ups. As outlined in Key 4, Respect the Span of "Happily Awake Time" (page 131), your baby is programmed to nap frequently throughout the day, and missing naps causes disruption to the formation of a working biological clock.

The key to proper newborn naps is to pay close attention to your baby's sleep cues (see Key 3, page 117), and, when you see these, to make sure she has a snooze, even if she hasn't been awake for very long. By acting on early signs of sleepiness—before she gets overtired and overstimulated—you'll help your baby regulate her sleep system and fall asleep more easily and sleep more soundly.

Nighttime Bottle-Feeding with Ease

If you are bottle-feeding your baby, make sure that everything you need for night feeding is close at hand, organized and ready to use. Your goal is for your baby to stay in a sleepy state and nod right back off to sleep once he's fed. If you have to run to the kitchen to mix formula and prepare a bottle while baby fusses or cries, you'll just bring both of you to the point of being wide awake, and what might have been a brief night waking will turn into a long period of wakefulness.

Nighttime Diapers

If your baby is waking every hour or two during the night, you might not have to change her diaper every single time she wakes. Remembering back to when my firstborn child was a "newborn" and I was a "newmom," I dutifully changed her every time she woke up. Oftentimes I was changing one dry diaper for a new one.

I eventually learned that I was more "tuned in" to the diaper issue than *she* was!

I suggest that you put your baby in a good-quality nighttime diaper, or a doubled cloth diaper with an added insert, and, when she wakes, do a quick check. Change her only if you have to, and do it quickly, quietly, and as in the dark as possible. After all, once she is sleeping longer stretches, no one will be changing her diaper every hour!

Use a tiny night-light when you change the baby, and avoid any bright lights that can signal "daytime." Have your changing supplies organized and close to Baby's bed, and make sure you use a warm cloth to wipe that sleepy bottom—there's nothing like a cold, wet cloth on a warm bottom to fully wake your baby up!

Pay attention to both the diaper and your baby. Some newborns cannot sleep with even the smallest amount of wetness, so change your baby when needed, of course, but don't fully rouse a groggy baby just to change a dry diaper!

KEY 8

Ensure Adequate Daily Naps

Newborn babies sleep a lot, but here's the challenge: they don't take one or two long, defined naps the way that older babies or toddlers do. Their fifteen to eighteen hours of daily sleep are distributed evenly over four to seven (or more!) brief sleep periods—day and night, which means they could have four, five, or more naps every day, depending on how long they sleep during each nap. The length of their naps varies throughout the day; some are as short as fifteen minutes, while long naps can last several hours. Premature or sick babies will likely sleep more overall hours, but they sleep for shorter spans, so they divide their daily sleep into six to ten sleep periods.

During the first three months or so, newborns nap anywhere from five to as many as eight hours in a day, and these daytime nap hours are critically important to their health, growth, and happiness.

The Importance of Naps

Most people accept that babies need naps, but they don't realize the many benefits that daytime sleep provides. Napping is an important component of a child's healthy mental, physical, and social growth throughout babyhood and the early childhood years. Science tells us that naps benefit a child in a number of ways:

- **Naps are a biological necessity.** Children have natural peaks and dips in energy and alertness during the day. The peaks tend to occur after a baby awakens fresh in the morning or after a nap, and the dips occur at the end of each "happily awake" time span (see page 131). Those dips happen regardless of the quality or length of sleep that occurs prior. Even if a baby were to sleep ten straight hours overnight, the dips in energy would still happen because they are related to the length of time spent awake. When a baby lands in the dip, he desperately needs to sleep. A lack of response to this natural craving for a nap results in a biological misfiring that can lead to emotional and physical breakdowns. Naps that correspond with these energy dips fill a child's inherent need for rest, which allows the body and mind to function properly all day long.
- **Naps reduce the day's fussiness and crying.** Naps enable the body to release cortisol and other hormones that combat tension brought on by the normal process of learning about and engaging with the world. Without the release of these hormones, they build to uncontrollable levels that create inner pressure that erupts as fussiness and crying. Infants who do not get enough daytime sleep tend to cry more and are more difficult to console then those who are getting a nap every few hours.
- **Naps increase learning capacity for babies.** Babies who have adequate daily naps spend more of their waking hours in a relaxed, alert state. They learn more, they enjoy life more, and their parents are provided with added relaxed time for engaging, teaching, and bonding with their babies.
- **Naps improve brain development.** Adequate sleep is crucial to proper brain development. Studies indicate that daytime napping may play a role in learning by helping to move new information into a more permanent place in the

Anke, two months old, with Daddy

memory. Naps allow a baby important pauses to review and store new information and make room for the remainder of the day's learning. Sufficient sleep is also thought to help young brains develop the ability to achieve high levels of abstract thinking later in life.

- **Naps create an increase in attention span.** Research shows that children who nap have longer attention spans and are better able to interpret and absorb new information. Conversely, children who lack appropriate sleep tend to be more fretful and less focused.
- **Naps ensure proper growth and development.** Growth hormone is released during the deepest stages of sleep, and children who sleep well during naps and night sleep are assured their necessary sleep-assisted growth. Naps provide a baby's body with important downtime that is needed for

rejuvenation, cell repair, and growth. Naps also fuel the dramatic developmental surges that occur when children are
learning to master major physical and mental milestones
during babyhood.

- **Babies' nap times give caregivers a needed break.** No
matter how much you adore your precious newborn, it's
hard work to care for an infant. Babies require constant
attention, and this is particularly challenging when you are
sleep-deprived. Sometimes parents need their little ones to
nap just as much as their babies need the nap. During nap
time caregivers can reenergize, do a few things for themselves, or take a much-needed rest or nap themselves. These
breaks relieve adult stress, reduce the risk of postpartum
blues, and assure that caregivers can enjoy their sweet little
nappers more when they wake up.

Sleep Benefits Fade Over Time

As you can see, naps provide your newborn with an amazing array
of benefits. However, from the moment that your baby wakes up
each time, he is slowly using up the benefits that accumulated
during the previous sleep session. He wakes up refreshed, but, as
the time passes, little by little, the benefits of sleep time are used
up, and an urge to return to sleep begins to build. This is like a
phone or computer battery that slowly drains with use, and then is
filled to the top once plugged in—or, in the case of a baby, once a
nap has occurred.

When you catch your baby during these energy dips by observing and responding to early tired signs with a nap, you help to
build up a reservoir of sleep-related benefits, allowing your infant
a "fresh start" after each sleep period.

The Newborn Nap Pattern

To understand your newborn's sleep pattern, it can help to consider that not many days ago your baby was nestled in the sleep-inducing womb. The environment was perfect for sleep, so before birth your baby slept twenty hours a day or more. Waking periods were random, and for very short periods of time. (The kicking and poking that you felt when pregnant were often from movements made during sleep—just like a newborn, a fetus is a very active sleeper.)

The moment after birth, your baby doesn't drastically or instantly change—your newborn will continue the same sleep/wake pattern that occurred in the womb for weeks. At the same time, you will be adjusting to life with a new baby in the house, which takes a tremendous amount of energy, and perhaps you will be recovering from childbirth, as well. (This, by the way, is more justification for you to sleep when your newborn sleeps!)

Newborn Sleep Cycles

Newborns have shorter sleep cycles than adults do, and they wake easily between those cycles. Even short naps can be broken into yet smaller segments. This pattern is thought to act as a protective device—babies need lots of care and feeding, and they need to gain the attention of others to tend to their needs. Infants require food every few hours, so their light sleep cycles accommodate their need to wake up to eat. Babies who are born prematurely or with special needs may sleep *even more lightly* with shorter sleep cycles, which is nature's way of stepping in to be sure these special babies get the extra care that they require, and why it is important to respond to these needs.

New Babies Need to Eat Frequently

In the womb, babies don't need to think about eating because their nutritional needs are continuously met—they never feel hunger. After birth, babies must adjust to a different reality. Hunger is a new sensation, and likely not a pleasant one. Furthermore, they are growing rapidly, their tummies are small, and their diet is liquid and digests quickly. To fuel their amazing growth, newborns need to eat every two to four hours—and often more frequently—day and night. Breastfed newborns may sometimes need to nurse in as little as an hour after their last feeding. (If anyone argues this point with you, then I suggest you ask for an opinion only from the person who matters the most—your newborn.)

In the majority of cases it isn't necessary to wake your baby for a feeding, as a healthy baby will set her own feeding schedule. Even if she is taking a much longer nap than usual, just keep an eye on her. If your baby is an exception (such as premature babies or those with special needs), your healthcare provider will let you know if your baby should be awoken from sleep for a feeding.

The one time you might want to rouse a sleeping infant is when he is sleeping a majority of hours during the day but then waking up and staying awake in the middle of the night. For that baby you might want to wake him after four hours or so from his late afternoon or early evening nap so that he has an hour or two of playtime before it's bedtime for the night. This can help get your little one on a better day/night pattern of sleep. (For more tips on this see Key 7, page 163.)

The Happily Awake Span

If you've read through the previous Keys, you'll remember from Key 4 (page 131) that your newborn baby can only stay happily awake for very short periods of time. An infant can only stay awake for one to two hours before needing to sleep again. By three months of age, your baby can stay awake for one to three hours at a time; by six months most babies stay awake for two to three hours at a time, and that remains steady until about eight or nine months of age or later when your baby can begin staying awake for longer spells. (See the sleep chart on page 50.)

Keeping track of this happily awake span can help you to better gauge when your newborn needs a nap. It's useful to keep an eye on the clock and then watch your baby for sleepy signals when the happy span is nearly over. Take another look at Key 3, Learn to Read Your Baby's Sleepy Signals (page 117). The happily awake span should be your guideline, but your baby's signs of tiredness are the indicator of exact nap times. Every baby is unique, but all newborns need their daily nap time and will demonstrate their need for sleep in many ways. Refer back to Key 3 for a list of common newborn sleepy signals (page 92).

Safe Places for Naps

Whenever your baby naps, make certain it is in a safe place for sleep, and that your newborn is always placed to sleep on his back, except when held in your arms, of course. The safest locations for newborn naps are:

- In the arms of an awake adult
- Baby carrier or sling made for infants, and used properly
- Crib, bassinet, Moses basket, or cradle that meets all safety rules (See page 324.)
- Family bed that meets all safety rules (See page 326.)
- A baby swing made for infants that has a cradle-type bed that allows for Baby to lie flat
- A stroller made for infants that allows for Baby to be secured properly and to fully recline to lie flat

Test Parent Question

When I put my baby in our sling carrier she ALWAYS falls asleep. I work around the house or we go for a walk outside. She's sleeping pretty well at night in her bed, but this has become our routine for daytime naps. Is this a bad idea?

It's actually a fantastic idea! Babies love sling naps. You get to cuddle your precious baby, you get two hands free to do other things, *and* you get some fantastic exercise! It's a win-win-win-win!

What's most important for sling naps is that you make certain that you are using your sling correctly. Be sure that your baby is secured properly, and that you follow all the rules for safe sling use, such as keeping Baby's legs and hips in the M-shaped frog position, being able to see your baby's face, and holding your baby up high on your body—"close enough to kiss." Often I see new parents holding their baby in a cradle hold inside the sling. While this may seem correct, you actually want your baby upright, belly-to-belly with you, legs bent, with the top of his head under your chin. (See sling safety information on pages 272–274.)

One thing to consider here is if you love holding your baby for naps enough to do it for every nap—every day. If you can do this, and you want to, then enjoy holding your newborn for naps and come visit one of the other No-Cry Sleep books whenever you are ready to make a change.

However, if you don't want to sling your baby for every single nap for the next six to eighteen months, make sure at least one good nap each day occurs in your baby's bed, so that it becomes a familiar, comfortable place for her to sleep. (For more information see Key 10, page 205.)

Unsafe Places for Naps

The following places are *not* safe for an infant to nap because your newborn can shift into a hazardous position and possibly become entangled, or slump down, which can impede breathing.

Do *not* place your newborn to sleep in these places:
- Car seat, except when you're driving in the car, and it's installed properly and Baby is buckled in correctly. (If you're alone with Baby in the car, use a rearview baby mirror that hooks to the backseat headrest to keep an eye on your little one. These are available wherever baby products are sold.)
- Baby swing, seat, or bouncer where baby sits upright, or nearly upright, and/or is unsecured
- Nursing pillow, cushion, or beanbag pillow
- A sling or baby carrier that has not been specifically made for infants, does not fit your baby well, or is not used properly
- An adult bed that has not been made safe for an infant (see page 326)
- Bedding contraptions that are marketed for infant sleep that don't meet federal safety requirements
- Beside an older sibling, friend, relative, or pet
- On a sofa, recliner, or chair
- In a room where people smoke

Helping a Reluctant Napper to Sleep

There are times when your baby just doesn't feel like napping—even though he should! If you are watching the clock for the end of that "happily awake span" and also watching your baby for signs of

Parent-Speak

"I think the best idea for me has been that you don't have to have your baby nap only in one specific place all the time. I love that you can use a sling and have in-arm naps, and sometimes have your baby sleep in a crib alone—and value the freedom when he does that, and not feel guilty about it!"

—Laura, mother of five-month-old Martin

sleepiness, you should be able to tell if it's time for a nap. However, there are times when all signs point to nap time, but your baby is reluctant to nap. At times like these it can help to create conditions that mimic the conditions of the womb, which are sleep-inducing.

Holding your baby on your chest or carrying your baby in a soft sling are wonderful nap-inducers. You can enhance the benefits by resting your baby's cheek against the warm skin of your chest. The skin-to-skin cuddles and the sound of your heartbeat are very soothing to your baby.

Another option for a reluctant napper is to place your baby, snuggly swaddled and secured, in a flat-lying rocking cradle or baby swing or hammock, while using pink-hued white noise and adding a pacifier if your baby uses one—all of these things together can help your baby nap.

Here's an idea that has worked for many reluctant nappers, which also has the benefit of being easy to wean from when the time comes. Bring your stroller into the house. Walk your baby around for naps until he falls asleep. You can even do this in a small apartment; just roll back and forth over a small hump (like a doorway threshold), which enhances the relaxing effect. When your baby falls asleep, park the stroller near you for the remainder of nap time (don't leave your baby unattended). If your baby starts to move about or make noises before he's had a good nap, then

Thea, seven weeks old, with Mommy

walk and bounce him a bit to help him fall back to sleep. I did this frequently with my grandbaby. I parked him next to my desk and rested my foot on the stroller wheel. He slept, while I wrote. If he stirred, I rocked him with my foot. When he awoke, Nana was right there to play!

Once your baby gets a little older and is used to taking a nice, long nap in the stroller, then you can make the transition to your baby's bed, if you wish. Start by parking the stroller right next to your baby's bed (near you or while you listen in with a baby monitor), then work toward letting him fall asleep in the stroller and then moving him to his bed when he's totally asleep. Eventually, try a nap in the crib. To make it more inviting, use soft flannel or jersey fabric sheets in the crib and have white noise playing in the room. Step by step—this nap plan can work!

Test Parent Question

My baby is starting to notice the world so even when she's tired she starts to look like she's falling asleep, but something will catch her eye and her head bobs back up and she's fully awake!

It's a baby's job to learn all about the world. And some take this assignment so seriously that they never want to miss a minute, so any small thing can prevent them from sleeping. You can help a curious baby to sleep by removing distraction. Put your baby down for a nap in a darkened room, or hold her in a sling or your arms while pacing in a boring hallway or sitting in a darkened room with little for your baby to look at but blank walls. Humming softly or using white noise can also help muffle outside noises that can create a distraction from sleep.

Limit Any Long, Late Naps

If your baby is taking long afternoon or early evening naps, but then staying up too late or resisting bedtime, work on shortening those late day naps. This is sometimes a very hard idea to follow. When you are sleep-deprived, and when you have gotten behind on your own chores and responsibilities, it's easy to take advantage of your baby's long daytime nap to catch up. While this may be helpful in the short run, it can interfere with nighttime sleep, which makes it harder for you to function during the day. It also delays the time when your baby organizes her sleep into short daytime naps and long nighttime sleeps.

This is one of the few times when we can break that rule of never waking a sleeping baby. If your baby has napped more than three or four hours in the late afternoon or evening, wake her gently and encourage her to stay awake for a short while and play, even for twenty minutes or a half hour. It doesn't have to be rowdy playtime, but a bit of open eyes and then back to bed for the night is fine.

To determine if a nap is going on too late in the day, review the sleep chart on page 50, particularly the span of happily awake time:

Age	Endurable awake time between sleep periods
Up to 4 weeks	45 minutes–2 hours
1 month	1–3 hours
3 months	1–3 hours
6 months	2–3 hours

Ava, four days old, with Daddy

Review these numbers and consider the amount of time your baby typically stays awake between sleep periods, keeping in mind that often a baby will stay awake longer after a good long nap. So, if your three-month-old baby usually stays awake for about two to three hours and has been taking a three-hour nap, and now it's 4:00 p.m., I'd say you might want to wake him up so that he won't be up and alert past 7:00 p.m.

Some babies are such sleepy newborns that it seems an earthquake can't wake them! Here are a few tips for waking such a sleepy baby when it's time to get up and eat:

- Try to wake your baby during a lighter stage of sleep. Watch for movement in arms, legs, and face. If your baby's limbs are dangling limply, she'll be especially hard to waken.
- Unwrap your baby if she's swaddled.
- Turn off the white noise.
- Hold her in a more upright position.
- Talk and sing to her.
- Move Baby's arms and legs in a gentle exercise pattern.
- Place your baby in an infant seat or stroller in the middle of the family's activity. (If you keep her snuggled in your arms, she may not wake up easily.)

Learn to Incorporate Baby into Your Activities

Newborn babies sleep for a large portion of the day. But this will change very soon! It can be a challenge to learn how to go about your usual daily routines with a baby along, but it's helpful to begin to see your baby as a little person who keeps you company throughout the day.

Test Parent Question

My baby is eight days old. Everybody says I should nap when he naps. Should I?

Yes, absolutely! The more rest you can get, the happier you will be. You don't have to nap every time your baby sleeps, but when you feel tired, drop everything and take a snooze, or at least a quiet rest break. Being a brand-new parent can be one of the most overwhelming times in your life—so be patient with yourself and give yourself permission to take a rest when you can.

New mothers are more likely to suffer from the baby blues and postpartum depression if they don't take care of their own sleep needs. As new parents, you can find that taking care of a baby in addition to other responsibilities can take a toll on your mood, your health, and even your marriage and other relationships. Take your own daily nap can help you combat fatigue, and it can help you to be a better parent. Even a twenty-minute catnap can rejuvenate you and help to offset your disturbed nighttime sleep, so definitely give it a try.

Don't feel that you must save every task for the times when your baby is sleeping. Begin now to include your baby in your everyday chores. After all, babies love to watch and learn, and you are your baby's most important teacher. He will enjoy becoming a part of your daily life, and you will enjoy his company, too.

KEY 9

Understand and Respect Your Baby's Sucking Reflex

B abies are born with an incredibly strong sucking reflex that is possibly their most important instinct as it is their only way to eat. Newborns typically double their birth weight in the first three to six months, and they do this incredible amount of growing on a liquid diet with a teaspoon-sized stomach. Frequent feedings are the means to their survival, so the need to suck is an unstoppable instinct.

In addition to being their only means of nourishment, your baby's sucking reflex is a method of stress release and relaxation. Most babies need the soothing effect of sucking in between feedings, and you may even spot your baby making sucking motions during sleep! Sucking is a baby's most powerful soothing mechanism. Sucking activates the release of calming hormones in a baby's nervous system, which bring on relaxation, drowsiness, and, ultimately, sleep. When coupled with the warm, snug, and safe place within a parent's arms, this is a potent and addictive sleep inducer.

Falling Asleep at the Breast or Bottle

Feeding is hard work for your new baby! It requires complete and focused attention, and it takes time to complete a full meal. Because of this, it's very likely that your baby will fall asleep after

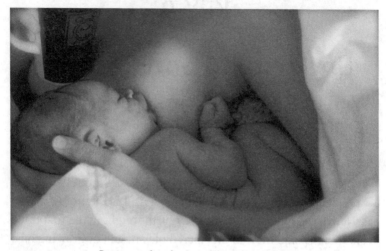

Paxton, a few hours old, with Mommy

expending the energy that feeding requires. It's nearly impossible to prevent your baby from becoming drowsy as she sucks, particularly if you are breastfeeding, since a biological benefit of breast milk is that it contains a number of sleep-inducing substances.

Some sleep methods suggest separating feeding times from sleep times with playtime in between. I don't suggest you even try this, because you'll be fighting against your baby's natural tendencies and can agitate your baby by forcing him to wake up when he's been blissfully falling asleep, and it can alter your own natural instincts as you are learning to read your baby's sleep and hunger cues.

If you are a breastfeeding mother, it makes even less sense to try to separate nursing from sleeping, as the two are intricately bound together. The nurse-play-sleep sequence is nearly impossible to achieve, as a newborn's natural sequence is more like this: *nurse, sleep, nurse, play, nursesleepnurse, play, nursenursenurse, sleep, nurse, play, nursenursenurse, sleep, and repeat (in no particular order).*

As many as 80 percent of newborn nurslings fall asleep at most of their breastfeeding sessions! When you consider that many hours of your time in the first month or two are spent breastfeeding, it's important that you understand how normal this is. Nursing your baby is meant to not only feed him, but help him sleep, as well. Even while respecting this natural process and allowing it to unfold naturally, you can still learn how to identify developing patterns as the weeks pass and understand how they will affect the coming months.

Point to Remember

If you are willing and able to let your baby fall asleep at the breast for every nap and throughout the night, then proceed as you are. There are no dangers or risks for your baby, and, as long as your baby is happy and healthy and you are happy and getting enough rest to get through your days, then enjoy this precious and fleeting life stage. I would still scan this chapter now, and then revisit it later when you are ready to make a change.

The Greatest Joy but Potentially the Greatest Problem

As we've been discussing, newborns nurse, feed, and suck a lot, and it is very natural for them to fall asleep while sucking at the breast, a bottle, or a pacifier. It's inevitable that many newborns barely stay awake until the end of the meal! However, when a baby

gets past the first month or two and continues to *always* fall asleep
this way, for every nap and every bedtime and every night waking,
she comes to associate sucking with falling asleep. This isn't a bad
thing, but, over time, there is a very good chance that she will not
be able to fall asleep any other way. A large percentage of parents
who are struggling with older babies and even toddlers who wake
them for assistance to fall back to sleep every hour or two all night
long are dealing with this issue. Because their children cannot
fall asleep or stay asleep without a nipple in their mouth, they are
fighting this natural and powerful sucking-to-sleep association that
lingered long after the newborn stage.

So this chapter will help you to find the best balance for respecting and honoring the natural needs of your newborn baby with an
eye on building the best patterns for the future.

Averting a Sucking-to-Sleep Necessity with Pantley's Gentle Removal Plan

Yes, it's true that some newborns can fall asleep for every nap
and night sleep while sucking at the breast or bottle, and then nap
well and sleep through most of the night. These babies also wean
themselves from this need on their own, naturally and easily. However, they seem to be the minority, and unless you have a crystal
ball, I can't tell you which babies those are. So, to prevent you
from struggling with a strong "suck-to-sleep" association that lin-
gers until your child's first or *second* birthday, you may consider
this idea an important one to try. This is something you can do
to prevent your baby from developing such a strong suck-to-sleep
association that it becomes an absolute necessity for sleep, and a
firmly ingrained habit that is very hard to change. The beauty is
that this plan also respects your baby's current needs to suckle to
sleep.

Pantley's Gentle Removal Plan works on this principle: if you want your baby to be able to fall asleep without your help later, it is essential that you *sometimes* let your baby suck on the nipple until he is very sleepy, but not totally limp-asleep.

The Removal is simple: After the first few weeks of life, and after breastfeeding is firmly established, for about one-third or more of your feedings, remove your baby from your breast or the bottle when he is done feeding, but before he begins the fluttery, on-and-off pacifying sucking that is nonnutritive but sleep-inducing. Before your baby is totally limp-limbed and snoring, remove him from the breast or bottle. (You can then replace this with a pacifier if your baby uses one for sleep.)

If you are aiming for some independent sleep, you can then transfer your baby to bed to finish falling asleep there (as discussed in Key 10, which is about bassinet sleep). You will likely need to pat, rub, jiggle, or shush her to help her fall asleep, but having her do this without the nipple in her mouth will show her that she can, indeed, fall asleep without it. The value of this idea is clearest among breastfeeding mothers who must nurse their *toddlers* fully to sleep for every single nap and bedtime. So, to avoid that scenario, start with this idea early, but remember, you don't have to do this at every feeding—just enough so that your baby knows sleep is possible without a nipple resting in her mouth.

Patience with Your Baby, Patience with Yourself

At any time, if you feel too frustrated with this idea, just let your little one nurse to sleep, and try again at the next nap or at bedtime, or even take a break and start up again next week. Don't feel you must succeed quickly. If you become frustrated, your baby will pick up on your tension and may cry or have difficulty transitioning to sleep. This process may take some time: weeks, or even months. Be patient. There are no awards for being the first parent on your block to have your baby fall asleep without your help!

Remember too that all the solutions in this book can work together like pieces to a big sleep puzzle. Make sure that you are applying all the other information you've learned about your baby's sleep in other parts of this book.

Point to Remember

Enjoy and respect your baby's desire to nurse to sleep, but make sure it's not the one and only way your baby sleeps, because it can become very difficult to change later.

To prevent a complete dependence on sucking for sleep, at least several times a day, and several times during the night, remove the breast or bottle from your baby's mouth and let him finish falling asleep without something resting in his mouth. Or, as recommended by the AAP, and if your baby enjoys it, you can replace the milk source with a pacifier. (Just don't put it back once your baby falls asleep and it falls out of his mouth.)

This doesn't mean that you should obsess about this idea, since newborns easily and frequently fall asleep while sucking. It does mean you should be aware so that it is not the way your baby falls asleep 100 percent of the time, since suck-to-sleep dependence is by far the most common problem among parents of babies over four months old.

If your baby is already over four months old and firmly established in this ritual, you can check out *The No-Cry Sleep Solution: Gentle Ways to Help Your Baby Sleep Through the Night* or *The No-Cry Nap Solution* for a more detailed and advanced version of the Gentle Removal Plan.

Julian, six weeks old, with Mommy

Consider Offering Your Baby a Pacifier for Sleep

Once breastfeeding is firmly established (typically three to eight weeks after birth), or if your baby is exclusively bottle-fed, it is fine to offer your baby a pacifier to help him fall asleep. There is no evidence that using a pacifier creates any health or developmental problems for young babies. On the contrary, new studies show that pacifier use might possibly reduce the risk of SIDS, although it is unclear why the connection exists. At this time, medical organizations no longer discourage the use of pacifiers for naps and nighttime sleep for babies up to one year of age. They do not make a recommendation of pacifier use for all babies, but if your baby benefits from having a pacifier for sleep you can now rest assured that it is fine to use one, as long as it doesn't interfere with your breastfeeding relationship.

Scientists and breastfeeding groups feel that more research needs to be done before any specific recommendation of pacifier use should be made, since this might interfere with the quantity or length of breastfeeding for some babies. There are a few professionals who believe that a breastfeeding baby who sleeps close to the mother and wakes frequently to nurse has this same protection against SIDS, but it is all conjecture at this point. So watch the news and talk this over with your healthcare professional as you make decisions about pacifier use.

> **Professional-Speak**
>
> "If used sensibly and for a baby who has intense sucking needs—in addition to, not as a substitute for, human nurturing—pacifiers are an acceptable aid."
>
> **—Dr. William Sears, author of *The Baby Book***

Using a Pacifier Safely

Professionals encourage parents who do decide to use pacifiers for their babies to use them judiciously, which often means keeping the pacifier linked specifically to sleep times, car rides, and colicky periods only, and avoiding having it become an all-day attachment. Keep these important tips in mind when it comes to using a pacifier:

- Never use a pacifier to replace or delay feeding when your newborn is hungry. Remember that some babies can breastfeed every hour, and that is a *need*. With any baby, but most specifically with a newborn, a pacifier should never postpone breastfeeding or bottle-feeding for a significant amount of time.

- Don't use the pacifier as a first choice when calming your crying baby—try holding, slinging, rocking, or singing to your baby first.
- Introduce the pacifier gradually and let your baby become accustomed to it on her own timetable.
- Never use a string, ribbon, or other device to tie a pacifier to your baby or the crib.
- Use only a clean pacifier. (Keep them clean by popping them in the dishwasher.)
- Offer your baby a pacifier for falling asleep, but don't replace it once your baby is sleeping and has pushed the pacifier out of his mouth.

What About Thumb and Finger Sucking?

Once your baby gets a bit older and is able to locate and position his hands and fingers, he may come to rely on sucking his thumb or fingers for sleep. If your baby falls asleep with the comfort of sucking his own fingers, this is an entirely different situation from using a bottle, pacifier, or your breast. Your baby is in control of his own hands and able to use them whenever he wishes. He's also not depending on someone else to help him every few hours all night long.

Current philosophies disagree as to whether letting a baby get into this habit is a good idea or not, but most experts agree that letting a young baby suck his own fingers poses no harm in the early months. The biggest issue, as you may expect, is that some children don't give up this habit on their own at any age, and you eventually have to step in when sucking could affect tooth, mouth, and speech development, nothing you need to think about in the newborn months.

KEY 10

Help Your Baby Make Friends with the Bassinet

One of the first things on the wish list families make when expecting a baby is a bassinet, cradle, or crib. The majority of people have these in place before their new baby arrives. They create a beautiful baby bed and envision their baby sleeping peacefully as they gaze lovingly into the crib.

There are many families who proceed along this road and find that having their baby sleep exclusively in his own crib works for them from the start—even if they have to go from their bed to his seven times each night for feeding and nurturing. If this describes your family, you probably don't need this chapter now. I suggest that you review the crib safety list on page 324 and make sure that you create a perfectly safe sleeping spot for your newborn. When your baby sleeps in a crib, you will, of course, be taking him out several times each night for feedings. An important point to keep in mind is that it is extremely risky to fall asleep with your baby on a rocking chair, sofa, or recliner, so make certain that you stay awake and return your baby to his crib after every night waking. You'll want to return to this chapter if sometime down the road your baby resists being put back into his crib as you hoped he would.

For the rest of you, once Baby arrives, that beautiful cradle or crib becomes a great place to hold stuffed animals or extra diapers. This happens once Mommy and Daddy realize how incredibly cuddly a newborn feels in their arms at nap time and lying beside

them in bed at night, and how much said newborn resists being put
into bed alone. Even if you think you won't fall prey to a squishy,
snuggly newborn, there's a good chance you'll turn to putty the
first time your seven-pound prince or princess protests the "putting
down in bed" ritual. This chapter will be very important for you.

You may even be the type of family that decides right from the
get-go that it's the family bed all the way for you. But don't stop
reading this chapter just yet! Even if that's your plan, and even
if that's what you did with your older child, there are reasons to
introduce your baby to a bassinet or crib, even if it's not your baby's
main sleeping location. Read on, and I'll explain why and how.

Where Your Newborn *Wants* to Sleep

Given a choice, your brand-new baby would sleep in your arms, in
a sling, or at your side for every single nap and all night long, every
night. That's because your baby is one smart cookie! What's not to
love about the warmth and security of loving arms and the comfort
of a familiar heartbeat, not to mention delicious, comforting milk
at the ready, especially if Mommy is breastfeeding? Your newborn
has some very strong instincts that direct every fiber in his being to
recognize that his adult humans provide the most comfortable and
safest place in the world to sleep, so that's where he wants to be.

Your bone-deep instincts are at work here, too. There is
nothing—absolutely nothing—as endearing and delightful as a
newborn baby falling asleep in your arms or at your side. When
your newborn falls asleep in your arms, your hormones breathe
a deep sigh of relief and contentment. I've held all four of my
children, my grandbaby, and countless friends' new bundles for
many, many, *many* naps! I can tell you that I am an expert at typing
with one hand. I can do, and have done, just about anything with
a sleeping baby in my arms—including coaching my daughter's

softball team (dugout baby in team-colored sling), chairing a PTA meeting, and even using the toilet. (Oh, you thought you were the only one to do that?) There appears to be a heavy-duty biological magnet that switches on when a newborn falls asleep in your arms or at your side that prevents you from putting the baby down!

Breastfeeding mothers are particularly affected by this phenomenon because the act of feeding is a natural sleep-inducer for both baby and mother. And, once both parties are relaxed and drowsy, it's easy and natural to simply keep the connection, close your eyes, and drift off to sleep.

Choosing to Honor the Instinct

Many parents of newborns give in to their basic instinct to hold their sleeping babies for naps and to bed-share at night. This is a perfectly natural and normal situation the world over, and is much too lovely of an experience to pass up. There are plenty of times when you should relish this lovely experience, and I encourage you to do so, at least occasionally. Newborns aren't newborns very long, and in a blink they will be toddling off on wobbly legs, and in another blink after that they will be on the school bus, and soon after driving off in their own car. As a mom of four grown children, trust me when I say the days are long but the years are short. So, some of you will choose to honor the instinct to keep Baby in your arms or at your side throughout the newborn months, and, if it suits you, carry on! (Please do read the safety list on page 326 if you choose to bed-share.) Even if you are one of these parents, you may want to take a shower, exercise, or use the toilet without a babe-in-arms once in a while, so I suggest you read on for a few tips.

If you have the time, energy, and ability to safely nurture your newborn for sleep, and never put your baby down, then, by all means, enjoy this very special time! However—and this is a Grand Canyon–sized *however*—a baby who *always* sleeps in your arms, at your side, or at your breast will . . . you guessed it . . . *always* want to sleep in your arms, at your side, or at your breast, and will resist heartily any attempts you make to change the sleeping conditions.

Mother-Speak

"Thank you for giving me the confidence to trust my parenting instincts and create a sleep plan that works for our family. I have gained a more confident understanding of my baby's psychology, sleep patterns, and needs, and a better understanding of how to create a safe sleep environment in our bedroom. With guidance from this book, nighttime went from my most dreaded time of day to my absolute favorite and most treasured time. My baby, my husband, and I are all so much happier!"

—Renee, mother of five-month-old Soren

It's a rare mother or father who has the time or ability to cater to an in-arms sleeper baby for every single nap, and all night long, every night for the next one, two, three, or more years! Babies need much more sleep than adults do. I've worked with many parents whose babies are so accustomed to a parent's presence in bed that Mom or Dad has to go to bed at 7:00 and *stay there* because their baby has built-in radar that won't allow them to leave the room. A parent also has to take daytime naps, whether he or she wants to or not, or hold a gangly toddler for a two-hour on-the-lap nap! A better idea is to enjoy the in-arms and bed-sharing times with your baby, when it works for you, but teach your little one that he *can* sleep by himself, too. It may be a good idea to build in this option for yourself even if you don't think you will need or want it, because you never know how things will change in a few months.

Your Baby's Bassinet or Cradle—Why It's Important Even If You Bed-Share Full-Time

My inbox is daily filled with letters from parents who are struggling with sleep issues. Here are a few genuine reader letters I have received lately. I get *thousands* of letters that sound exactly, precisely identical to these. The theme you see here defines one of the most common and challenging sleep issues in the first year or two. So, let me have these parents tell you why you should help your baby love his bassinet, cradle, or crib—right from the start, even if you plan to have a full-time family bed:

"My baby is ten weeks old, and I have a really hard time trying to get him to sleep by himself. He slept in his crib only twice since birth. I have been holding him or sleeping with him, but the only time he goes to sleep is in my arms or on my chest. Every time I put him down he immediately wakes up and cries. I really need your help as I cannot go on like this."

"My oldest daughter would not sleep unless she was being held. She would wake up the minute she was laid down in bed. The first two months she actually only slept in my arms, in Daddy's arms, or on my chest with me lying rigidly on my back afraid to move. Even though it wasn't safe, I did it out of sheer exhaustion because of a total lack of sleep."

"Two kids, two experiences. The first time, our son woke up four or more times every single night. He wouldn't ever go to sleep unless we were holding him! This continued until he was TWO YEARS OLD. With our second baby, we read *The No-Cry Sleep Solution* from the start, and applied the principles in the book, including using the crib for half of his naps and part of the night. Our second baby slept through the night by six months old and sleeps equally well in his crib or with us! They are both extremely happy, loving, confident and social children, so, given the choice, I'll take the track with better sleep, thank you very much!"

A Forward-Thinking Suggestion

So, there you have it. As glorious as it is to hold a sleeping infant, and as wonderful as it is to sleep beside your baby, this is a decision you should make with the future in mind, since the newborn months pass by in a speedy haze, and before you know it you have a one-year-old who is still sleeping like a newborn. So, as difficult as it may be, I recommend that when your baby is asleep, at least once every day, and once during the night, *put your sleeping baby down in a cradle, bassinet, or crib.*

Don't deprive yourself completely of the precious pleasure of infant sleep—I mean that, do make sure that you enjoy this treat—but not for every single sleep session. A balance between cuddle-sleep and having your baby sleep independently will probably bring you the best end result.

If you think you want to (and have time to) spend hours each day with a one-year-old on your lap, and tucked next to you from *his 7:00 bedtime* until *his wake-up time* (and yes, there are some parents who are truly fine with this!), then by all means continue on and enjoy this little slice of heaven! If this isn't you, though, it is better that you let your baby get used to sleeping in his bed now, since newborns seem to accept this process much more easily than older babies or toddlers. So whether your baby is a few months old, or has yet to be born, read on for some specific tips for getting your baby to feel comfortable sleeping alone.

Parent-Speak

"Putting her down in bed or in her swing for some naps and the first sleep of the night has been a game changer. This gives us time alone together and as the parents of four this has been HUGE for our marriage. This is the best we have ever done right after having a baby."

—**Dwain, father of two-month-old Jaclyn**

Get Your Baby to Love the Bassinet or Crib— The Four-Part No-Cry Plan

Now that you know *why* you should get your baby accustomed to sleeping in his own space, either full-time, part-time, or from time to time, let's talk about a few of the important aspects of this plan. You can use any of the ideas that suit you, or use all of the ideas. No matter which route you take, it helps to have an actual plan of gentle ideas outlined, because not having a plan and just putting your unwilling baby into his crib and letting him cry doesn't sound like any method I would be willing to use!

Make a Conscious Decision

This is an area that is prone to accidental parenting. Meaning that your cuddly newborn is so teeny-tiny that you get in the routine of

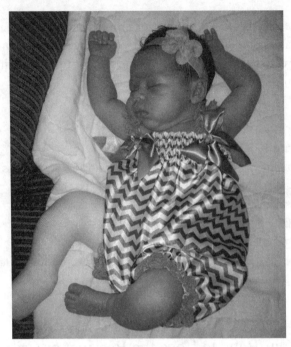

Brooklyn, six weeks old

holding her for every nap and letting her sleep squished beside you all night. But then, one day, your baby is a toddler and still sleeping in your arms or by your side or outright refusing to sleep at all. This pattern *can* be changed then, but it's challenging to convince a toddler to leave a parent's loving arms and sleep alone in an unfamiliar bed when he's slept beside you his whole life. If you totally love those in-arms naps and all-night cuddle-fests, and you feel it's worth it to deal with making a change in the future, then proceed, and come back to my books when you are ready to make the change, and I'll have lots of ideas for you then (because the number of parents in this boat could fill a fleet of cruise ships). However, if you feel you want to painlessly avoid this future challenge, consider the following four-part plan for introducing your baby to crib sleep.

Part One: Create a Cozy and Welcoming Bed

First things first! Make sure you have a cozy, comfortable cradle or bassinet for your baby. Many gorgeous baby beds are remarkably uncomfortable. Make sure the mattress isn't hard as a rock (which is oddly typical). If necessary, purchase a better mattress and mattress pad that fit the bed exactly, and that are firm enough to be safe but soft enough to be comfortable. (Use only a mattress that matches the exact size of your baby's bed, as any gaps can create a hazard.) Use soft sheets (such as jersey or flannel) that are warm and soft to the touch. Situate the crib in your bedroom, not far from where you will be sleeping, so your baby can see and hear you.

To help your baby accept this cradle or crib willingly, it needs to be comfortable and welcoming. Keep the following tips in mind as you set up a sleeping place for your newborn.

Make It a Small Space

Many newborns feel overwhelmed in a large, empty crib. Your baby may find that a smaller cradle, bassinet, or baby hammock is more to her liking.

There are cradles made especially for use alongside an adult bed, which is very helpful for ease of night feeding and for reaching over to settle your baby. A bedside cradle is a perfect choice because it keeps your baby at arm's reach but still in her own little space. A convertible bedside cradle that turns into a crib is a great choice since it can help your baby adjust to sleeping in a separate room eventually (after six to twelve months of age), as it can be unhooked from your bed and moved to the other side of the room, and then eventually down the hall. A cradle that rocks or sways is a nice option for newborns, since the movement can help your new baby sleep better.

If you have a large crib, it can help to use a crib divider inside the crib. (These are often marketed towards parents of twins to turn a crib space into two smaller areas. Make sure you select one that has a safety seal and that it doesn't leave any gaps in which your baby could become stuck.) This provides your baby with a smaller, cozier area, while letting him get familiar with the feel and location of the crib, which will make it easier when he outgrows the small space.

There are many style options for newborn beds, and it can be useful to shop around to find the perfect space for your infant.

Create a Nest

Because newborns spent nine months free-floating while curled in the fetal position, many are uncomfortable lying flat on their backs on a firm mattress. However, back-sleeping on a firm mattress provides the most important protection against SIDS. If your newborn only naps well in a sling or in your arms, this aversion to flat, stiff positioning on a hard surface may be part of the issue.

An idea that helps many newborn babies is to place them to sleep for naps in a bassinet-type swing or stroller—one made especially for newborns. (Don't use a device with a seat, because you don't want your seated baby to slump over with his head tilted down, as this can lead to breathing problems.) Safety dictates that you keep your baby next to you at all times if using this suggestion and don't use it for every nap. I personally like to park the sleeping baby next to my desk so I can see him throughout the entire nap and get some work done while he's snoozing.

As a safe option for your newborn's nest, check into a baby hammock. These gently embrace your baby and allow a free-floating 3-D type of movement similar to that felt in the womb. Baby hammocks have a slight angle, raising the head of the bed, and are attached to either a ceiling cable or a stable base and can be rocked either by the baby's movement or with your gentle nudge. Hammocks are especially soothing for a baby with reflux, colic, or extreme fussiness. They can be wonderful for a baby who resists back-sleeping, and helpful for preemies or babies with special needs. Hammocks are also beneficial as a way to avoid flat-head syndrome since the surface is more flexible than a crib mattress. There are a variety of styles available, so shop around for a safe one with high ratings, and get the okay from your baby's doctor for this type of sleep surface.

A slight potential drawback to this idea is that your baby may get used to sleeping in his little nest and resist future attempts to have him sleep in his flat bed, but you'll have many months of nice, long naps before you'll have to address this possible issue. Many parents decide that it's worth it since newborns spend so many hours sleeping. Once your baby has passed the newborn stage, you can begin to intersperse nest-naps with sleeping on a flat crib surface to help make the transition.

Consider the Temperature of the Bed and the Room

Cold sheets can be shocking to a baby who fell asleep in warm arms, so it helps to create a warmer surface. You can purchase fitted flannel or fleece crib sheets to fit your baby's mattress. These soft fabrics work better than plain cotton while you get your baby accustomed to sleeping in her own bed. Some people also pre-heat the bedding with a hot water bottle, heat pack, towel from the dryer, or heated blanket, then remove it—and place Baby down in the warmed bed. (If you do this, always lay your arms all along the surface before putting your baby down to be sure it's not too warm. Don't ever lay your baby directly on the heat source.)

Also make sure that the room temperature is optimal for the baby. It should be neither too warm nor too cold, and your baby should be comfortably dressed for sleep or properly swaddled. (See page 229 for swaddling information.)

Part Two: A Crib for the First Sleep Cycle of the Night

Now that you've created a perfectly welcoming bed, it's time to let your baby try it out. No matter where you plan to have your baby sleep full-time, I recommend that you try the following idea with your newborn from the first few days at home, or at least in the first

---

Test Parent Question

I am wondering if it is okay for my baby to sleep in a car seat brought into the house, in a bouncy seat, or on a crescent-shaped nursing pillow. He sleeps better in these than in his crib.

These are places that lots of babies enjoy napping in—but sadly, no; they are not a good idea since they have some significant and scary risks. It's fine for your baby to fall asleep in the car as you are driving, but the car seat is not a safe place for napping at home. A seated position is unsafe for newborn sleep because your baby can slump over and this can compromise his breathing. In addition, several studies show that spending too much time in this semi-upright position can put a strain on a baby's developing spine. Furthermore, spending awake time and nap time in the car seat, together with awake time in other baby carriers, increases a baby's chance of developing a flat area on the back of his head.

Pillows of any kind, such as a bed pillow, sofa pillow, or breastfeeding pillow, or any soft surface like these, also present a suffocation risk. Even if you are "right there," things happen—you could fall asleep (since you're probably exhausted!) or you could be tempted to get up "just for a minute" to get a cup of tea, answer a phone, or use the bathroom. It's much wiser to either hold your sleeping baby in your arms or a sling or put the little one down in a crib, cradle, or safely arranged family bed.

few weeks. This is because it's very easy to change your mind later and bring your baby full-time into your arms and family bed at any point, but it is *very hard* to reverse the plan and take Baby out of your bed and into a crib. You can always modify this later as you and your baby settle into life, but it is extremely difficult to start this routine once you've become entrenched in different bedtime rituals. (Not impossible, but much more difficult.) So, until you've settled in and gotten comfortable with your new family member, you may want to follow this routine for your baby's bedtime:

Have your first bedtime nursing or feeding session for the night in a chair or on a sofa that is *not* in your baby's sleeping room—make sure your baby is very relaxed and drowsy or even fully asleep—and then put your baby to sleep in a cradle, crib, or bassinet for the first sleep segment of the night. The first segment of the "night" happens any time after 6:00 p.m. when your baby is showing you clear signs of being tired. Since it's early enough, it's likely you'll then get up and do a few things around the house, watch television, or just have a peaceful few minutes before your own bedtime routine. Be sure that you are either in the same room as your baby or have a reliable baby monitor and check on your newborn from time to time. When using a baby monitor, have some white noise or soft music playing so you can tell that the monitor is working properly. Newborns should never be left sleeping alone for any great length of time.

If your baby is brand-new or if you've been following a different routine, when you first attempt to take your baby out of your arms and put your infant into bed, he might only sleep five or ten minutes in the cradle. Or you may have to stay and pat, rub, or shush him to keep him relaxed and prevent him from fussing himself awake. It is okay if your baby squirms or snorts or even crumples up his face and peeks at you a little bit. (But there is no need to ever, *ever* let your newborn cry!) He's just saying, "What the heck! I'm tired. Why didn't you keep me in your arms? What is this

Test Parent Question

When I breastfeed and then swaddle my four-week-old and put him in the cradle he only naps for about ten minutes. If I pick him up, feed him again, and then re-swaddle him he often sleeps two hours or more that second time. What should I do about it?

Do exactly what you are doing—that sounds perfect! Sometimes babies fall asleep midmeal, and they just need a brief snooze before finishing. Since your baby goes right back to sleep, then you've obviously read his tired signs correctly. (If he doesn't go right back to sleep, and his eyes are wide open and he looks alert and peaceful, perhaps he isn't ready for a nap yet.) But if he really is tired, then yep—sometimes it takes two tries, or maybe even three, but your end result—a nice, long nap in the cradle—is what you are aiming for!

place? How do you expect me to sleep *here?*" But your baby will soon figure out that, "Hey! My bed actually is quite comfortable. It's a really nice place to sleep!"

So, at first, if your baby lies in his own bed for *even five minutes,* this is success! Yep. Even five minutes for the first few times is success. Keep it up. The length of time your baby sleeps alone will increase. Within a week or two you may be surprised and delighted to see this first sleep session of the night last three or four hours . . . or more! This will be the time you get to yourself—or with your husband or partner—or to take a shower—or watch TV—or read a book—or even, go to sleep yourself!

By having her very first sleep cycle in her own bed, your baby becomes accustomed to this routine and will, over time, accept being put into bed at night-night time, even if later in the night you bring her into bed with you.

CAUTION

A word of warning to new parents, especially breastfeeding mothers—it is dangerous to fall asleep in a chair or on a sofa or recliner with your newborn. Your baby could slip into a posture that impedes breathing or get lodged between you and the side of the chair, or even fall to the floor. You need to stay fully awake until your baby is safely in bed. If you are exhausted and want the freedom to nod off, make sure there is someone in the room who can watch over you and make sure you both get safely to your beds. This is a great job for Daddy or a grandparent or other trusted family member, and a nice job to offer those who ask what they can do to help.

Part Three: At Least One Nap a Day in the Cradle

Babies are delightful, and there is nothing as wonderful as holding a sleeping newborn in your arms for naps. Don't ever deny yourself or your baby's grandmother (wink wink) or anyone else who loves your baby this glorious privilege. However, don't let your newborn have every single nap in someone's arms, because it will become the *only* way your baby will be able to nap. Yes, yes. I have already said this, but I want to be sure you got that point, since it's at the root of so many older baby problems. It only takes one or two naps per day in his bed for your baby to learn to welcome this as an option for naptime.

Even five or ten minutes of sleep in the cradle is a win when you first use this idea, whether your baby is four days or four months old. That time span will build, and before you know it your baby will be capable of doing a two, three, or even four-hour nap in his bassinet while you have time to catch up on the few things that are easier to do without a baby in your arms—like playing a game with an older sibling, exercising, or shaving your legs. If your baby

Marissa, three weeks old

does wake after five or ten minutes, you can either settle him back to sleep and return him to the crib or hold him for the remainder of his nap. What you choose to do depends on both your long-term and short-term goals. There are no rules here! Do what's best for you and your baby.

It's always important that your baby nap in the same room as you, so you can keep an eye on your infant. For short naps, you can use a reliable baby monitor system to keep one ear on your baby. (Keep white noise or soft music turned on to know the monitor is working properly.) Or get a portable bassinet that you can take with you into the kitchen or family room for nap time, or take with you to your mother's house or to a friend's when you go for lunch, or even take on an overnight trip.

> **Test Parent Question**
>
> *Is it okay if my baby naps sometimes in a bassinet, sometimes in a sidecar co-sleeper, sometimes in a pack-n-play and sometimes in the sling? It's a lot of different places, but it seems to be working fine.*
>
> Not only is it okay—it's absolutely perfect! Many babies need very specific conditions in order to sleep. If yours is flexible about sleep locations, it's a blessing. This way your baby will be able to sleep in many different places—a benefit for a family on the go!

Part Four: Early Morning Cradle Snooze

If you bed-share all night with your baby, or if you bring your little one to your bed at some blurry point in the middle of the night, here's a simple but effective idea to encourage your baby to have one final early morning snooze in his own bed. This "book-ends" the night so that your baby's first and last sleep cycles are in his own bed.

Some babies will sleep longer in the morning than their parents do. If this describes your little one, then gauge at what time she usually wakes for the day. If that's 9:00 a.m., then you'll want to aim for the cradle session any time after 6:00 or 7:00 a.m. Once it gets closer to that time of morning, and your baby wakes for a nighttime feeding, place your baby in the cradle after the feeding. Even though it's early morning for you, it's the last sleep cycle of the night for your baby. You can then go back to bed, or get up and on with your day.

If your baby is an early bird, waking up with the sun, then locate your bassinet time about two to three hours before the early waking time of the day. In some cases, this can even help your early bird sleep a bit later, as your own morning movements and sounds won't wake him as easily as when you're lying beside him.

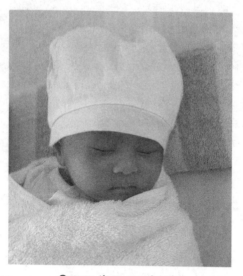

Quyen, three weeks old

A note that, if your baby primarily bed-shares with you, then you may have to leave the room so that your sounds don't announce your presence to your baby (but have that reliable baby monitor clipped to your belt.)

If you follow this early morning snooze routine, then you might be able to take a shower, get dressed, have breakfast, or tend to your other children while your baby sleeps his last few hours in the bassinet first thing in the morning.

Helping Your Newborn Accept the Crib or Cradle

Every baby is unique, of course. And you'll figure out your little one soon enough. However, the basic process of putting your newborn down to sleep in his own bed looks something like this:

- First, make sure you have a cozy, comfortable cradle or bassinet for your baby. (See page 213 for ideas.)
- Turn on white noise in the sleeping room. (See page 149 for white noise tips.)
- Feed your baby until he is done "actively sucking." Don't continue nursing or bottle-feeding for too long after your baby is clearly done feeding but still lingering with the nipple in his mouth. If there is no mouthing movement or swallowing, your baby is just enjoying the feel of the nipple in his mouth. (Check the chapter on the sucking reflex for ideas on this, page 195.) Swap breast or bottle for a pacifier if your baby uses a pacifier and seems to need this extra sucking as she falls asleep.
- Burp Baby, if necessary. (Breastfeeding babies don't usually need a burp. I know many people think that all babies must absolutely be burped after feedings, even at the risk of waking them up and interrupting that calm sleep process, but your breastfed baby may not need burping at all. Check with your lactation consultant if you aren't sure.)
- Swaddle your baby if she enjoys that. (See page 229 about safe swaddling.)
- Place your baby in her warm, cozy, and wonderful bed.
- Pat, rub, or "shush" your baby, if necessary, to help her settle to sleep. You might even gently lay your hand on your baby's tummy to help her settle into sleep.
- Keep Baby's cradle close by, or turn on the baby monitor. Respond to your baby as soon as she is awake, whether it's been ten minutes or three hours, so that she knows that you will come whenever she needs you. Do read the section about sleepy noises versus awake noises (page 139), and make sure that she really, truly is awake, and not just being a noisy sleeper!

Point to Remember

If your baby totally resists being put into the crib and cries the moment you begin to walk *near* the crib, try something different. Wait until your baby is asleep for ten to fifteen minutes and *then* put him into the bed. Stay close by so you can get immediately to your baby when he wakes, before he gets confused or upset. If he wakes happily, don't immediately pick him up. Lean into the crib and show him a toy or sing him a song or tickle his little tummy, just for a couple of happy minutes, and then pick him up. This shows him the crib is a pleasant place to be. Follow this pattern for a few days or a week and then try putting him into the crib awake for just a few minutes of playtime. Build a happy relationship with the crib, and then gradually try using it for sleep.

- Every day, have a few short, relaxed playtimes while your baby is in her cradle or crib, with you hovering above—talking, smiling, and singing to her. These short sessions can help build a positive association with the crib and encourage your baby to accept that this is a nice place to be.

Tips for Transitioning a Bed-Sharing Baby

If your baby is currently full-time bed-sharing, and you want to transition him to his own bed at least part of the time, here are a few extra ideas for you.

- You may want to start by putting the cradle or crib directly beside your bed and letting your baby fall asleep with your hand reaching over to pat or rub or just laid gently upon him. Once he gets used to that you can gradually move your hand away.

- Don't push yourself to go from full-time bed-sharing to independent sleep in one day—or even one week. Be patient and calm. It takes time to make any sleep-related change, but, if you are like me, taking the time necessary for a peaceful transition is a better prospect than letting your baby cry!

Parent-Speak

"A few weeks ago I was feeling VERY discouraged. I felt as though I could never set my daughter down during the day—ever. Naps were only happening in the sling. Naps were stressing me out and I felt like my toddler wasn't getting any of my time! Then you sent a group update that urged us to keep trying for naps in the crib if it was something that was important to us. You also said that it's okay to stop trying for a bit and begin trying again in a week or two. I immediately relaxed and felt like I wasn't the only one struggling with it. I took a few days off then began to again try to put my daughter down for one afternoon nap as well as the first stretch of nighttime sleep in her crib. After one week of sometimes needing three attempts to put her down, my daughter began sleeping up to two hours in her crib for naps! Now she does it for the first nighttime sleep while I bathe our toddler and get him ready for bed! I feel proud and happy that we did all this so gently and never once let her cry. And now I feel like I really can be a present mother to both of my children."

—**Kate, mother of two-year-old Justin
and three-month-old Lexi**

Dance Your Sleeping Baby into Bed

If your newborn always falls asleep in your arms or at your breast, it doesn't give him a chance to get accustomed to his cradle at all. For some babies, if you put them into their bed once they are asleep and later they wake up in that different place, they still wake up happily—and if that's your baby, keep doing what you are doing! Other babies, though, wake up crying when they realize they are alone, so it's better to "show" these babies that they are being placed into bed and change their "falling asleep point of view." You might try this:

As you are putting your sleeping baby down into his crib or cradle, very gently give him a small wiggle and say "night, night, Baby" so he becomes slightly aware of his location ("Oh, I see . . . I'm in my bed . . ."). Then give your baby a pat or rub, or provide a pacifier if necessary so he'll fall back to sleep quickly.

This is often what happens when an older child falls asleep in the car. They have a vague notion of being carried up to bed from the car (and they typically enjoy the trip), but they never fully wake up. Experiment with this as you want just a very slight, brief peek of awakeness—you certainly don't want your baby fully awake and fussing!

If you notice your baby starting to wake up after you've put her in bed, try to jiggle or rock her cradle and making soothing sounds and see if she falls back to sleep. If not, it's okay to pick her up, breastfeed her, or rock her, and help her fall back to sleep. Just try again at the next nap or tomorrow.

If this idea works for your baby, it can be a game-changing idea—since your baby will see the cradle before falling asleep, it won't startle him when he finds himself between sleep cycles in the middle of the night, and he may just fall right back to sleep.

Test Parent Question

Sometimes my seven-week-old just absolutely doesn't want to nap in her cradle. She just won't sleep at all until I put her in the sling. What's more important, then, making a point that the cradle is her sleeping place, or getting her enough nap time?

Getting good nap time is of the first importance, but you may be able to have her fall asleep in the sling and then move her into bed. Some slings and carriers are easier than others when it comes to the process of getting Baby in and out. A one-sided ring sling, for example, is an easier style for slipping Baby off your body and into bed. So, if you have several types of carriers, experiment to see which one is easiest to work with when your baby is sleeping, or borrow a friend's different-style sling to test it out. Keep in mind that, if your baby is ensconced in the sling and lying on it in bed, then you'll have to stay near your baby during the nap because of all the fabric surrounding her. So stay close and either do some paperwork or read a book or enjoy a session of yoga as your baby practices some crib sleep.

It's most important to your baby's health and well-being to be getting ample nap hours. The location of those hours is irrelevant when it comes to the actual benefits of sleep. A well-rested baby is a happy baby, no matter where naps take place. So, if your baby wakes up anytime you even try to get her out of the sling, then today isn't a cradle day—so don't force it. Just pop her back into the sling and let her snooze happily. Just try again tomorrow . . . and the next day, and the next, until it begins to work for both of you. Infancy passes more quickly than you can imagine, so be patient.

If You Simply Can't Put Your Sleeping Bundle Down

What if you love holding your sleeping newborn and simply cannot put her down, and end up holding her for an entire nap? No worries! Enjoy the in-arms naps and don't fret about it! Here's another idea that you can try once or twice a day, instead: When your baby has had a nice, long nap in your arms and just begins to stir and wake up, put her in her cradle! Stay right there and talk soothingly to her as she begins to wake up—"Hello, Baby! Did you have a nice nap?" As she looks around at her bed she might think, "Wow! I slept here? This is a pretty nice place. I had no idea." Then it won't be so foreign if you put her there for a future nap.

KEY 11

Swaddle Your Baby at the Right Times in the Right Way

You probably think that stretching out on a comfortable mattress is the perfect way to sleep, but your newborn would definitely disagree. Your baby has just arrived from a place that he felt was the epitome of comfort—and it was the complete opposite of stretching out on a mattress. You baby was folded up like a pretzel and squished on all sides inside a soft and pliable nest. His arm and leg movements drifted through a fluid-filled space, so they were in slow motion and confined to very tight quarters. This snug place was your baby's home for nine months. After this close-fitting, body-hugging space, your newborn might find it unsettling to be put on his back on a flat surface—yet this is the safest way for your newborn to sleep. Now that your baby is out of the womb, his own wildly flailing and totally uncontrollable arms and hands can easily wake him from even the deepest sleep.

There is a solution for helping your baby transition from the confining sleep space of the womb. Many babies are comforted and sleep better and longer when parents recreate the womb-like experience for sleep by wrapping them up securely: swaddling. It is a common and popular way to help newborns to cry less and sleep better.

Babies are unique individuals, and, while some love to be snugly swaddled, others adamantly reject anything that restricts their movement. In addition, just like so many baby care practices, it has supporters and critics. Let's unwrap the controversy over swaddling and listen to both sides of opinion on this baby care technique, and then discuss safe and appropriate ways to swaddle.

What Are the Pros? What Do Supporters Say?

Many hospitals, birth centers, and midwives swaddle newborns soon after birth, and many parents continue to swaddle their babies through the newborn months. Those who believe in the practice point to the fact that it helps to soothe fussy babies and promotes better sleep. Since sleep is one of a newborn's most important jobs, and promoting and protecting sleep is one of a parent's most important jobs, swaddling is often praised for its role in encouraging good sleep. The following list shares more of the reasons swaddling is a common practice.

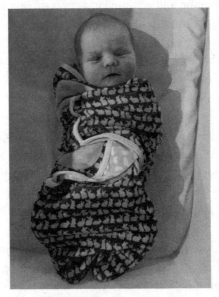

Mackenzie, two weeks old

"Pros" in support of swaddling:

- Swaddled babies have better naps and sleep for longer stretches at night with fewer spontaneous awakenings.
- A baby's startle reflex is blunted so that his own flailing limbs don't wake him.
- A swaddled newborn may accept back-sleeping more easily than one who is not swaddled, and the baby stays in that safe-sleep position. It prevents a baby from rolling over into the riskier stomach-sleeping position and makes parents more likely to consistently put their baby to sleep in the safe back-sleeping position.
- Swaddling can help to regulate Baby's temperature when sleeping in a cooler room.
- It is an effective sleep aid for a baby who only sleeps well when being held in someone's arms, so it provides an alternative to holding such a baby for every nap.
- Swaddling can often calm a restless, fussy, or crying baby if nothing else works.
- It can provide comfort to babies who suffer from colic or reflux or have special needs. They are soothed and calmed, and they fall asleep more easily.
- Swaddling might reduce the risk of postpartum depression for mothers of very fussy or colicky babies who only sleep well when routinely swaddled.
- It provides parents of twins and higher-order multiples a way to keep all of their babies calm at the same time.

What Are the Cons? What Do Critics Say?

As with many baby care approaches, there are differing opinions on this topic. Those who disapprove of swaddling frequently cite the following reasons for why they feel parents should not swaddle their babies:

"Cons"—arguments against swaddling:
- Swaddling could potentially be overused by parents as a substitute for a parent's arms, and babies should be held often throughout the newborn months. Babies should primarily be soothed in a parent's arms or held in a soft carrier, rather than lie swaddled in a bed.
- Since swaddling can reduce the amount of a baby's crying, it can also reduce some of a baby's method of communication. Habitually swaddling a baby beyond just sleeping times could lessen parents' ability to read their baby's fussing, and to respond with appropriate feeding or holding.
- There is a risk of hip dysplasia if a baby's legs are pulled straight and not free to move and bend in a natural position.
- If a baby rolls over when swaddled, it can create a breathing hazard and increase the risk of SIDS.
- Babies' arms and legs are not free to move, limiting natural movement. In addition, when they are tightly wrapped they cannot push away and protect themselves when in an uncomfortable or dangerous position.
- Babies who are swaddled may sleep too deeply and for too long, and waking up through the night is a protective device for babies. Babies are meant to wake up throughout the night, and their startle reflex is one way they rouse, so reducing wake-ups may not be in the baby's best interest.
- Babies may sleep through necessary feedings, and newborns need nourishment throughout the night.

- It can be difficult to wean a baby from swaddling, causing sleep disruption during the transition away from the swaddle.

Should You Swaddle Your Baby?

Once you review the pros and cons and research the topic, you can make an informed decision. There are a large percentage of parents who do use swaddling in an appropriate and safe way to aid sleep in the early months of life.

Swaddling is right for many babies, but others don't require it. It's important for you as a parent to figure out what is best for your unique baby. What's most important is that your little one is safe, content, sleeping enough, feeding well and often, and growing appropriately.

It's important to do your own research and discuss swaddling with your spouse or partner and with your healthcare provider and then make the right decision for your little one. Research is ongoing on this issue, and new information is always being released. As of now, there isn't just one definite answer about how swaddling fits into newborn care, so watch the news and decide what is best for your baby and you. If you think swaddling is a practice you'd like to explore, read on for tips, safety information and some important dos and don'ts.

Point to Remember
Swaddling does have some downsides, so it's better if you don't automatically assume that your baby is one who needs to be swaddled. Try first having your baby sleep without being swaddled to see if he is someone who does fine without it.

Your Baby Isn't Here Yet? It's the Perfect Time to Practice Swaddling!

If your baby hasn't arrived yet it's a great time to learn how to swaddle! Even if you decide not to swaddle once your baby is born, it's easier to learn this skill before those bewildering first days arrive. I suggest that you purchase a muslin swaddling blanket *now* and practice on a doll, a stuffed animal, or a friend's baby. It's best to practice *a bunch of times* before your baby is even born. If your baby enjoys being swaddled, it can help him from the very first day of birth, and it can be a tremendous burst of confidence if you already know how to wrap your baby up.

Many hospitals, birth centers, and midwives swaddle newborns, and they will be happy to show you how. However, it often takes many days of practice to keep your little Houdini snugly wrapped, so you'll be way ahead of the game if you know how to swaddle before your baby arrives. Plus, during those early days you may be feeling a bit overwhelmed and exhausted, since you'll already be learning so many new things. Anything that you can master ahead of time will be helpful!

Professional-Speak

"[A significant number] of babies are still placed face down to sleep, despite a massive education campaign. One of the main reasons parents give for this dangerous choice is that their babies cry more on their backs and don't sleep as well. If swaddling babies reduces crying and improves sleep, it might help promote sleeping on the back, further reducing SIDS, while making life more pleasant for babies and their parents."

—Dr. Alan R. Greene, pediatrician and author
of *Raising Baby Green: The Earth-Friendly Guide
to Pregnancy, Childbirth and Baby Care*

Amari and Azari, twenty-one days old

Swaddling Your Newborn

If your newborn has already arrived, your pediatrician, nurse, midwife, doula, or childbirth educator, or a veteran parent, can teach you how to swaddle your baby, and they'll often teach you right at the hospital or birth center. You can also find step-by-step instructions for swaddling your baby in a baby care manual or in a wide assortment of articles and YouTube videos. When learning how to swaddle, be certain you learn from a qualified person who knows the safest method. Old-fashioned swaddling techniques were often done incorrectly and can create safety issues or developmental problems for your baby. Check out the recommendations for swaddling techniques provided through the International Hip Dysplasia Institute. (Read more on this in the next section.)

Professional-Speak

"Reducing crying and exhaustion are key goals because these problems often trigger a terrible cascade of dysfunction and death, including postpartum depression (which can lead to lifelong depression, suicide and even infanticide); child abuse/neglect; breastfeeding failure (which can increase SIDS); dangerous sleeping practices (which can increase SIDS and suffocation); marital stress; cigarette smoking (which can increase SIDS); car accidents; overtreatment with medication; and perhaps even maternal and infant obesity. . . .

"The upstream issue is crying, exhaustion and feeling incompetent, and that's where we need to focus our efforts. . . . If we can teach families to be better at calming babies and getting more sleep, we have a real chance at making a dent in these other serious issues.

"Another SIDS expert [Bradley T. Thach, MD] wrote, 'All in all, it would appear that the advantages of swaddling supine-sleeping infants outweigh the risks, if any.' "

—Harvey Karp, MD, pediatrician and author
of *The Happiest Baby on the Block*

How to Swaddle Correctly and Safely

Swaddling is used worldwide with newborns, but not everyone does it properly. It takes practice to master the art of baby-wrapping, so be patient as you learn how. In addition, some babies take a week or so to adapt to swaddling, so if your baby resists the first few times it doesn't mean you should abandon the idea. At first, swaddle your baby when your newborn is calm and relaxed. Don't have your first few attempts happen when your baby is fussing or crying. This is something new for both of you, so relax as you learn.

Keep these important things in mind as you master your swaddling technique:

- **Swaddle only a full-term, healthy baby.** Unless your doctor tells you otherwise, don't swaddle a premature baby or one with special needs. Your special baby *might* benefit from swaddling, but your medical care professional should approve this and guide you on the specifics for your baby.
- **Swaddle only when Baby sleeps in the same room as you.** Swaddled babies can sleep deeper and longer, so you want to be sure someone is nearby for monitoring. Ask your doctor how long a span is safe for your own newborn to sleep without feeding, and, yes, wake your baby up for feeding if he sleeps too long. Always unswaddle him for feeding, especially if you are breastfeeding, but you can reswaddle him if you wish, as soon as he is finished nursing and ready to go back to sleep.
- **Begin swaddling well before three months of age.** Start swaddling with a newborn, but wait at least a few hours postpartum to swaddle if skin-to-skin with Mommy, Daddy, or another family member is possible. After three months of age, a baby is too old to adapt to the restricted sleeping that swaddling creates. New babies swaddled from the start will learn how to sleep comfortably within their swaddled space.

  Continue plenty of skin-to-skin cuddling in between swaddling times and allow Baby to stretch out and explore her limbs during the windows of alert times.
- **Don't overuse swaddling—keep it for sleep or colicky times only.** A baby who is awake should be free to explore her world with all her senses. If your baby is fussy or crying, your first line of defense should be holding her in your

arms or feeding her. During feeding times your baby should have the freedom move her hands and touch you. Reserve swaddling for times when your baby is clearly showing signs of tiredness, or when crying doesn't stop with other efforts.

Parent-Speak

"We think that swaddling regularly is helping develop sleep cues. He will fall asleep more quickly if he's been swaddled, or if he's being really fussy he will calm down once he is swaddled. And when we add the white noise it's like magic—full belly, change, swaddle and noise and Baby is off to sleep, and that's pretty great considering we have three noisy older siblings in the house!"

—**Annie, mother of Kate, Alexander, Eleanor, and baby Jacob**

- **Use a light, breathable fabric, such as lightweight muslin.** A great choice for swaddling is a blanket made of lightweight muslin (cotton with a breathable weave), bamboo fiber, or soft cotton flannelette that's big enough for a complete, secure swaddle, without the bulk of excess fabric. You can find swaddling blankets in most baby stores. It takes a bit of practice to get this right, but once you get the hang of it you can control exactly how it fits around your baby.

  As an alternative, you can use a specially designed swaddle wrap with Velcro tabs, snaps, or a zipper, a swaddle-type sleep sack, or baby sleep sack pajamas. However, some of these are not as safe as a lightweight blanket, particularly if they do not fit your baby properly. So, pay attention to package instructions on weight, size, and use. If the sack is too large, your baby can slip down inside it or become tangled in the extra fabric. A baby can also wriggle out of these if they are too big, which defeats the purpose of swaddling them securely in the first place. In addition, some are too thick and heavy, and could overheat your baby, so look for lighter-weight choices. Your baby's tummy, back, neck, and chest should always feel warm and dry, not sweaty or cold. Contrary to great-grandma's advice, "the warmer, the better" is not a good theory when it comes to babies, since overheating is a risk factor for SIDS—making sure your baby is *just warm enough* is the goal.

- **Make sure the fabric of your swaddling blanket cannot become loose.** Loose fabric can be pulled up over your baby's face or create excess fabric in the bed that your baby can become entangled in. Stick to the smallest blanket that does the job.

- *Always* **put your swaddled baby down on his or her back.** *Never* leave a swaddled baby sleeping on his side or stomach. (This goes for an unswaddled baby, too, unless your doctor specifically advises otherwise.) Studies show that swaddled babies who are placed on their stomachs are at a high risk of having their breathing impaired and that it may increase the risk of SIDS.

- **Leave chest-area room for breathing.** There should be space for two or three of your fingers to slide between Baby's chest and the fabric—plenty of room to breathe, cough, or sneeze. It should be snug enough that it doesn't come loose, but not so tight that it is affecting circulation or breathing.

- **Consider the best placement of your baby's arms and hands.** The traditional location for babies' arms is at their sides, and this is still a common placement, but it may not be best for your baby. Many infants like to have their arms positioned slightly bent and over their stomach or chest, and some prefer their hands out of the blanket so that they can suck on them. Keeping their hands out could mean that they could unravel the blanket more easily, and might be rolling over sooner, so you'll want to wean from the swaddle before your baby can escape the swaddle or push over onto his stomach. (And trim those little fingernails so your baby doesn't scratch himself.)

- **Keep the blanket away from your baby's head and face.** Tuck the edges down securely so that they cannot creep up. This can wake your baby up if it touches her face, and could bring on the rooting reflex, or it could move up over your baby's mouth or nose and impede breathing.
- **Keep the swaddle snug enough on top to prevent unwrapping, but secure it loosely around the legs and hips.** Your baby should be able to move his legs into the "frog" position—up and out—while swaddled. This allows important mobility for hip development. Swaddling the legs and hips too tightly can cause hip dislocation or hip dysplasia (abnormal development of the hip joint). In the womb your baby's legs were pretzel-shaped and overlapped. Binding your newborn's legs fully straightened can damage the joint and soft cartilage of the hip socket. And, furthermore, babies usually prefer this froggy-style position and may get irritated if they can't pull their legs up comfortably.

Point to Remember

Froggy up those little legs! To protect hip development, make sure your baby's legs can bend up and out whenever swaddled.

- **Consider using a pacifier for naps and bedtime.** Allowing a newborn to fall asleep with a pacifier when he is swaddled has been found to reduce the risk of SIDS. There is no need to replace the pacifier once your baby lets it fall out of his mouth, and actually that's what you want. A baby who can only sleep with a pacifier in his mouth will be calling out for help all night long when he gets a little older. Ideally a pacifier should be used to help the baby drift off to sleep rather than as something to suck on all night long.
- **Don't put your swaddled baby in a hat.** Immediately after birth your baby might be given a hat to help regulate her body temperature. However, after that first day, it's likely your baby's head should be uncovered. There are a few possible exceptions: if your newborn has special needs; weighs less than eight pounds; the room is cold; and in all cases, if your healthcare provider gives a thumbs-up for use of a hat during sleep. Putting a hat on your baby when she's swaddled could add to overheating, or it could slip down and cover your baby's face. Skip the hat unless your doctor tells you otherwise.
- **Don't put anything else in the crib.** Don't add extra blankets, bumper pads, crib wedges, stuffed animals, toys, positioners, or pillows. Any extra item placed in your baby's bed could present a safety risk.
- **Keep your baby's sleeping room smoke-free.** Exposure to secondhand smoke can create breathing issues and is a SIDS risk. Whether swaddled or not, your baby's sleeping room should always be smoke-free.
- **Swaddle only when your baby sleeps in your room.** Don't ever swaddle a newborn and leave him to sleep for a nap or all night alone. Always stay close by and check in regularly on your swaddled baby.

Declan, ten days old, with Mommy

When *Not* to Swaddle Your Baby

Although your newborn may love to be swaddled, there are times when it's not a good idea—and times when it can be downright dangerous. So, make sure you know the right times to swaddle your baby.

Do not swaddle your baby in the following situations:

- **If your newborn is premature or has health issues.** Some babies are not good candidates for swaddling, so check with your baby's healthcare provider about this. It may be fine for your special baby, but with some adapted points, such as keeping his arms bent and up on his chest, so ask this important question.
- **If your baby is sleeping on his side or stomach.** These are typically unsafe positions for sleep, even when unswaddled,

Parent-Speak

"Swaddling and white noise together is a genius combination! We swaddle him every night at bedtime and he falls asleep to his ocean waves sounds. We also swaddle for those naps when he's not in his sling. It helps him sleep so much better. He's in a cradle right next to our bed. I can tell the difference between his waking up noises and sleep noises usually, and when he does wake up he's very peaceful and never crying."

—Lucia, mother of two-month-old Juan

but when you add swaddling to the side or stomach sleeping positions you increase the risk of SIDS even more. If your medical provider has approved letting your baby sleep in a position other than on his back, then make sure you discuss swaddling as well, and unless given specific, detailed instructions, skip the swaddling.

- **Don't swaddle a baby if the room is too warm.** While all people, adults and babies, have their own preferences for the right temperature, sleep research shows that the majority of people sleep best in a cooler room. "Cooler" has a different definition for different people, but generally the range from 60 to 72 degrees (15.5 to 22.2 degrees Celsius) is cited as best for sleeping. A warmer room, plus swaddling or excess clothing, puts your baby at risk of overheating.

Overheating is one of the risk factors of SIDS. If it's a warm night, you might be able to use a light muslin blanket and dress your baby in only a diaper and T-shirt. Feel your baby's neck and back to be sure she doesn't feel overly warm or sweaty, and watch for flushed cheeks or rapid breathing, which are also signs that your baby is too hot. As a general guide, professionals recommend dressing your baby in no more than one layer more than an adult would use to be comfortable in the same environment.

- **If your baby is sick with a fever.** Swaddling could increase your baby's already overly warm temperature. If your baby is dependent upon swaddling, ask your doctor if your baby can be wrapped in a very lightweight blanket while dressed only in a diaper in a cooler room—and then keep your sleeping baby near you for constant supervision.

- **When you are bed-sharing.** As you've probably already discovered, sleeping next to your baby keeps you both warmer, so you don't want your baby to overheat by adding swaddling. In addition, you'll always want your baby to have hands, arms, and legs free to prod away anything that causes discomfort. In addition, bed-sharing provides the ultimate womb-like experience, so swaddling isn't necessary for a bed-sharing baby.

Point to Remember

Never swaddle your baby when bed-sharing. It can be dangerous.

- **To delay a meal.** Newborn babies need to feed frequently. Swaddled babies might remain calmer when they are waiting for a meal—but that's not necessarily a good thing! You baby needs to be alert enough to voice an opinion about mealtime, so don't swaddle your baby as a delay tactic. Reserve swaddling for your well-fed and sleepy baby.

- **During feeding, especially breastfeeding.** Your baby should have hands and arms free, and be able to freely move his body to adapt to different feeding positions. Also,

your newborn should have lots of body contact during feeding, and being snugly swaddled prevents a normal amount
of touch. Breastfed infants use all their senses to locate and
latch onto the breast. They love to touch and hug the breast,
and swaddled arms don't allow that normal and precious
connection between Mommy and Baby.

- **When your baby is in a car seat, stroller, or infant seat.**
  Swaddling prevents proper positioning of safety straps,
  which are meant to keep your baby securely in the seat. A
  swaddled baby will not fit the seat properly, since belts are
  designed to go between and around arms and legs, so your
  little one could slip out of position. In addition, your baby
  must be free to move his arms and legs when strapped into
  a seat.

- **If your baby is over three months old and has never
  been swaddled before.** Babies who are swaddled from
  birth adjust the way they sleep to align with their swaddled
  environment. Babies who are accustomed to having body
  freedom at night likely won't take to swaddling, and it
  could even be dangerous if they attempt to escape the blanket or roll over while wrapped. In addition, a baby who is
  not accustomed to swaddling may have a harder time waking up, which increases the risk of SIDS.

- **In a daycare, childcare, or babysitting situation, especially when your baby is not routinely swaddled at
  home.** Caregivers could use a different style of wrapping,
  which can pose a hazard. Some caregivers don't know or
  follow all the safety requirements of swaddling, or they may
  leave your baby in a separate unsupervised room, creating a
  potentially dangerous situation for your child.

  If, however, your baby is swaddled at home daily, and your
  caregiver uses the same type of blanket and the same exact
  wrapping technique that you use, and follows *all the safety*

precautions, all the time, including not leaving your baby without direct supervision, then this situation could be safe.

- **When your baby is awake, alert, and content.** Swaddling is intended as a practice to aid sleep and calm crying. Swaddling an awake and alert baby can restrict natural movements necessary for physical and mental development. Your baby needs full freedom to move when awake, including some short daily "tummy time" sessions to aid developing muscles. Use swaddling as a sleep aid only, and allow your alert and awake baby the use of all his limbs and a full range of motion.

Customizing Swaddling to Suit Your Baby

Just like anyone else, your baby is unique in her preferences. So, for example, even if everything you read says to tuck your baby's arms at her sides or on her chest, your little one might clearly prefer to have her hands out near her face. So, if you're sure that's what she is telling you, then honor her request! (And trim and smooth her sharp little nails with an emery board—skip the baby mittens!)

It's not always easy to know what your baby really wants when it comes to swaddling, though. Sometimes it takes a week or so for your baby to become accustomed to being swaddled. Also, there are many other factors involved in your baby's sleep, so it's not always easy to decipher the bits and pieces—it can be a bit of a Sherlock Holmes mystery. However, as the weeks unfold, you'll figure out how swaddling fits best for your baby.

If your baby enjoys swaddling, you can use it every day for naps and at nighttime, right from the day of birth, provided you adhere to all the safety items listed previously and wean at the proper time—this will be covered on page 249.

Parent-Speak

"My firstborn was colicky and she cried for hours every night and nothing would help. Nothing! Many times she cried so much she wouldn't even nurse. I just paced around the house holding her because I didn't know what else to do. I tried swaddling a few times but thought that she hated it because she didn't immediately stop crying. Now I suspect that may not have been the case. It's possible that I could have helped her cry less and we all could have gotten more sleep if I had learned how to swaddle her and added some white noise as well. These things are working so well with our new baby, and so far no colic, but if it happens I'll be more prepared."

—**Diana, mother of three-year-old Grace and six-week-old Jack**

If your baby is one of those very sleepy newborns who want to take super-long daytime naps but then keep you up all night, you might pass on the swaddle for naps and use it only for night sleep, thus encouraging longer nighttime sleep stretches and shortening those excessively long daytime naps. Another option is to swaddle for the first nap of the day, and allow your baby to nap unswaddled for naps later in the day.

Not all babies want or need to be swaddled, so, if your baby sleeps fine without this, don't feel you must try this idea. However, parents who have babies who are colicky, fussy, or sensitive resistant sleepers may find swaddling to be a lifesaver, especially when paired with the other techniques in this book. Many new babies do enjoy the womb-like security of being swaddled for sleep. If swaddling helps your baby to sleep better, follow all the safety guidelines and enjoy your little wrapped bundle.

When to Wean Your Baby from Swaddling

Every situation is unique, but there are a number of critical factors to watch for in deciding when to end the swaddling.

Most experts say that once your baby begins to move, roll, and squirm around, he could flip over onto his belly while swaddled and then be unable to safely position his head and body, which could affect his ability to breathe. In addition, the loose fabric of a swaddling blanket could become a hazard during the night. Trailing fabric can become entwined around your baby's limbs or face. Also, having mobile babies wrapped up prevents use of their limbs to extract themselves from an uncomfortable or hazardous position. Therefore, many groups recommend weaning from the swaddle when your baby *begins* to make efforts to roll (around three to four months) when he is placed on the floor unswaddled. Other groups recommend that you use swaddling only for the first two months, and then wean your baby before mobility even becomes an issue.

A few experts, such as Dr. Harvey Karp, author of The Happiest Baby series, say that swaddling can be done up to six or more months of age, if done properly. It's important that you discuss this topic with your healthcare provider and do your own research into the safety aspects of swaddling older babies if you wish to continue to swaddle your baby after infancy.

Professional-Speak

"Parents should stop swaddling when the potential risks outweigh the potential benefits."

—**Jennifer Shu, MD, FAAP, medical editor of the AAP Healthy Children website**

Alternatives to Swaddling Blankets During Weaning

If you have a squirmy baby who continues to wiggle out of the blanket, yet doesn't sleep well when unswaddled, you might consider a premade swaddling blanket that uses Velcro, zippers, or snaps rather than tucking long pieces of fabric. Shop carefully, though. Some commercially available swaddling blankets are very thick and warm and could contribute to overheating, depending on the temperature in your bedroom.

Another option for a squirmy baby who still enjoys being swaddled is to wrap your baby snugly around the torso only with a lightweight muslin blanket, or Velcro swaddler pajamas, but keeping both his arms and his legs untucked, so that your little one has freedom to move plus the ability to push himself up or shove blankets out of the way.

Step-by-Step Weaning from Swaddling

If it's time to wean your baby from swaddling, you can begin by leaving only one arm out of the swaddle. Then, a few days or a week later, leave both arms out. Keep your baby's middle snugly swaddled and legs loosely swaddled as usual for a week or two, and then experiment with letting her sleep fully unswaddled. This gradual approach often works better than just stopping the swaddling suddenly.

Keep in mind that once your baby's arms are free it will be easier for your little one to roll over onto her stomach, particularly if she's trying this feat during the day during tummy time, so always keep an eye on her and swaddle only for supervised naps, not when you are all sleeping at night.

A great transitional sleep solution for a baby when you wean from swaddling is to dress your baby in an armless sleep-sack style sleeper (like a sleeping bag with arm holes). These sacks give a little one who likes to be swaddled a similar tactile sensation, rather than going straight to normal pajamas or bare legs. A pair of socks can also help your baby feel more contained.

The time for weaning from swaddling often occurs when other big things are happening in your baby's life—turning over, sitting up, scooting on the floor, and teething. To reduce the stress on your baby when everything happens at once, keep all the other parts of your bedtime routine the same. If you've been using white noise, for example, continue to use it in the same way you have been.

Build a New Routine—Minus the Swaddling

Weaning from any bedtime-related factor is a time when a bedtime routine shines. If you don't have a specific bedtime routine for your baby, begin using one prior to weaning. Follow the same sequence of prebedtime for a week or two. It doesn't have to be complicated or long, but a few consistent steps help create an expectation for sleep. (See Key 14, Develop a Hint of a Bedtime Routine, page 293.) Then keep all the other facets of the routine intact and work on eliminating just this one feature a bit at a time, as described previously.

Any transition related to sleep often takes a few months to really settle in. So please be patient with your baby and with yourself. Also keep in mind that weaning from swaddling may not be the cause of more frequent waking for a baby who is also going through developmental leaps. Teething, rolling, sitting up, and scooting all tend to disrupt sleep patterns as your child grows and masters these new milestones.

Key 12

Give Your Baby Opportunities to Fall Asleep Unaided

Newborns are precious and unbelievably cuddly. Having yours fall asleep in your arms, at your breast, or in your sling is one of life's greatest pleasures. It's easy to keep these exquisite little people in your arms long after they have fallen asleep, and it is a joy you should treasure every time it happens. This chapter is about understanding how this lovely ritual can affect your baby's sleep and suggests ways to enjoy a balance between holding your baby as he sleeps versus allowing him some opportunities to fall asleep on his own.

The reason that this concept is important is not about today. It's about next month and the month after that, and the months after that. Babies love being nurtured to sleep, and you should do plenty of that; however, if you *always* hold or nurse your baby to sleep, your little one will very easily become accustomed to being held as she falls asleep, and as she moves between sleep cycles as well. After months of these delightful falling-asleep experiences, she'll accept it as the way that sleep arrives, and she'll actually be *unable* to fall asleep on her own. She'll cry to protest the minute you place her in bed, as if to say, *"Why am I here? I'm tired and need to sleep, and I can't do it here! Pick me up please so that I can sleep!"*

There are some parents who are perfectly fine with being the sandman for their little bundles, and actually welcome and relish the job of helping their baby fall asleep, and stay asleep, for every nap and nighttime sleep well past the first birthday party. And some babies can fall asleep in your arms and then sleep a full nap or night's sleep in their own bed once you put them down. If you have one of these babies, or if you are one of these parents, then this chapter is not for you. Skip it, or skim it and move on to the next idea, and come back to this at any time if you decide you'd like to have your baby fall asleep on his own once in a while.

For those of you who know that, no matter how lovely the experience of holding your sleeping baby is, you cannot possibly be the full-time "bringer of sleep"—read on.

You can avoid creating the almost inevitable scenario of a child who is totally sleep-dependent on you. The key is to place your baby in her crib, cradle, hammock, or cradle-swing when she is comfortable and drowsy, but not entirely asleep—*some of the time.* Most infants will accept being put down awake much more easily than an older baby who has come to learn that sleep only comes when Mommy, Daddy, or another important adult is there to provide it. So, if you think you like the sound of this, there is no harm, no risk, and no tears involved in giving it a try.

The surprise for many parents of a newborn is that a tired, well-fed, cozy newborn will often accept being put into his crib or cradle for sleep when he is tired, but still awake, where he will then fall asleep peacefully on his own, without any fussing or tears. This can be a shock for second-time (or third-time or sixth-time)

Mother-Speak

"I think one of the most helpful ideas was to put him down when he was tired but awake—he surprised me by allowing it so often!"

—Judith, mother of three-month-old Harry

parents who spent many months (or years) parenting their previous children to sleep only to find that trying this idea actually works with their newest baby!

How to Put Baby Down When *Sleepy* Instead of *Sleeping*

How this idea works will depend on how old your newborn is, what you've been doing so far at sleep times, and, of course, that significant wild card: your baby's unique personality.

The success of this strategy is also based on this critical factor: putting your baby down for sleep at exactly the right time—the magical moment when she is well-fed and perfectly tired. That means not overtired, not crying, and not too wide awake and alert.

Finding this magical moment is a mystery that unfolds over the early weeks as you learn about your baby. The way to determine "perfect tiredness" is twofold. First, learn to read your baby's tired signs—this point is defined in detail in Key 3, Learn to Read Your Baby's Sleepy Signals, page 117. The second factor is making sure your baby is getting enough sleep at the right times; you can read about this in the description of typical newborn sleep patterns outlined in How Much Sleep Does Your Newborn Baby Need? on page 47.

When you feed or hold your baby to sleep, typically your baby requires no other factors—you can nurse or cuddle your baby at a baseball game, a concert, or in the middle of a busy party, and your baby can still fall asleep. But, if you are attempting to let your baby fall asleep unaided, it's important to provide the right sleeping environment that is primed for sleep. The room should be darkened—see page 163 about setting your baby's biological clock. It should also be quiet except for quiet music or white noise—outlined on page 149, about using pink-white noise to enhance sleep.

Your baby's bed and sleeping particulars must be comfortable and cozy and fit her personality. Depending on your unique baby, this could include a sleep-sack, swaddling (page 229), or a pacifier (page 201).

> **Point to Remember**
>
> Getting your baby and the environment ready is really as simple as this:
>
> - Be sure your baby is fed, dry, and perfectly tired.
> - Verify that your baby's bed and room are comfortable, cozy, and welcoming.
> - Turn on white noise or soft lullaby music.
> - Help your baby to relax with feeding, holding, or rocking.
> - Swaddle or provide a pacifier, if your baby uses these.
> - Place your baby in bed when drowsy and ready to sleep.

The Flexible "Sleepy Instead of Sleeping" Guideline

There is no risk or danger in holding your baby as he drifts off to sleep, of course! I would never advise you to miss out on this unique and beautiful experience. Believe me, I have a long and delightful history of holding my four children and my grandbaby as they slept. The idea is to balance this with plenty of times when you put your baby in his bed when he is drowsy and relaxed, but not yet fully asleep. When your baby has the ability to fall asleep in his bed, it will give you the freedom from being absolutely required to parent your baby to sleep for every single nap, every single day, every night at bedtime, and every night waking throughout every night. This means you might actually be able to take a shower, put an older child to bed, or have a few moments alone with your husband or partner. Even if you are an adamant bed-sharing attachment family, these small bits of baby-free time can be refreshing. This idea will also set the stage to allow other people, like grandparents, aunts, uncles, or babysitters, to be able to put your baby to sleep if you are not home, and these caregivers will be happy they can help.

The ratio for parenting your baby to sleep versus letting him fall asleep on his own will be different for every family, but I suggest that you work to give your baby a chance to fall asleep on his own at least a quarter of the time for any lasting effects. If you don't do it frequently enough, your baby will come to resist every time you even try, because every time it will seem like something new.

> **Point to Remember**
>
> What if you plan to put your baby down awake but your newborn falls asleep while nursing, being fed from a bottle, or being cuddled in your arms? What should you do? . . . Enjoy the experience! Then either gently put her in bed or keep her in your arms, as you choose. Your baby will only be a newborn for a short time, so relish these exquisite moments.

Even if your baby accepts being put down drowsy at times, it's unlikely that it will work every time. Sometimes your baby will go to sleep on her own, and sometimes she won't. That's perfectly normal. When your baby *doesn't* settle and fusses instead, you can rock her, pat her, or even pick her up and give her back the breast/ bottle/pacifier or rock and cuddle her. Perhaps start over in a few minutes, or not. It's perfectly okay to let her nap in your arms for now and try independent sleeping for her next nap, or tomorrow. There are no rules—do what works best for you and your baby.

What If Your Baby Isn't Sleeping, Yet Isn't Crying to Be Picked Up?

If your baby is peaceful and enjoying his time alone, you can leave him to his solitude—a bit of quiet personal time can be a blessing for a baby, too, you know. Some little ones relish a few minutes here and there to just "be." Of course, always keep an ear and eye on him to be safe. Even days-old newborns can enjoy a few moments of solitude provided that the rest of their life is filled with the warmth of human interaction.

If you put your baby to bed, and she seems fitful or tired but can't sleep, it's perfectly fine to offer help if she isn't getting the hang of why you've put her there! Particularly if this is a new idea, you might need to hum or sing to her, shush her, jiggle her cradle, or rub her tummy as she drifts off. Gradually make your touch slower and softer, until your hand is lying still on her, and she's asleep. Then slowly remove your touch. You can also use your baby's cradle-swing for these independent nap times, if your baby enjoys sleeping there. (See Key 13 for tips on this idea.)

What If Your Baby Only Has a Short Snooze After Falling Asleep Alone?

It doesn't matter how long your baby naps when you first begin to use this idea. Even five minutes counts as a win—your little one

Valexia, three months old

fell asleep in bed instead of your arms! Hooray! If you continue this routine, your baby will likely sleep for longer spans on her own. This can be a blessing that grows as time goes on, because many babies who eventually fall asleep on their own then sleep a nice, long nap or nighttime sleep stretch with this peaceful routine.

If this was a too-short nap, you can scoop your baby up and get her back to sleep using other methods that you know will work. If you choose to, once she's back to sleep you can then try to lay her back down or just keep her in your arms and try again next nap time or tomorrow.

What If Your Baby Falls Asleep in Your Arms or at Your Breast?

This isn't a "what if" question, it's a "when it happens" question. Newborns are sleepy people, and when they are tired they easily fall asleep when being fed or carried. In addition, breast milk and the act of breastfeeding are sleep-inducing. This is normal! So, oftentimes, your baby will be asleep so quickly you will miss the window of putting him down into bed. That's perfectly, beautifully fine. There's no pressure here; this is an idea to keep in the back of your mind to set you both up for easier sleep routines in the future weeks.

Guess What? Not Every Newborn *Can* Fall Asleep Alone!

You may have tried this idea a number of times, and every single time your baby's eyes pop wide open and the fussing begins the moment you even lean over the crib with the intent of putting her there. You may be wondering what the heck you are doing wrong. Perhaps the answer is: nothing!

There are some newborn babies who simply *cannot* put themselves to sleep easily. These babies will stay grumpily, unhappily, miserably awake until you do *something* to make sleep happen: nursing, rocking, holding, or bouncing. These babies honestly need your help. It appears to me, after working with many thousands of newborns, that these babies have a harder time adjusting to life outside the womb, where they had 24/7 holding, rocking, swaying, and shushing. Anything less than the 24/7 care they are accustomed to is unacceptable! These precious little ones need more assistance to fall asleep.

News flash! Don't assume *you* have one of these babies unless you have tried the ideas previously outlined in this chapter a number of times over a number of weeks, along with ideas from the other Keys. Some babies are slow to get the idea, but they do eventually. So give it a good college try!

If you have attempted to lay your baby down sleepy instead of sleeping a dozen or more times and it never, ever works, then you may have to admit that yours is one of those little ones who needs more help, at least for now. Pause this idea and come back to it in a couple weeks, or even a month or two—babies change rapidly, and they can make drastic changes in a month's time.

Should You Use This Idea for Naps or During Middle-of-the-Night Feedings, or Both?

You can use this idea at any sleep, daytime or nighttime. Experiment with this to see what brings the easiest results for you and your baby. Some babies cluster feed in segments at some point in the evening, in a pattern of feed-sleep-feed-sleep, which sometimes tanks them up for longer stretches of sleep in the night ahead. Some fall asleep so quickly when feeding that getting them placed in bed awake is nearly impossible. Yet at other times of the day they seem totally content to nurse and cuddle, and then fall asleep in their crib. Some babies need more help to initially fall asleep at bedtime, but are in such a sleepy state in the dark of night that they accept being put into bed at midnight. You just need to figure out the best match for you and your baby.

Try a Little Jiggle

If your baby always falls asleep in your arms, and you have no idea how to get him to accept being put into his crib, you might want to change the way you place your baby into bed. Many babies absorb their surroundings as they fall asleep (i.e., being held in your secure embrace and drinking warm milk), and if they are in a light stage of sleep (which is often for newborns), they may feel the motions of being put down, and they immediately jolt awake and protest. If your baby always falls asleep in your arms like this, it's hard to introduce the idea of the crib. One method is to change his falling-asleep point of view and make his final moments before sleep crib-friendly.

First, make sure the bed is warm and cozy—I suggest soft flannel or fleece crib sheets that feel soft and warm to the touch. When you put your sleeping baby in his crib, very gently give him a jiggle so he slightly wakes and peeks at his location ("Oh, I'm here in my bed."). Then begin "shushing" him and pat or rub so he'll fall back to sleep quickly. Experiment with this as you want just a very slight, brief peek of awakeness—you certainly don't want your baby fully awake and fussing! Some babies require a more elaborate ritual to become comfortable with falling asleep in their own bed, and that is The Pantley Dance.

Gliding baby down, vs putdown

The Pantley Dance

It's common for a baby to fall asleep in your arms, but then to wake up the moment the crib is touched, and the jiggle isn't enough—then you have to dance. The reason for this is the drastic difference between being cradled in warm, cuddling arms and lying on the flat, still surface of a bed. The difference is so dramatic that Baby instantly wakes up. So, instead of "putting down" your baby, try gently *gliding* your baby into bed using *The Pantley Dance*. This is not just a method of preventing waking; it can also help set the stage for other ideas to make crib sleeping easier to adapt to.

Step One

Prepare your baby's bedroom and bed using ideas from the previous sections. (For example: shut the blinds, turn on the white noise, unplug the phone, put soft flannel sheets on the crib, and swaddle your baby, if that's how he sleeps.)

Step Two

Hold or feed your baby as usual, and allow him to *become calm and sleepy* in your arms. Let him settle into the state where he is relaxed, but not totally limp-limbed and asleep. This is when you'll begin the "dance" to glide your baby into bed. For the first few times, you might wait until your baby's eyes first close and he is just beginning to drift off to sleep. After a few days of practice, make the move sooner, and a few days later, sooner still.

Experiment with the position in which you hold your baby in your arms as he is falling asleep. If you now hold him upright or belly-to-belly with you, and then you lay him flat on his back (the safest position for sleep), the flip-over radical change in position might contribute to his waking up. Try holding him in a more reclined, upward-facing position, similar to how he'll be lying in the crib. So, after feeding, roll him slightly away from your body so that he's lying on his back in your arms.

Step Three

Begin to softly sing, hum, make shush-shush sounds, or murmur quietly as you rock, bounce, pat, or jiggle your baby in your arms. Create a full sensory experience of movement and sound. Do this for a few minutes, and then stop and remain perfectly still and quiet for a few minutes. Then resume movement. Continue to alternate movement and sound with stillness and quiet as you carry your baby to her bed. Alternate a few steps of movement, then stop and be still. Repeat. Get it? You are dancing your way to the crib.

Some babies do well if you alternate sound and quiet along with movement and stillness, but others will need you to keep singing or humming consistently during both movement and stillness—the sound creates a common thread for both experiences. Experiment to learn which combination of movement and sound work best for your baby.

If you use the same song, humming style, or monologue each time you put your baby down to sleep, this can become a consistent part of your routine and become a signal that it is time for sleep.

Step Four

Continue The Pantley Dance—alternating movement and sound with stillness and quiet (or stillness plus sound) as you lay your baby down.

Place your baby in the crib so that only her legs touch the mattress, and then pause. (You may need to keep humming at this juncture.) Then begin movement again as you slowly ease her to the mattress, from bottom to top: feet, legs, bottom, back, and head.

Step Five

Gently touch your baby with your free hand. (You might need to add some rubbing or patting, or simply put gentle pressure on his chest, belly, legs, or head.) Continue your song, and alternate patting or rubbing with stillness. Move the other hand out from under your baby.

Mother-Speak

"My three-month-old, Sammy, would *never* let me put him down for a nap without immediately crying, so I held him in my arms for every nap. I used many of your ideas and have been doing The Pantley Dance for about a week, and today was a milestone day! He took a two-hour nap in his crib! Two hours! Alone! I barely knew what to do with myself! Sorry for all the exclamation points, but it's a very big day around here!"

—Jenny, mother of three-month-old Samuel

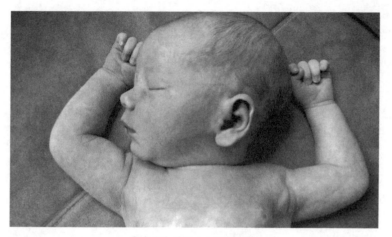

Gabriel, three weeks old

With physical contact broken, continue your song but slowly reduce the volume. Prior to this you should have had your white noise sounds or lullaby turned on, if you use these for sleep, so it is now background noise.

If your baby wakes or fusses—either now or twenty minutes from now—put both hands on him and jiggle or pat while you continue the same song or humming as before to see if he will settle back to sleep.

Step Six

Set up a reliable baby monitor or stay close to your sleeping baby—if he wakes up before a full naptime you can use the same technique to help him fall back to sleep and prolong the nap. The minute you hear your baby waking up, return quickly and resume the same patting and quiet humming or singing sounds. (Do take care that your baby isn't simply making noises in his sleep! Remember Key 5—Differentiate Between Sleeping Noises and Awake Noises. Wait and listen. And, of course, if your baby is awake and hungry, it's feeding time again.)

Note: If at any point you get tired or frustrated, or your baby fully wakes and begins to cry, of course you should pick him up and start again at Step One, later. Or, maybe tomorrow. Or the next day. You want this process to develop into a soothing presleep routine, and not let it turn into a trigger to cry.

It will take persistence, but you can build this into a new bed-sleeping ritual. This gentle dance will teach your baby that the transition from arms to bed is a peaceful, pleasant experience, and not one to be feared or resisted.

What If Your Baby Won't Go Along with This Idea at All?

If you've identified your newborn as one of those who needs help to fall asleep, this doesn't mean you should throw in the towel and resort to holding your infant for every single nap and letting him sleep in your embrace all night long, unless, of course, you want to. (Don't change a thing if you are both happy!) But a look into the future tells us that, if you do this, then your newborn could soon be a six-month-old . . . eight-month-old . . . twelve-month-old who fully relies upon you to fall asleep, and stay asleep, and can't do it any other way. Sometimes it's all about the timing. Your baby might fight you on this today, but a week or two from now accept the idea cheerfully. So try this out every week or two, or cross it off your list entirely. You can always deal with this issue down the road when you are ready.

If you do want to set your baby up to be able to fall asleep somewhere other than your arms, it's wise to provide the minimum aid necessary for your baby to fall asleep and stay asleep—some of the time. You'll need to find the delicate balance between helping your baby fall asleep and encouraging her to accept sleep when she's tired, without always having her wage a battle to keep those little eyes open.

> ### Point to Remember
>
> I want to mention again that not all babies will take to this idea, and not all parents want to make this a goal—some will be happy to always parent their baby to sleep. And some children will need a little bit of help falling asleep up until they are three or four or five years old. If you are okay with settling your little one off to sleep, and your baby sleeps well all night, then don't sweat this one for now. Come back here at any time in the future if you want to make changes.

Any combination of parenting to sleep and falling asleep alone is effective. Babies—even brand-new babies—are individuals, and your most important key for great sleep is to read your baby and follow your little one's lead. I don't want anyone to think he or she needs to "work" at sleep too hard right off the bat! Any little thing you do will make the weeks and months that follow easier. So, relax and keep getting to know your baby!

It's amazing how often I hear surprise that in the first month or two a baby can be put "sleepy but awake" in her cradle and then go to sleep. But I also know how quickly you can pass that window of opportunity and have a baby that won't accept being put down awake. Ever. At all. However, as I've mentioned, some people don't care about this—they are happy to always parent their baby to sleep—and that is okay too! As always, do what is best for you and your baby.

KEY 13

Provide Motion for Peaceful Sleep

Prior to birth, 100 percent of your baby's sleep occurred in a bed of fluid that sloshed and moved with your every step and motion. You walked, you bounced up stairs, and you may have even jogged, biked, or attended aerobics class. And if you loved your rocking chair—imagine how that moved your baby around! Even during the typically disjointed sleep that pregnancy so kindly provides, you likely shifted and moved your baby around throughout the night. If you'd like to really understand how much your motions rocked your baby, stand up, put both hands firmly on your belly, and walk around the house, go up and down the stairs, bend up and down as if folding laundry or loading dishes, and jog in place. This was the environment your baby slept in—each and every day before birth. Can you understand now why lying flat on his back on an unmoving, rigid crib surface can be unsettling to your new baby? The fluid sway of movement was a constant, soothing sleep-inducer.

Your baby didn't magically transform into a different life form at the instant of birth—he was the same person he was just a minute before. That's the reason that the first three months of life are often referred to as the fourth trimester. There is a time of transition from womb to world that takes months, usually even lingering long past this fourth trimester. After this transition time, the comforts of motion sleep can become a happy habit. Ask any adult who loves rocking chairs, gliders, hammocks, or a ride on a train or boat—she will tell you that motion can be comforting and restful.

Human beings have been rocking babies to sleep for as long as there have been babies—it's a very natural way to help them relax and sleep. Parents instinctively search for ways to provide their babies with movement to settle them because it works so well. During the early weeks, adding motion to the sleep process can help your infant fall asleep and stay asleep.

How Motion Sleep Mimics the Womb

Motion naps are incredibly popular with infants since they mimic the experience of the womb environment in four distinct ways:

W—Whooshing sounds. When motion happens in your arms or a soft baby carrier or sling, your baby is pressed against your body and can hear the pleasant, memory-invoking thump of your heartbeat and gurgles of your digestive system. In a baby swing, the pleasant-wooshing white noise sounds of the motor, the ticking back-and-forth of the swing, and the addition of white noise or soft music are akin to the constant sounds of the heartbeat and fluids heard in the womb. Not only do they soothe your baby to sleep, they also block out outside noises that can interfere with sleep, and they combine to create a very powerful sleep cue that says *time to sleep.*

O—Orderly, predictable events. Diaper changed, fed, into the sling or cradle, buckle clicked, music on, swaying begins, sleep time! It's exactly the same every single time—a very predictable and memorable routine.

M—Movement. The gentle, consistent sway creates a pleasant rocking that mimics the movement of the womb, as described previously. This rocking is the same instinctual movement that parents have used to soothe babies since the beginning of time.

If you rock your baby often, you might find yourself swaying at times even without your baby in your arms!

B—Buckled. Snugly tucked into a sling or buckled into a seat, your baby's limb movements don't startle her awake. In addition, she isn't free to move around, explore, and thus evade sleep. She's cradled in a cozy space, much like being encased in the womb.

Those four components together create a sleep-inducing environment for your newborn—they soothe him and help him relax and fall asleep. Additionally, every time a baby shifts between sleep cycles (every hour or two), or if noises wake him up, these components can lull him back to sleep before he fully wakes, resulting in a nice long nap.

We often add a fifth item to this list without even realizing it— the gentle hum of humanity. If you are babywearing, your little one is hearing the gentle singsong of your voice and others' along with the sounds of the world. A swing or cradle is usually placed in the main part of the house near *people*, while the big crib is often off in a room by itself. Since babies are naturally drawn to being with the people they love, it adds another advantage over the crib. You may not realize it, but your presence and the quiet voices and noises of the household can be a very soothing addition to your baby's nap environment.

Professional-Speak

"Throughout time, parents have had kith and kin to lend hands of support. In today's mini-families, a swing can help replace that missing extra pair of hands you need to comfort your baby."

—Harvey Karp, MD, author, *The Happiest Baby on the Block*

Babies often nap better when we recreate some of these experiences from the womb. This explains why young babies enjoy a sleeping place that is warm, closely held, slightly noisy, and gently moving.

Additional Benefits of Motion for Babies

Our instinct to rock our babies in our arms or a cradle may actually help with our child's development. The rocking motions we

Katherine, four months old, with Daddy

commonly use with babies help their developing vestibular system, which controls balance. This system begins its development in the womb and continues after birth. It coordinates movement, and, among other things, it links the nervous system connecting the inner ear, eyes, arms, and legs.

There is no question that children want and need more vestibular stimulation than adults do. They love to swing, spin, roll, jump, twirl, and somersault! Children have their own personal preferences for the type, amount, and intensity of movement they need—starting as newborns. Some enjoy gentle rocking, while others need a stronger, more intense experience. So, while you might find the constant rocking, swaying, and jostling to be annoying, your baby is likely loving every single jiggle. If you have any concerns about this movement, you can rest assured that it's actually good for your baby.

Babies who suffer from colic, reflux, colds, or other medical ailments can benefit from motion sleep, which can alleviate some of their discomfort. Babies with special needs and sensory integration issues can often benefit from daily naps in a swing, rocker, hammock, or bouncer—ask your medical care professional for more information.

Types of Motion for Newborns

There are a wide variety of ways that we can provide movement for our newborns—especially when calming their crying or trying to help them fall asleep or stay asleep. Some of these are perfect and pretty much cannot be overused for your infant, others are great when used in moderation, and a few should be avoided altogether. Let's discuss the various methods of adding movement to your newborn's life.

Your Arms or a Soft Carrier or Sling

The most obvious place for your baby to find that swaying, rocking, womb-like feeling is in your arms or a baby sling or soft front-pack carrier; this is a newborn's ideal happy-sleep place. As long as you are comfortable and willing, an in-arms/in-sling nap is pure joy to your baby, and a real endorphin boost for you, too.

Many parents relish the experience of holding their sleeping newborn, but it's a rare parent who would like to continue doing this for the next year or more. Therefore, the only caveat here is to avoid holding your newborn for 100 percent of naps, plus for falling asleep at bedtime every night. It's very easy for this to become routine and morph into the only way your baby can fall asleep, making you the permanent sandman. Do give your baby the regular opportunities to fall asleep in other ways. (See Key 12, page 251.)

Carriers can be a great way to hold your baby while still being hands-free. Baby gets the experience of being held, and you get freedom to move about the house or run errands while you are recreating that womb-like experience. Walking with your baby in a carrier is a great way to soothe her at the end of a long day, especially if your baby is colicky or if you are feeling worn down or tense. Babies can sense that tension in your body, and your arms, shoulders, and back can only last so long—the carrier helps provide a more relaxed method of carrying for any length of time.

It's important to be certain that you are using your carrier correctly and your baby is positioned properly within the sling or carrier to keep your baby safe. Here are a few of the most important carrier safety rules:

- Choose a sling or carrier that is intended for your baby's size and age, plus your height. Read and follow the instructions for use.
- Newborns should be carried upright (vertical) except when actively breastfeeding.

Augustyn, four months old, with Mommy

- The carrier should be snug enough to support your baby's back and keep your baby in place while allowing ample room for breathing.
- Your baby should be belly-up to your body, with his knees higher than his bottom in an "M"-shaped frog position. Babies should not be in outward-facing carriers until they are much older, if at all, since facing outward puts their body in an awkward posture. Piggyback carriers are great once your baby is sitting up confidently on his own.
- You should be able to see your baby's face when you look down. It should not be burrowed into your body or covered by fabric.
- Your baby's chin should not be curled down into his chest, as this position could impede breathing.

- Baby should be held high enough for you to be able to kiss his head. (Always: Close enough to kiss!)
- Double-check all aspects of the carrier at each use to make sure that everything is secure and arranged properly.
- Be careful when babywearing and trying to do other activities, such as cooking or doing yardwork. You don't want to accidentally fall, bump your baby, cause a burn, or otherwise accidentally harm your little one.

Your Lap + a Rocking Chair = Sweet Sleep

Rocking chairs were probably invented for mothers, fathers, and grandparents to have a place to soothe their babies to sleep! As long as you and your baby are comfortable and happy, this is a great option for helping your baby fall asleep. Parents often add a rhythmic pat on Baby's bottom or back, which adds a natural vibration to the mix.

Professional-Speak

"Rocking a baby to sleep in the first few months of life is often not only necessary but hugely rewarding for parents and baby alike. For your baby, it might feel close to being in utero— wrapped in the warmth of your arms, close to your heartbeat, and moving with the rhythm of your body motions. There is a precious short time when this is the most helpful way to get your baby to sleep."

—Jean Kunhardt, MA, author of *A Mother's Circle: An Intimate Dialogue on Becoming a Mother*

CAUTION: The potential danger with using a rocking chair or glider is that *you* might get so comfortable that you fall asleep— and this is a highly dangerous situation, as your newborn could slip out of your arms and become wedged beside you or slip into a position where his face is covered. As long as you are fully awake, or have someone beside you to watch over the two of you, rock on!

Bouncing on a Yoga or Birthing Ball

Believe it or not, this is a very popular way to soothe a fussy newborn! Holding your baby while getting a bouncing rhythm going can be an effective cry-stopper. Putting your baby into a sling or carrier and bouncing gently is a great way to watch your favorite TV show and get some exercise, too!

Just don't let this become your baby's go-to bedtime routine. Many a parent who is stuck bouncing in the middle of the night has regretted relying too much on this method.

Rocking, Gliding, Swinging, or Vibrating Cradles and Swings

Being held in a parent's arms or in a soft carrier or sling creates the perfect place for motion naps, but many busy parents cannot possibly hold a napping baby for the many hours a newborn sleeps every day—that can be as many as seven to nine nap hours each day! The next best solution for a movement-loving baby is a swing, glider, hammock, rocking cradle, or vibrating infant seat. These are often a baby's favored location for napping over a stationary cradle, crib, or bed.

There are a number of devices available for providing motion for newborns. You can find a vast array of rocking, gliding, swinging, and vibrating cradles—but should you use them? The answer is yes—with conditions! If you have a fussy sleeper and if you can use this type of sleep aid wisely and selectively, it can be a big help during the newborn stage. These can be especially helpful for parents of multiples or those with other young children in the house, and for those with babies who have special needs, reflux, or colic, or babies who take very short naps or outright refuse to nap.

When used properly these devices are not only safe and help-ful—they can be sanity-savers. The biggest risks are the temptation to overuse them and the possibility that your baby will become so accustomed to them that you'll be battling a set-in-concrete sleep association six months from now. The fact is that at some point you will have to wean your baby from these motion naps. For some parents of colicky infants, or for those who are desperate for a way to help their newborn sleep better, it can be a trade they are willing to make.

Mother-Speak

"My daughter had colic. I tried everything under the sun to get her to nap in the afternoon, but all she did was cry. And cry. And cry some more. Even carrying her in my arms didn't work—I would pace the house with her for an hour or more and she never stopped crying. This made me feel drained and helpless. I found that the only thing that helped her to sleep was swaddling her and securing her in her swinging cradle— she would fall asleep easily and sleep for two hours that way. There was absolutely no way I would have been able to sur-vive the colic without the swing. We are slowly weaning her now and it is taking a lot of patience. But those months of peaceful sleep were definitely worth it for both of us."

—Natalia, mother of seven-month-old Eva

Here are some of the most important points to keep in mind when using any type of motion device as a sleep aid for your newborn:

- Don't overuse any device or carrier for your newborn. The primary place your infant belongs is in your warm and loving arms. Use other options sensibly and selectively, and mainly for sleep. Your wide-awake baby should not be left in a swinging or rocking cradle.
- Use only a cradle that lies flat like a bed. It is risky to have infants sleep in a sitting position, as they can slump forward, and this could impede their breathing, which can lead to a higher risk of SIDS.
- Check the packaging (or the manufacturer's website) and use only a device labeled to fit your baby's age, size, and weight.
- Take care to secure your baby with a five-point safety harness to prevent falls or entrapment. (If the device only has a lap belt, it should not be used for an infant.)
- Make sure that there is always an adult nearby. These are not meant to be used for a baby who is alone.
- Check with your baby's pediatrician to be sure motion sleep is safe for your baby.

Buying the Right Product

When shopping for a swing, glider, hammock, or bouncer, take plenty of time to choose the right product. If possible, shop in person instead of online, and bring your baby along and place him in the floor model. He may not take to it immediately (especially in the store environment), but it will give you a good idea of how he fits and how easy it is to use. Consider borrowing one, renting one, or letting your baby take a test ride in a friend's. Babies don't always take to these immediately, but you might get a sense of whether this will work for your baby with a trial run.

Take time to compare various options and consider these points:

- Purchase only a new product, as safety features are improved constantly. Used swings or older model bouncers and seats may not be safe for your sleeping baby. If you acquire a used product from a friend or family member, check the manufacturer's website or contact the manufacturer for information to be sure it's safe to use.
- Check to be sure the base is stable and that all parts have sturdy construction.
- Read the package to find the size and weight restrictions so that your baby won't grow out of it too quickly.
- Look for a certification from the Juvenile Products Manufacturer's Association or another formal safety organization.
- Consider neutral colors and fewer frills, since bright colors and toy attachments can be interesting for a playful baby but distracting if your baby is trying to sleep (which is the primary purpose of these items, right?).
- Choose a product that has soft lullaby music, white noise nature sounds, or no sounds at all. Avoid swings with loud or harsh sounds. Whether a swing has built-in sound is a minor consideration, though, since you can use another source for this; it doesn't have to be part of the device.
- Pick a model with easy-in, easy-out access, especially for a sleeping baby.
- Listen for a pleasant sound while the motor is running. Listen for one that will be soothing to your baby and to you. (Don't purchase a swing or seat until you've turned it on, watched it run, and listened to it.)
- Pick a product with a volume button for the music or sounds, *plus* an on/off button to turn off the sounds

independently of the motion so you can have your baby swing without the sound. If you don't like the sound that comes with the swing, you can use a different source for your baby's white noise or lullabies.

- Shop for a product with a secure five-point harness system that will keep your baby safe from becoming entangled or falling out of the swing.
- Consider a model with variable speeds and possibly several swinging directions so that you can adjust it to suit your baby. Some models include various movement directions— side-to-side, back-and-forth, and even up-and-down.
- If possible, choose a model with a timer that can turn the swing or vibration off after your baby is sleeping.
- Look for a model with a removable, machine-washable cover.
- Find out if the motor is electrical or runs by batteries. If it's battery-operated, have a supply on hand or consider two sets of rechargeable batteries.

Stroller Nap

Many babies love stroller naps; they provide a delightful way for them to fall asleep, and the ride lulls them into a nice, long nap. The side benefit is that it is great exercise for you.

If you can take regular outside stroller walks, try to schedule these to coincide with typical sleep times aimed to match your baby's signs of tiredness. Using a stroller is also a great way to get a tired baby who's reluctant to fall asleep to drift off peacefully to dreamland.

If your little one doesn't easily settle to sleep in the stroller, try finding some uneven ground to stroll over, instead of a smooth walkway. Check your neighborhood for a grassy area (perhaps a park), gravel path, cobblestones, or wooden boardwalk. The gentle thumpity-thump of a rough surface is a great baby soother. If you can't find a rough surface to stroll over, give the stroller a slight side-to-side jiggle as you walk, or put a few plastic zip ties around the front tires to create that bumpy ride.

If going outside isn't an option, simply bring your stroller into the house. Walk your baby around for naps until he falls asleep. (You can even do this in a small room or apartment—just roll back and forth, over a "bump" like a doorway, or make your own bump with a couple of folded towels. This is often relaxing for a baby.)

When your baby falls asleep, you can continue your walk or bring the stroller into the house and park it near you. If your baby starts to move about, make noises, or open an eye and peek at you before a long-enough nap, immediately walk around or jiggle the stroller in place.

Once your baby gets a little older and is used to taking a long nap in the stroller, you can make the transition to a bed, if you wish. Start by reducing the amount and length of motion. Work toward letting your baby fall asleep in a nonmoving stroller, and perhaps moving him to his bed when he's totally asleep so he can get used to that location.

Car Rides

There are many babies who hate being in their car seat, and you can't get them out of it quickly enough. Others, however, fall asleep as soon as you drive off. If you have a baby who is lulled to sleep in the car, you may be tempted to use that advantage for nap time. However, there are risks involved, since car seats are not intended as a regular napping spot.

When a seat is installed correctly, and your baby is properly secured with the straps, it is a safe place for your little one to nod off while you drive—although you should always be aware of how he's doing back there. Use a specialty rearview mirror clipped onto to a back headrest for keeping an eye on your sleeping baby when the two of you are alone in a car. Once you have arrived at your destination, however, your baby should be taken out of the car seat. Prolonged, frequent naps in the seat could present risks of your baby slipping down or slumping in the seat, which could impede breathing. It also adds the risk of putting excess strain on an infant's developing spine. If you feel stuck because your baby will only sleep well in the car, then check the chapter on helping your baby to make friends with the bassinet, page 205.

The Negative Aspects of Motion Naps

As is always the case in parenting, no matter how great something seems, there is always another side to the story—the problems or complications. Motion naps are not perfect; they do have a negative side. Here are the potential problems, and a few tips to overcome them:

- *If your baby gets accustomed to napping in her swing, rocker, or glider, then you may be forced to either stay home at all nap times or deal with an overtired, cranky baby who won't nap away from home.*

  The good news is that most often babies who sleep in these devices will also sleep well in a sling or in your arms. So, if you are willing to hold or sling your napping baby in a restaurant, at a movie, or at a friend's home, then you've solved the majority of issues related to this potential problem.

- *Convincing your baby to nap while traveling can be complicated if you can't bring the swing or cradle with you on your trip.*

Ireland, three months old, with Daddy

There is a possibility that you can borrow or rent a similar swing—check with rental companies that rent lawn mowers, garden equipment, and party supplies, as they often have baby swings. A travel-sized swing, cradle, or small bouncer or vibrating bed is a good option to take along with you on a trip. You can also bring along a stroller—a folding stroller can even be used indoors. Or bring an easy-to-pack sling and carry your baby for naps.

- *You'll have to make a change at some point. All swings, cradles, and gliders have size, weight, and age limits for good reasons. A baby who is too big can cause the apparatus to tip over. A baby who is too old might roll or climb out, or reach out to pull down an attachment or connection.*

Very often, by the time babies outgrow their swings, they are developmentally ready to move to a stationary bed for their naps. Later in this chapter you'll find many ideas for making the change once you are ready.

- *If your baby is content and quiet in his swing or glider, there is the danger that you'll overuse the device. Even if you believe that excess time spent in these baby holders is not in your child's best interest, overuse can sneak up on you.*

One of the ways to avoid being drawn into the overuse of these baby soothers is to decide that you'll *only* use them for naptime, and avoid having your baby there whenever she is awake: that's the time for parent-baby interaction, especially since newborns have such a small amount of alert time each day.

Protecting That Sweet Little Head

When your baby sleeps strapped into a swing or cradle of any kind, he may have less ability to move his head into different positions while he is sleeping. If your baby also spends daytime hours in other seats (bouncers, car seats) or even lying on his back in a crib, he may be at risk for developing a flat area on the back of his head (called positional plagiocephaly or flathead syndrome.) By being aware of this, you can take steps to protect your baby. The best ways to avoid positional plagiocephaly are:

- Reduce the overall number of hours your baby spends in reclined seats of any kind, or lying on his back *during waking hours.* (Your baby should always *sleep* on his back.)
- When you put your baby down to sleep, vary the position of her head; slightly turn her head to the left, right, or center, instead of always laying her nose up.

- Move the location of the cradle every day or two so that the things your baby sees before she falls asleep and when she wakes up are on the opposite side of her. Vary the locations of your baby's toys so that your baby isn't always looking in the same direction.
- Be certain that your baby has plenty of time every day being held upright, since when you carry your baby there is no pressure on the back part of the skull. Being held also strengthens your baby's muscles, preparing him for when he'll hold himself upright. Plus, it is nature's preferred way of baby-carrying!
- Make sure that your baby has some tummy time for play during the day. This not only avoids pressure on the back of the head but also helps your baby develop her neck and back muscles so that she is more able to move around on her own.
- Alternate the direction of your little one when you change your baby's diaper, since this is an activity that you'll be doing many times every day. Learn how to change diapers in both directions, because if you spend the early weeks doing it only one way it will be hard to do the reverse.

Safe Sleeping in a Swing, Rocker, or Glider

If you choose to have your baby sleep in a swing or glider, there are some important safety factors for you to be aware of. Keep the following information in mind (along with those tips from the safety chapter on page 321).

- For naps, always use a cradle-style bed in lieu of an upright chair-style seat. You want your baby lying in close to the same position she would in a crib: flat on her back. Daily naps in the seated position can negatively affect physical development of the back, hips, and legs. A seated position can also present a breathing problem if your baby slumps forward. Look for a swing made specifically for infants—many include a built-in head support cushion for newborns.

- Keep your baby near you or invest in a quality baby monitor and check on your baby frequently. (When you do this, leave some white noise or music turned on so you can hear it and be sure your monitor is always working.) Safety experts recommend that you don't leave your baby alone if he is sleeping in a cradle, swing, or infant seat of any type, unless it is specifically made for solitary sleep.

- Use the slowest, gentlest speed that settles your baby. If your baby requires a higher speed to be able to fall asleep, you can reduce the speed after your baby is asleep and work toward slowing this down over time. Every week or so, experiment with a lower speed. When you make changes by small increments, it's likely your baby will accept the change, particularly if all other parts of his routine remain the same.

- Turn the swing or vibration off, or to its lowest setting, once your baby is asleep so that he isn't swinging or vibrating for long periods of time. Turn the swing back on if your baby begins to wake up before an appropriate length of nap time. If he's moving between sleep cycles, this will help him fall back to sleep.

- Always use the five-point safety harness and straps properly, according to the directions provided with the product. (If there is no five-point harness, then it's possible the device is not safe for a newborn.)

- Never place a swing on a table, counter, or other elevated surface.

- Don't put any blankets, cushions, or toys in the cradle with your baby.

Parent-Speak

"My son sleeps so well in the swing that I use it every day for naps. While he swings, I make phone calls, cook, and do other things I can't easily do when he's awake. When he wakes up, we play. After listening to some other dads complain about their non-napping babies I got to feeling guilty about how easy it is for us: swaddle, snap, swing, snooze. But then I had an epiphany. He's happy and healthy, we both benefit from his naps, and we have plenty of playtime and cuddle time when he's awake, so why not?"

—Jay, father to four-month-old Maxwell

- Never leave a baby in a swing alone in a room with a dog or a toddler—even for a minute. The dog might "chase" the moving swing, or try to play with the baby or the attached toys. A protective dog might respond and try to help the baby if he cries. A toddler might attempt to play with him, climb into the swing, or knock the swing over.
- Read and follow the instructions and safety information that come with the product, including weight limitations.

How Much Motion Sleep Is Wise?

As with so many other things in these early months, your baby will be the leader on this one. However, it's important that you don't get totally swept away into thinking that you are helpless and must provide motion for all your baby's sleep times. The problems with that are many, as described previously on page 281—"The Negative Aspects of Motion Naps."

What is the ideal balance between motion naps and bed naps? This answer is different for all babies and the adults who care for them. Clearly, having all naps be motion naps can lead to dependence on these, but, other than that, every baby benefits from a unique balance of the two.

No matter your newborn's preferences, aiming for at least one good nap per day, plus part of the night in the stationary bassinet or crib, is a great idea, if you can make it happen. If your baby can fall asleep in several different ways, that can give you more flexibility and will likely make it easier if you wish to modify sleep locations down the road.

One idea that can often help prevent long-term motion dependence is to use the motion only until your baby is relaxed and sleepy, but turn it to its lowest setting, or even completely off, just as your baby is falling asleep. That way the motion helps soothe your baby, but your little one is getting used to sleeping in a stationary bed.

Finding the Right Balance

For the first weeks of life you can use motion naps as often as your baby enjoys them, if your doctor gives a thumbs-up. After the first few weeks of your baby's life, I recommend that you balance motion naps with crib naps. (See Key 10: Help Your Baby Make Friends with the Bassinet on page 205.) A large number of babies who spend their early months of life being rocked to sleep and swinging to sleep are unwilling to give this up for a flat, still bed. So plan ahead!

Newborn babies often sleep better in swings or gliding cradles. If that's the only way your newborn will nap, then don't fret, and don't let the concern taint these precious first weeks. Just wait a few weeks or a month or so and then make another effort at stationary sleep.

When to Wean Your Baby from Motion-Naps to Stationary Sleep

During the newborn months there is no need to wean your baby from motion sleep, if it works for your infant and you, and if you are following safe motion-sleep practices whether your baby sleeps in a sling or swing.

Establishing your unique bond, keeping everyone calm and happy, and genuinely enjoying your time together should be your priority, and if some motion naps enhance this, then enjoy them. Gradually, over the early months of life, most babies will adjust to a motionless sleeping surface, but some need a bit more time and some help to make the transition. There is no absolute rule for when you must wean your baby from motion naps to stationary sleep. The right decision is different for every child. The following questions can guide you as you determine if you should continue naps as they are or if it is the right time to move your child to stationary sleep:

- How do your child's daily sleep hours match up to the chart on page 50? Is she getting enough sleep and napping often enough throughout the day?
- Is your baby safe? Is your baby within the stated age and size for the device, or have they been outgrown?
- Is the motion sleep becoming troublesome or complicated, or is there another reason that your baby must be transitioned now?

How to Wean from Motion Sleep

If motion sleep is not working for your family, for whatever reason, it's perfectly fine to transition your baby to stationary sleep. Once you decide it's time to wean your baby from motion sleep, you can do it gently without any tears. Here are a few ideas to help this along.

Move Your Sleeping Baby

If your baby falls deeply asleep in the swing, try letting her fall asleep there and then moving her while she sleeps. Set up her bedroom to be inviting for sleep: pull down the shades, turn on soft music or white noise, warm up the soft flannel sheets with a heat pack or warm towel (remove these and test the temperature before you lay your baby down).

It can help to locate the swing in the bedroom adjacent to the crib so that you aren't traveling a long distance between the two places. This helps Baby get used to her bedroom.

Point to Remember

Any time you change what you are doing at nap time, your baby may resist the whole idea. This is typical whenever you modify a sleep routine that your baby is happy with. Stay with any new idea for a week or two to allow your baby to adjust before you judge its true effectiveness.

Watch for Tired Signs and Happily Awake Spans

Remember to watch the span of wakeful time between sleep sessions. Be sure your baby has been awake long enough, yet not too long, and is showing some signs of tiredness before you head to nap time. A baby who isn't quite tired enough can be lulled to sleep with motion, but this benefit is lost when moving to a stationary bed—this requires you to be more observant regarding tired signs.

The Step-by-Step Plan for Transitioning from Motion to Bed Sleep

If it's time to transition your baby from his swing, stroller, or rocking cradle, try this step-by-step plan. You can customize it to suit you and your baby.

- **First: slow it down.** An easy way to begin the transition from motion to stillness is to keep your routine exactly the same, but gradually reduce the speed, intensity, or length of time over a period of several weeks.

- **Analyze your current sleep routine.** Even if you don't realize it, you do have a "bedtime routine" that precedes nap or bedtime sleep. What actions (including feeding and diaper changing) do you take, and in what order do they occur?

- **Add more sleep cues.** Babies who love motion sleep typically don't need any other sleep cues, except perhaps a full tummy and a dry diaper. It can help to create a bedtime and nap time routine so that your baby expects sleep to follow the steps that you take.

    What are all the technical parts of your sleep arrangement other than motion? These are important. If you don't have them, add them to your routine consistently for a week or two to help create sleep cues other than motion. These might be: a darkened room, white noise or soft lullaby music, a pacifier, or swaddling.

- **Set up your baby's new sleeping place.** Where would you like your baby to sleep? Is it a bassinet, a crib, or your baby-safe family bed? Make sure the location is prepped (see the safety charts on page 322). Do what you can to make the bed cozy, for example, by getting a softer crib mattress or using soft flannel or fleece sheets.

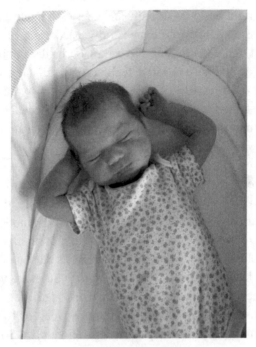

Rosa, two weeks old

When it's time for sleep, follow these steps:

- Prepare the room for sleep (dim the lights, turn on the white noise).
- Be sure that your baby is well fed and tired. (Follow the tips in Key 3: Learn to Read Your Baby's Sleepy Signals, page 117.)
- Follow your exact routine—except when it comes time to place your baby in the swing or other motion device, put your baby in the stationary bed instead.
- When you put your baby in bed, slightly move or jiggle the mattress or bed until your baby's eyes close.

- Stay right beside your baby and begin the jiggle again if necessary. Once your baby is fully asleep, stay close enough to get to her the minute she wakes so she doesn't become startled and have negative feelings about the new location.
- Over the next week, continue the routine. As your baby gets accustomed to the new routine you can reduce the amount and intensity of your jiggle. Soon this new location will be a happy napping place!

Be patient, as the transformation from motion to stationary sleep could take anywhere from a week to several months, depending on your baby's age, how deeply ingrained the motion habit is, the actual reasons your baby is attached to motion naps, and how well the solutions you pick match your baby's personality.

If your baby totally resists all attempts you make to have her nap in her crib, or if you are becoming frustrated, then sometimes it's best to leave well enough alone for a week or two, or even more. Then try again, perhaps with a different plan. Sometimes a slight change to your approach, along with another week or more of maturity, can make a big difference in the end result. All babies eventually outgrow the need for motion during naptime. Be patient!

KEY 14

Develop a Hint of a Bedtime Routine

A newborn baby does not need a bedtime routine. A one-year-old toddler might, and a two-year-old almost certainly does. So, why did I include this Key in a book about newborns? Because your baby is not Pinocchio! In the classic children's story, Pinocchio turns into a real boy in a magical moment. Your baby, however, will gradually, day by day, transform into a toddler, and if you aren't paying attention (because you're exhausted and busy), then the first birthday will pass you by, and you'll still be handling bedtime the same way you do now. By casually incorporating a bedtime routine into your home now, you'll glide seamlessly into toddlerhood . . . well, maybe. Toddlers are unpredictable and move through many physical and cognitive leaps that affect sleep—but at least you'll have the foundation of a good bedtime routine that can help you through the bumps of toddler sleep a little more easily.

There is a benefit to incorporating a bedtime routine now: it can help you to pinpoint and strengthen your baby's perfect moment of "tired-but-not-overtired" by including factors that help your baby to become perfectly tired at bedtime.

But What If I Hate Routines?

Some parents avidly reject the idea of any kind of routine for babies. This is usually because when they hear the word *routine* they think of a rigid English nanny demanding a clock-driven schedule with feeding and sleep charts. This isn't at all what I mean here! This is a soft routine, if you will. A guideline that helps you to gently create patterns that help your baby nap effortlessly and ease into bedtime each night. It's important to have a flexible routine that is adapted each day to your baby's life and needs. Use your intuition and your baby interpretation skills to customize the routine each night to best suit your baby.

I do want to add that if you truly, totally hate the idea of any kind of routine, then skip this chapter entirely. Instead, watch your baby from dinner time onward—very closely—and head for bed whenever the signs are there. You can keep up this same approach throughout childhood, if you remain diligent about your child's individual sleep needs. Children change their own sleep needs from time to time, and you can help yours be happier and healthier by making certain they get all the sleep they need.

Bedtime Routine for a Newborn

Newborn babies don't require much of a bedtime routine, since they sleep and wake all through the day and night, so it's hard to actually pinpoint when it's "bedtime" versus another nap. But there are many simple things you can do to help the sleep process flow more easily, and to gradually build a good bedtime routine over time. Here are some things to consider:

Pick a Bedtime Based on Both the Clock and Your Baby

Choosing a bedtime is not an exact science with newborns because their day and night sleep blurs together. Over the next few weeks, though, you'll start seeing a more defined day/night pattern, and when you do it's great to already have at least the start of a bedtime routine in place. Many young babies have a bedtime around 6:00 to 7:00 p.m., after which their longest sleep spans occur. This time frame can give you a good starting point to work with. Watch your baby's tired signs and sleep patterns over a few nights and settle in on an approximate time. Each night, pinpoint the right moment around that time based on your baby's daily signs of fatigue. This will of course be a rough estimated time, as it will be affected by prior naps and the amount of activity and the feedings your baby has had.

Parent-Speak

"Thank you for the early bedtime idea! We were putting our three-month-old to bed when we went to bed at 10:00 or so, but in the hours before bedtime he was always so cranky. We'd spend the night passing him from one to the other trying to keep him peaceful until bedtime. I never in a million years would have considered 6:00 as a bed time, but since we've started putting him to bed then he falls asleep more quickly and actually sleeps better all night long. Plus, we get to have a grown-up dinner together every night! Granted, we're often so tired it's just a bowl of cereal!"

—**Brian, father of three-month-old Evan**

Wind Down Time

Remember that your newborn can only stay happily awake for forty-five minutes to two hours in the early weeks, one to three hours at one month of age, and possibly up to three hours by six months (see the sleep chart in Key 4, page 50). If you are keeping one eye on the clock and one eye on your baby, you'll see some early indications of tiredness when sleep time draws close. Your baby will likely find it easier to fall asleep if you help him "wind down" for ten to twenty minutes before sleep time. If you go from an active, noisy room with people, television, musical toys, or sibling noise and their accompanying blurs of activity, for example, and then expect him to go directly to sleep, it's likely that he'll be too revved up to relax. Quiet play, a sling-walk, cuddles, book-reading, and soft music will help your baby to transition from activity to the restful state required for sleep.

Dim the Lights

Bright lights are an alerting factor in the biological clock process, whereas darkness brings relaxation and sleepiness. It's easy to take advantage of this natural process by dimming the lights in the ten to thirty minutes before a nap or bedtime. (See Key 7, Set Your Baby's Biological Clock on page 163.) Keep an eye on how much light is surrounding your baby when nap time or bedtime is near. If she's lying in her cradle and looking up at the lights on the ceiling, she'll be drawn to stare at that bright spot. If you're walking her in the stroller on a sunny evening, daylight can signal her brain to be more awake when she really needs to sleep. So dim the bedroom lights or throw a small blanket over the top of the stroller and let the darkness work its magic.

Use Pink-Hued White Noise

The use of white noise to aid newborn sleep is popular because it is soothing and masks noises that prevent your baby from falling asleep, while providing a soothing background hum to fall asleep to. This also creates a very effective and specific cue that lets your baby know that sleep time is here. The use of white noise can be a very effective and simple part of your bedtime routine. These soft

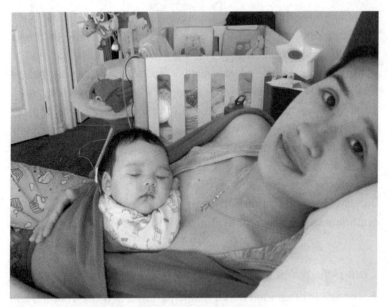

Thea, three months old, with Mommy

sounds make a perfect addition and are defined in detail for you in Key 6, page 149.

Cuddling or Massage

Newborn babies are very in tune to your touches. Studies show that simple massage can help your baby relax, and it promotes more restful sleep. Massage can also help to relieve the pain of colic, gas, illness, and teething. In addition, giving your baby regular massages provides you an opportunity to become more competent in reading your baby's bodily cues and some extra time to enjoy the feel of your baby's miraculous little body. With all these benefits, and no known risks, adding a bit of baby massage to your prebedtime routine makes sense.

Very young babies who are new to massage are sometimes uncertain about it. Keep the room warm and lay Baby on a soft towel or, even better, on your lap. Vary the pressure and location of your touch depending on your baby's reactions. Watch your baby's face and body language for feedback; where does he like to be stroked? Does he respond better to light touches or a firmer pressure? This is a learning experience for both of you. Many hospitals and private organizations offer baby massage classes. These are beneficial because a certified infant massage instructor can show you all the how-tos, step by step. An instructor can give you a hands-on demonstration and answer your questions to help you feel confident in this very gentle and soothing art.

Bath Before Bed—Yes or No?

Bath time is often touted as a magic part of a bedtime routine, and when your child is a toddler it may be something worthwhile to consider, if it relaxes your child. However, this isn't a good idea for your newborn. New babies don't need—and shouldn't have—daily baths. Daily bathing can dry out your baby's delicate skin or even cause skin irritation. Excess use of even the gentlest baby soaps can increase the chance of cradle cap (a scaly buildup on the head) or eczema. Newborns don't get that dirty, so keep your baby's face and diaper area clean, but give him a bath only once or twice a week.

A great place for massage, as we discussed previously, is in the bathtub—bring your baby into the tub with you (not for a scrub, but just for the cuddles and massage, and make sure the water isn't too hot for your little one), and add the soothing feel of water to the experience. Breastfeeding moms, be prepared—as soon as your baby notices the milk is close by he'll want to nurse, and this is a lovely place for a relaxing nursing session! (Stay awake!)

Routine Sequence of Events

It can become a calming ritual if you create a short but peaceful presleep routine, possibly including a change into pajamas, specific bedtime music or white noise, dimming the lights, and a quiet diaper change. Over time the predictability will help ward off bedtime resistance. It can also help you get through the process on autopilot during the time of day when you are most tired. A planned bedtime routine that includes these factors will help your little one transition easily from awake to asleep because it builds a series of predictable sleep cues. It will alleviate any stress that comes from dealing with a baby who refuses to sleep when tiredness is clearly present. It will also begin to build the routine that will be invaluable as your baby gets older.

Fill Baby's Tummy Before Sleep

To help make sure Baby's first sleep of the night is a longer one, try to make the last feeding before bedtime a complete one. If baby nods off after feeding from one breast or after taking half a bottle, shift her around, untuck the blanket, and encourage her to finish the feeding; otherwise, she may doze off for a short break and then wake up very soon to finish her feeding.

Be Conscious of Your Own Bedtime Routine—or Lack Thereof

It's not uncommon for a parent of a newborn to finally get the baby settled for the night and then zip into high gear to clean up, do laundry, or catch up on the computer. And then, finally, by the time you hit the bed, you are wide awake, and perhaps just nodding off when your baby wakes for a feeding. It's hard to handle nighttime parenting when you are not getting adequate sleep yourself, and this can actually increase your risk of getting the baby blues or postpartum depression.

This is one time in your life when you really need to be taking better care of yourself so that you can take care of your baby. Give yourself permission to take some wind-down time and to go to bed earlier. This can help you to be better equipped to handle night waking and enable you to enjoy the newborn stage. Maybe even tuck yourself in after the soothing ritual of your baby's bedtime routine on some nights. A 7:00 p.m. bedtime once in a while can be a mood-enhancer for a tired parent.

Bedtime Versus Nap Time

Naps don't need the same kind of bedtime routine as nighttime during the newborn months. Daily naps should happen frequently whenever your baby shows signs of tiredness. Over time, it can be beneficial to have this different routine to signal the longer, deeper sleep of nighttime.

Be Thoughtful About Creating Patterns

Newborn babies don't have habits . . . but they don't stay newborns for long—they are growing older day by day. Before you know it, your newborn becomes a baby who is accustomed to a specific routine. Babies get used to a certain pattern that becomes a very strong sleep cue, and then they are reluctant to accept change. The things that we do daily for bedtime now can easily become very strong habits over the next year or two.

For example, if you rock your baby in the living room rocking chair before sleep, then that is the pattern that your baby comes to expect before sleep. It becomes a very comfortable—and very strong—sleep cue. If your baby falls asleep nursing or sucking a

Point to Remember

When you notice that your baby is broadcasting clear signs of tiredness, do not launch into a long prebedtime routine. Doing so delays her needed sleep and can give her a second wind, and you'll end up with an overtired-wired baby who won't fall asleep easily. Instead, if your baby is clearly tired, pop on a clean diaper, feed your baby, and put her to bed!

Perfectly tired baby?
Skip the bedtime routine
and just go to bed!

bottle or pacifier, it is this action that becomes the strong sleep cue. Pay attention to the bedtime routines that you are creating with your newborn baby today. It is, of course, absolutely fine to construct patterns that you will be comfortable continuing for the next three to six months or more—such as nursing or rocking your baby to sleep—and lots and lots of parents do this. But as time marches on, stay aware of how you will want things to go after the newborn period ends—for example, while it works for your two-month-old, it's unlikely you'll want to bounce your one-year-old on an exercise ball as part of your nightly bedtime routine! Stay alert to signs that your baby's sleep biology is maturing and make appropriate changes then, instead of waiting until it becomes a problem for you. If you miss the transition from *newborn* to *baby* or from *baby* to *toddler*, you may look up to find that today's routines are set in stone and much harder to modify, though not impossible. It makes sense to be aware and thoughtful about your baby's changing bedtime needs, to keep bedtime as a peaceful, happy time for both of you.

KEY 15

Live by the *No-Cry Philosophy* and Enjoy Your Happy Family

Whether you are currently pregnant, awaiting adoption, or already have a newborn in your life, no matter if it's your first baby or your sixth, this new little person starts you on a whole new journey. This baby gives you an opportunity to examine who you are as a parent, and who you are as a human being. This baby's fresh start in life is also yours. Your newborn has his eyes open to the world, but because babies are fully dependent on the people who care for them it is specifically the world that you provide. What world will you provide to your child? Now, as a newborn, and later, as your child grows?

Even when your baby is brand-new, it can be an eye-opening exercise to look ahead to the future and try to envision your baby as a child, as a teenager, and as a young adult. Try to capture the most important traits and values you hope to see in that beautiful person, and the relationship you will have with the incredible human being your child will become. Use your vision to help you make important decisions in your daily life today, and every day.

We cannot mold our children into the people we want them to be, of course, and we can't mastermind a lifetime relationship and have it be so just by wishing for it. However, the ways that we respond to our babies will directly affect the way they will be as toddlers, preschoolers, school-age children, teenagers, and adults.

The seeds of behaviors and future relationships are planted now. If you could get a glimpse of your babies as they will be in the future, it would provide enlightenment and give you tremendous guidance as you move through your days. You can't see the future, of course, but you don't really have to. Since children are remarkably similar in many behaviors, you can gain the benefit of those families who have gone before you to build a foundation for a positive and pleasant future.

Raising a child requires that we make many decisions every single day, from the insignificant to the life altering. Sometimes it's obvious that you've made the right decision, other times it's unclear, and from time to time it's apparent that you've made a mistake. It's likely that every mistake you make as a parent has been made by parents who have come before you. What is more important than any single action is your overall philosophy and approach to raising your child. Be a conscious, compassionate

Maddison, six months old, with Mommy

parent. Build a friendship with your child right from the start. When love is your foundation, and your goal is to raise your child to be a good human being with whom you can have a pleasant life-long relationship, then it is likely things will turn out as you hope.

Enjoy the happy moments and know that there will always be challenges, and that you can rise to them. Don't be so focused on sleep issues, or any other distraction, that you miss the glorious loveliness of your new baby—this time passes in a blink of an eye. When your baby is (finally) asleep, take a few minutes to bask in the breathtaking beauty of his soft hair, his tiny ears, his smooth-as-silk skin, the gentle rise and fall of his breath, or those adorable baby snores. These are the moments when memories are built and when the building blocks of your relationship are laid.

The No-Cry Philosophy

The parenting theme throughout all the books in the No-Cry Solution series is outlined for you here.

It all begins with basic promises you make to yourself.

- I will commit to being a kind, compassionate parent.
- I will be a knowledgeable parent. I'll read, listen, and learn.
- I will view my actions through the eyes and the experiences of my children and teach by both lesson and example.
- I will look for the real needs behind my children's behavior.
- I won't look for the easy way, I will look for the right way.
- I will make thoughtful, purposeful decisions.
- I will be a present parent, in both quality and quantity of time.
- I will focus on what is important, not what is convenient or easy.
- I will consider the future as I make daily decisions.

Tune out the outside advice or criticism that doesn't fit with your parenting style. Be confident in your decisions and stand up to those who would break down that confidence. Keep in mind that there are no absolute rules about raising children, and no guarantees for any parenting techniques. Be thoughtful and purposeful about your parenting decisions, do your homework, and then educate others. Raise your children how you choose to raise them and in ways that are right for you and for your family. Politely ignore those who feel they must provide their opinions, particularly when they do not align with yours. Don't create or imagine problems because someone else has a different lifestyle than you do—no matter if that person is family, friend, or expert. Be true to yourself.

Understand that raising a child is a complex lifelong commitment, and that you are, and always should be, the best expert on your own child.

How to Handle Unwanted Advice About Your Parenting Choices

When you have a newborn, the abundance of advice you get can make you frustrated and confused. Here is how to handle everyone's unwanted advice and find more confidence in your own parenting decisions.

Understand Their Motivation

Most often, the underlying motivation here bespeaks love and concern more than it does mean-spiritedness: just as your child is an important part of your life, he is also important to others. Most often, family members and close friends dispense advice from a position of love and concern for your child. People who care about you and your family are bonded to you in a special way that invites their counsel. Knowing this might make it easier to tolerate, might help you find your sense of humor, and may give you a reason to handle the interference gently, in a way that leaves everyone's feelings intact.

Regardless of who is giving the advice, how many times they give it, or why, it is *your* child, and, in the end, you will make your own decisions and raise your child the way that you think best. They cannot *make you* do anything. So it's rarely worth creating a world war over a well-meaning person's advice—no matter how *unhelpful* it may really be.

You can respond to unwanted advice in a variety of ways. The method that you choose for each situation will depend on your personality, your mood, the topic, and your relationship with the advice giver.

Listen First

It's natural to feel defensive if you get the impression that someone is judging the way you are parenting your own child; sometimes this gets in the way of really hearing someone else's idea. Chances are, you are not being criticized; rather, the other person is sharing what he feels to be valuable insight. Try to truly listen to the person giving his opinion—you may just learn something new and valuable. And maybe not. But unless you listen with an open mind, you might miss something helpful. Sometimes, reining in our own pride can result in learning something of great value.

Disregard

This is a helpful approach if you are confident in your choice and you know that there is no convincing the other person to change her mind—for example, a sister or close friend who's already raised her child and is imparting that "I did it this way

(continued)

and you should too" kind of advice. Simply smile, nod, and make a noncommittal response such as, "That's interesting!" Then go about your own business in your own way. It is rarely worth compromising your relationship over a differing parenting style.

Agree (Yes, Agree!)

You may be able to pick one point out of the advice that you actually agree with. If so, jump into the conversation with wholehearted agreement on that one point and take the conversation in that direction. If you can acknowledge the bit of advice that you value, you can shift the focus away from the other bits with which you disagree.

Pick Your Battles

This is a matter of perspective and importance. If your mother-in-law insists that your baby wear a hat on your walk to the park, go ahead and pop a hat on his head. This won't have any long-term effects except that of placating your mother-in-law. However, don't capitulate on issues of safety or those that are important to you or your child. In those situations, you can resort to the other options listed here.

Steer Clear of the Topic

If your best friend is pressuring you to let your baby cry to sleep, but it's against your belief and you know that you would never do it, then don't complain to her about your baby getting you up four times the night before. By bringing up the topic, you invite her to share her opinion! If the other person brings up the topic, then diversion or distraction is definitely in order. "Oh! Would you like a muffin? I just bought them and they're incredible . . . and how about a cup of coffee? Now where did I put that bag . . ." If she accuses you of changing the subject, admit that you are and offer another muffin.

Educate Yourself

The more secure and confident you are in your parenting decisions, the easier it is to let other people's comments slide by without concern. Knowledge is power; protect yourself and your sanity by reading up on your parenting choices, and rely on the facts that you know. It will build your confidence that you are doing your best for your family.

Educate the Other Person

If your "teacher" is imparting information that you know to be outdated or outright wrong, you might choose to share some of what you've learned on the topic. If done delicately, you may be able to open the other person's mind about the topic. Quote experts, or refer to a study, book, or report that you have read; the more complete the data you can cite, the more credible you will appear. For example, if Grandma is suggesting that you give your three-month-old a bowl of baby cereal before bed to help him sleep through the night, you can quote some of the information from a baby book or parenting program on the medical reasons why it's best to wait. Remember that Grandma is basing her opinion on information that was considered valid when she was raising her children, so a polite update on current scientific and medical thinking might help her understand your way of doing things.

Quote a Doctor

Many people accept your point of view if a medical professional has validated it. If your own pediatrician agrees with your position on the topic, simply say, "My doctor said to wait

(continued)

until she's at least six months before starting solids." If your *own* doctor doesn't back your view, then refer to another doctor— perhaps the author of a book about baby care. Then you can say, "*The* doctor says to wait until she's at least six months old before starting solids."

Better yet, present your "advisor" with a book or article that has most influenced your parenting philosophy so she can weigh the issues for herself based on current thinking. Don't *throw* the book at her—simply say, "I know the way I do things mystifies you. But I've read up on [insert issue in dispute here], and I've made my decisions based on what I believe to be good information. Here . . . see what you think of this."

Be Vague

If you are aware that your position on a particular topic is opposite the other person's, and you know that any discussion would just lead to a heated battle, you can avoid confrontation altogether with an elusive response to any question or com- ment. For example, "We're moving in that direction." Or, "Yes, we've considered that." Then change the subject.

Ask for Advice!

I'm sure that your friendly counselor is an expert on a few issues that are inconsequential or upon which you can agree. Search out these points and invite guidance. Go ahead and encourage the person to teach you in these areas. She will be happy that she is helping you and that you're actually listening, and you'll be happy because you've found a way to avoid a showdown about topics that you know you don't agree on. Plus, you just might learn something useful!

Memorize a Standard Response

Here's a great one-line replay that can be said in response to almost any piece of advice or criticism: "This may not be the right way for you, but it's the right way for *me*." This prevents the other person from having to be defensive about his point of view and is a nice way to agree to disagree.

Be Honest

If someone you care about is becoming a true annoyance to you because of constant advice or criticism, consider being honest and direct about your feelings. Pick a time when distractions are at a minimum, and choose your words carefully. You might say something like, "I know how much you love little Harry, and I'm glad you get to spend so much time with him. As much as you think you're helping me when you give me advice about his sleeping habits, though, I'm comfortable with my own approach, and I'd really appreciate if you'd understand that."

Search Out Like-Minded Friends

Join a support group or an online group with people who share your parenting philosophies. Talking with others who are raising their babies in a way that is similar to your own can give you the strength to face friends and family members who don't understand your viewpoints.

Do unto Others

When the time comes for *you* to be the one giving the advice, remember to present your idea in a way that you'd like to receive it.

Handling Future Sleep Problems with Gentle No-Cry Solutions

Wait! What was that heading? Future sleep problems?! Take a deep breath, and please don't get mad at me—but even if you do everything exactly right, even if you set up the perfect sleep situation for your baby, and even if you apply everything you learn so brilliantly that your five-month-old baby sleeps gloriously through the night and naps long, blissful naps during the day, it does not mean you are home free.

I'm sorry to be the bearer of bad news, but sleep issues are an ever-changing state of affairs, and there is no "finish line" when it comes to sleep and children. There will be many, many disruptions to your child's sleep in the years ahead, such as teething, milestones, growth spurts, illness, vacations, separation anxiety, daylight saving time, or starting daycare, just to name a few.

When real problems arise or issues need to be addressed in regard to your child's sleep, take a clear look at the problem and determine what it means to you, your child, and your family. Define the problem first, from the perspective of *your family only*. Then, do your research. And know that when sleep needs evolve and change over time and problems crop up, there is always an array of ideas and gentle solutions to address them.

Children are not like computers that can be programed a certain way and then function that way forever. Oh, wait! Maybe they *are* like computers—computers that freeze up, pop up error messages, or cease to function as expected, right when you need them to work. Just like computers that require service and ongoing maintenance to keep functioning smoothly every day, children need ongoing attention and action to maintain good sleep routines throughout their childhood.

Your newborn can be an amazing sleeper one day, and then suddenly dive into the up-all-night-and-won't-nap-all-day territory.

Darcia Narvaez, PhD, an infant sleep researcher from the University of Notre Dame, says, "A return to night waking after periods of sleeping through the night is entirely normal. In fact, researchers looking at sleep patterns have found that often between 6 and 12 months, infants who had previously been sleeping long stretches suddenly start to wake more frequently at night."

Why Good Sleepers Can Suddenly Change Course

So that you can be on the lookout for possible sleep issues down the road, let's cover some of the reasons why a good sleeper suddenly begins to resist sleep, refuse naps, or wake up more often at night:

- **Newborn sleepiness fades away.** Infants are wired to need massive amounts of sleep. If you read your newborn's cues properly and provide a perfect sleep environment, she will sleep and sleep . . . and sleep. But as the months pass, your baby's biology dictates the need for fewer naps, fewer hours of sleep, and longer awake periods. Many babies sleep much differently as newborns than they do after they pass through infancy.
- **Your sleepy newborn becomes a baby driven to learn.** Once infancy passes your baby enters the conscious world and develops an all-encompassing desire to learn about *everything*. There are so many new things to see, hear, taste, and explore and many milestones to summit. When your baby's eyes peek open (day or night), the world beckons: "Wake up, kiddo! Let's get busy. You have things to do!"
- **Major milestones can cause twenty-four-hour upheaval.** For many babies, leaps in development affect daytime

hours and sleep time, as well. Learning to sit, crawl, cruise the furniture, climb, walk, and run—along with cognitive growth that has your baby suddenly understanding how to push a button, color with a crayon, or stack blocks—keeps his brain and body far too busy to sleep.

- **The teething monster enters the picture.** Darn if it isn't the worst timing ever! Most babies begin teething at about five to seven months of age—just when you and your baby have graduated from the newborn stage and life is settling into your new normal. Teething can be difficult and painful, and it is a well-known sleep-disrupter. Teething can also affect your baby's mood and sleep for many weeks before a tooth even emerges because of growth and movement occurring under the gumline.
- **Swaddling loses its value.** If your newborn was calmed by swaddling, there will come a day when it suddenly becomes restrictive and annoying to your ever-active baby. Or you'll have to stop swaddling because your little one begins to roll over or wiggles so much in her sleep that you risk a wad of blankets wrapped in all the wrong places. Yet a baby who has slept well when swaddled will often struggle to fall asleep without it.
- **Your baby gets smarter.** As babies move out of infancy they become masters at figuring out their parents. Your little one learns that calling for you in the middle of the night or poking you in the ribs brings warm milk and a lovely cuddle.
- **Good habits formed in infancy become problems to you later.** It's a blessing to your newborn and to you when you hold your little one in a sling or your arms for naps. There's nothing sweeter than the sleepy, soft breathing of a teeny-tiny bundle in your arms. You can take a walk or complete household chores with your baby gently swaying in the sling. But when that bundle is nine months old and weighs

twenty pounds, yet still wants to spend every nap in your arms, you may find that impossible, so things must change.
- **It's your baby's temperament.** All facts considered, some babies are just better sleepers than others. Even if you do everything exactly the same with two babies, they may have completely different sleep patterns. I've had many parents of twins and triplets tell me exactly that. Sleep patterns are partially personality driven.

Point to Remember
It can be difficult to comprehend, but in many situations you do not control the outcome with your child, no matter how hard you try. And, when it comes to sleep, some children are born great sleepers and others are born believing that they don't need any sleep at all. Sometimes, a child's personality and preferences can trump any amount of efforts made by the parents!

- **And add one more possibility to this long list.** It's the mystery reason that even Sherlock Holmes cannot deduce. That's when everything seems to be right, but sleep is suddenly so wrong, and you cannot pinpoint any logical reason for the disruption. Chalk it up to the complexity of life and little human beings.

Parenting Isn't a One-Act Show

Your children will have needs that change from now until they become adults, and your responsibility in regard to these needs changes, but it never disappears. Yet, no matter what comes up, there are gentle, respectful, and loving ways to handle all aspects of parenting.

A wise parent understands that child-rearing is a fluid and ever-changing job. When problems arise, or issues need to be addressed, there are always solutions to be found. And when your child's sleep needs evolve and change over time, there are always gentle No-Cry sleep solutions to address them. So, when things do change, keep your problems in perspective and take ample time to plot the best course of action, designed for your unique child. Solve your problems by analyzing possible solutions and choosing those solutions that are right for you and your family. Know that there is rarely only one right answer, and that you will often take multiple routes before getting to the best destination. And always keep in mind that your child can teach you more about himself than any friend, neighbor, expert, book, or research. When you pay close attention, your child can be your best teacher about himself, and you have within you everything you need to be the best student.

Family life is complicated, and we often unknowingly make things more complicated by trying to force natural things into unnatural shapes. When things aren't going right, try to go back to basics and discover what is getting in the way. And, when things are going perfectly, then relax, enjoy, and savor every single blissful moment.

What Family Life Is Really All About

Life is made up of moments. One, plus one, plus one. When your children are young, the days seem to last forever and sleep deprivation makes most of those moments just slightly foggy. Then, before you know it, your children are in school, and the days are quiet and the house a bit emptier. And in a blink after that they drive away in a car filled to bursting with a teenager's possessions, heading toward college or wherever their young lives lead them. And you'll be standing in the driveway, a movie-loop of their childhood playing through your head as the tears roll down your cheeks and the gasping sobs take over your body. No-Cry isn't even possible. Hopefully, your movie will show memories filled with happiness and overlaid with confidence.

Raising your child only starts with the blur that is babyhood. This time now is only the beginning, the setting in motion of a relationship that will blossom from what you plant today.

Raising children brings plenty of challenging moments and more than a fair share of confusing moments. But the moments that really matter are those filled with love. When you can focus on enhancing those love-filled moments, and doing what you can to pull through the tough ones with your head held high, you will find that being a parent is the most frightening, challenging, beautiful, enriching, fulfilling, and marvelous experience of your lifetime. Now, go hug your baby, and start creating your own movie.

Part 3

Safety

Sleeping Safety Checklists

PLEASE MAKE SURE THAT
NO MATTER WHERE YOUR NEWBORN SLEEPS
FOR NIGHTTIME AND NAPS
YOU CREATE A SAFE PLACE FOR YOUR BABY.

As a parent, it's important to be aware of the many aspects of safety for your child. Making your home safe for your baby starts the day he enters your life, well before he ever starts to crawl or walk. The following safety information comes from a wide variety of reputable sources and authorities. Please read over these lists, and give your baby's safety serious attention.

Keep in mind that these lists cover safety issues relating to *the bedroom* and *sleep* at *home*. You should, of course, be aware of many other safety issues, whether your child is asleep or awake, at home and away. If your baby spends time with a childcare provider, babysitter, grandparent, or anyone else, insist that safety guidelines are followed in that environment, also.

Keep in mind that, because safety precautions are updated constantly, and because children, their families, and their homes are all different, no checklist is fully complete and appropriate for every household, so be diligent about safety for your child.

General Sleeping Safety Precautions for All Families

- Put your infant to sleep on his or her back for naps and night sleep, unless your doctor specifically says it's safe for your baby to sleep in other positions.
- Have your newborn sleep all night in *your bedroom* so you can keep an eye and ear on him. The American Academy of Pediatrics (AAP) says "*sharing a room with an infant can reduce the risk of SIDS by up to 50 percent.*"
- Keep the bedroom at a comfortable sleeping temperature, usually between 65°F and 72°F (18°C to 22°C). Be careful not to let your baby get overheated or chilled. If your baby comes home from delivery wearing a newborn hat, ask if this should be removed for sleep, as a hat can contribute to overheating.
- Do not allow anyone to smoke around your child, or in rooms where your child spends time. This holds true whether your baby is asleep or awake. Children exposed to secondhand smoke face an increased risk of SIDS and health complications such as allergies, asthma, sleep apnea, and other sleep disruptions. If you are a smoker, avoid smoking before breastfeeding. Nicotine levels peak in breastmilk 30 to 60 minutes after smoking and are gone after three hours, so the more time you can place between smoking and your baby's feedings the better.
- Do not use pillows, adult blankets, or comforters under or over your child as these can entangle him or become a suffocation hazard. Instead, dress your child in warm pajamas layered with an undershirt when the temperature warrants them, and use small baby-sized blankets. Hold off on using a child-sized pillow until your child is over eighteen months old.

- Dress your child in snug-fitting sleepwear, not oversize, loose-fitting cotton clothing. Billowy or cotton fabrics pose a burn hazard in case of fire.
- Do not allow your baby to sleep on a very soft sleeping surface such as a pillow, waterbed, beanbag, foam pad, nursing pillow, featherbed, or any other flexible surface. Babies should sleep only on a firm, flat mattress, with a smooth, wrinkle-free sheet that stays securely fastened around the mattress.
- Keep nightlights, lamps, white noise machines, and all other electrical items away from where your child sleeps.
- Make sure you have a working smoke detector in your baby's sleeping room and check it as often as the manufacturer suggests. Have a carbon-monoxide alarm in the home as well. Replace batteries as recommended.
- Do not put a child to sleep near an accessible window, window blinds, cords, or draperies.
- Keep your child's regular appointments for checkups. If your child is sick or feverish, call your doctor or hospital promptly.
- Never shake or hit your baby. (Child abuse often occurs when parents are sleep-deprived and at the end of their rope. If you feel like you may lose your temper with your child, put your baby in a safe place or with another caregiver and go take a breather. Ask someone for help.)
- Never tie a pacifier to your child with a string, ribbon, or cord, as any of these can become wound around your child's finger, hand, foot, or neck.
- Follow all safety precautions when your child is sleeping away from home, whether in a car seat, stroller, friend or family's home, or unfamiliar place.
- Never leave a child unattended while in a stroller, baby seat, swing, or car seat.

- Never leave a pet with access to a sleeping baby. Even the most gentle, protective pet can unintentionally harm your baby.
- Learn how to perform infant CPR. Be sure that all other caregivers for your child are also trained in CPR. (Check with your local hospital or fire department for classes.)
- Keep your child's environment clean. Wash bedding often. Wash your hands after diapering your child and before preparing food. Wash your child's hands and face frequently.
- Pay attention to your own health and well-being. If you have feelings of anxiety, panic, sadness, or hopelessness, you may be suffering from postpartum depression. Please talk to a professional (such as your doctor or midwife). This condition is common and treatable. Call someone now.

Safety Precautions for Cradles and Cribs

- Make certain your child's crib meets all federal safety regulations, industry standards, and guidelines of the U.S. Consumer Product Safety Commission's most recent recommendations (www.cpsc.gov). Look for a safety certification seal. Avoid using an old or used crib.
- Make sure the mattress fits tightly in the cradle or crib, without gaps on any side. (If you can fit more than two fingers between the mattress and the side of the crib, the mattress does not fit properly.)
- Make certain that your crib sheets fit securely and cannot be pulled loose by your child thus creating a dangerous tangle of fabric. Do not use plastic mattress covers or any plastic bags near the crib.
- Remove any decorative ribbons, bows, or strings. Don't use bumper pads.

- Be certain that all screws, bolts, springs, and other hard-ware and attachments are tightly secured, and check them from time to time. Replace any broken or missing pieces immediately. (Contact the manufacturer for replacement parts.) Make sure your crib has a sturdy bottom and wide, stable base so that it does not wobble or tilt when your baby moves around. Check to see that all slats are in place, firm, and stable—and that they are spaced no more than 2⅜ inches (60 mm) apart.
- Make sure that corner posts do not extend more than ¹⁄₁₆ inch (1½ mm) above the top of the end panel. Don't use a crib that has removable decorative knobs on the corner posts, or headboard and footboard designs that present a hazard, such as sharp edges, points, or pieces that can be loosened or removed. When you raise the side rail, lock it into position.
- Don't hang objects over a sleeping or unattended baby—that includes mobiles and other crib toys. There is a risk of the toy falling on your child.
- If you are using a portable crib, make sure the locking devices are properly and securely locked.
- Make sure your child is within hearing distance of your bed or that you have a reliable baby monitor turned on. It is rec-ommended that your baby sleep overnight in the same room as you during the newborn period.
- Check the manufacturer's instructions on suggested size and weight limits for any cradle, bassinet, or crib. If there is no tag, call or write the manufacturer for this information or check the manufacturer's website.
- Make sure that any place your child sleeps when away from home meets all of the above safety requirements.

Safety Precautions for Bed-Sharing

- It is much wiser to create a safe condition in an adult bed than to fall asleep on a sofa, recliner, or chair with your baby in your arms or lying on you, which carries a high level of risk.
- Bed-share only with a healthy, full-term infant or an older baby.
- If you choose to bed-share with your newborn it is likely better if you breastfeed your baby, as the breastfeeding mother-infant pair may be safest for infant co-sleeping. Dr. James McKenna, a leading authority on infant-mother sleep states, "Bottlefeeding newborns should sleep alongside the mother *on a separate surface* rather than in the same bed." A bed-side cradle adjacent to your bed keeps baby close enough to touch, but on a separate surface.
- Avoid bed-sharing with an infant if either parent is a smoker, or if the mother smoked while pregnant, due to the fact that secondhand smoke and smoke residue can affect a baby's developing lungs and increase the risk of SIDS.
- Your bed must be absolutely safe for your baby. The best choice is to place the mattress on the floor, making sure there are no crevices that your baby can become wedged in. Make certain your mattress is flat, firm, and smooth. Do not allow your baby to sleep on a soft surface such as a waterbed, beanbag, soft pillow-top, or any other flexible surface.
- Make certain that your fitted sheets stay secure and cannot be pulled loose.
- If your bed is raised off the floor, use mesh guardrails to prevent your baby from rolling off the bed, and be especially careful that there is no space between the mattress and headboard or footboard. (Many guardrails are designed

for older children and are not safe for infants because they have gaps that small babies can get stuck in.)

- If your bed is placed against a wall or against other furniture, check every night to be sure nothing has shifted to create a space between the mattress and wall or furniture where your child could become stuck. Make this part of your bedtime routine.
- The majority of professionals agree that infants should be placed between Mother and the wall or guardrail. Yes, of course Father, siblings, and grandparents love the newborn every bit as much as Mother does! Once baby is a bit older it will be safe, but science shows that others don't have the same instinctual awareness of an infant's location as mothers do. Mothers, pay attention to your own sensitivity to Baby. Your little one should be able to awaken you with a minimum of movement or noise—often even a sniff or grunt is enough to wake a mother sleeping next to her baby. If you find that you are such a deep sleeper that you only wake up when your baby makes a loud cry, you should consider moving Baby into a bedside cradle or crib.
- Use a large, firm mattress to provide ample room for everyone's space and movement.
- With a premature newborn, or a newborn with special needs, you might consider a sidecar arrangement in which the baby's crib, bed, or mattress sits beside or close to your bed. Many three-sided co-sleepers are now available to give Baby a designated space of his own attached to your bed.
- Well before your child reaches his first birthday, make certain that the room your child sleeps in, and any room he might have access to, is child-safe. (Imagine your child crawling out of bed as you sleep. Even though he's too young now, time passes quickly and he eventually will!)

- Do not ever sleep with your baby if you have been drinking alcohol, if you have used any drugs or medications that could make you drowsy or affect your senses, if you are ill and unable to respond to your baby's needs, if you are an especially sound sleeper, or if you are suffering from sleep deprivation and find it difficult to awaken.
- Do not swaddle your baby when bed-sharing. Your baby's arms and legs should be free to move about. In addition, swaddling during bed-sharing can increase the risk of overheating.
- Do not sleep with your baby if you are a large person, as a parent's excess weight has been determined to pose a risk to a baby in a bed-sharing situation. Examine how you and your child settle in next to each other. If your child rolls towards you, or if there is a large dip in the mattress, or if you suspect any other dangerous situation, play it safe and move your child to a bedside crib or his own bed.
- Remove pillows and blankets during the newborn period. (You might be able to use a small, firm pillow under your own head.)
- Do not wear any nightclothes with strings or long ribbons. Don't wear jewelry to bed, and, if your hair is long, put it up.
- Don't use any strong-smelling perfumes or lotions that may affect your baby's delicate senses.
- Do not allow other children or pets to sleep in a bed with your newborn. Save this treat for when your child is older.
- When your baby is not actively breastfeeding, he should be sleeping on his back, the safest position for newborn sleep.
- Never leave your baby alone in an adult bed unless that bed is perfectly safe for your child, such as a mattress on the floor in a childproof room, and when you are nearby or listening in on your child with a reliable monitor.

- As of this writing there are no proven safety devices for use in protecting a baby in an adult bed. However, as a result of the great number of parents who wish to bed-share safely with their babes, a number of new inventions are appearing in baby catalogs and stores. You may want to look into some of these nests, wedges, and cradles—but check the safety factors, watch the news, and do your homework. Just because something is sold does not ensure that it is safe.

Index

About the Author

Parenting educator Elizabeth Pantley is president of Better Beginnings, Inc., a family resource and education company. Elizabeth is frequently quoted as a parenting expert in newspapers and magazines worldwide and on thousands of parent-directed websites. She publishes articles that are distributed in schools, daycares, medical offices, childbirth educator programs, lactation centers, doula and midwife offices, and parent programs everywhere.

Elizabeth is the author of twelve popular parenting books, available in twenty-seven languages, including the bestselling No-Cry Solution series:

The No-Cry Sleep Solution for Newborns
Amazing Sleep from Day One—for Your Baby and You

The No-Cry Sleep Solution
Gentle Ways to Help Your Baby Sleep Through the Night

The No-Cry Sleep Solution for Toddlers and Preschoolers
Gentle Ways to Stop Bedtime Battles and Improve Your Child's Sleep

The No-Cry Nap Solution
Guaranteed Gentle Ways to Solve All Your Naptime Problems

The No-Cry Picky Eater Solution
Gentle Ways to Encourage Your Child to Eat—and Eat Healthy

The No-Cry Separation Anxiety Solution
Gentle Ways to Make Good-Bye Easy from Six Months to Six Years

The No-Cry Discipline Solution
Gentle Ways to Encourage Good Behavior Without Whining, Tantrums and Tears

The No-Cry Potty Training Solution
Gentle Ways to Help Your Child Say Good-Bye to Diapers

Elizabeth and her husband, Robert, are the parents of four children: Angela, Vanessa, David, and Coleton.

For more information, excerpts, and parenting articles, visit the author at:

Website
http://www.nocrysolution.com

Blog
http://elizabethpantley.com/

Follow her on social media:

Facebook
https://www.facebook.com/ElizabethPantleyNoCryAuthor/

Pinterest
http://www.pinterest.com/nocrysolution/

Blogger
http://www.kidsinthehouse.com/blogs/Elizabeth-Pantley

Instagram
https://instagram.com/elizabethpantley/

Twitter
https://twitter.com/NoCrySolution

Other No-Cry Solution Titles from Elizabeth Pantley

the no-cry sleep solution
0-07-138139-2

the no-cry sleep solution for toddlers and preschoolers
0-07-144491-2

the no-cry nap solution
0-07-159695-X

the no-cry separation anxiety solution
0-07-174077-5

the no-cry potty training solution
0-07-147690-3

the no-cry discipline solution
0-07-147159-6

the no-cry picky eater solution
0-07-174436-3

① TURN OFF WHITE NOISE ASAP ② WAKING

② Baby asleep... PAUSE to see if
he'll quiet down + fall back asleep

④ When awake, play, sing, carry,
no lying in a seat. ENGAGE!

⑤ Daylight naps, Blackout nights.
Expose to light 1st thing in morn.

⑥ Partly Dance.
A. Nurse him in arms. Detach
and roll back slightly away
so that on back, like how
lying in crib.

B. ~~Swing~~ Sing, hum, while
jiggle, bounce, pat, rock.

C. Pause! Repeat above.

D. Lower feet, but, back, head
while humming.

E. Gentle pressure? jiggle,
sing